M000302265

Hiking Utah's High Uintas

Second Edition

Jeffrey Probst and Brad Probst
Revised by Brett Prettyman

WITHDRAWN
BY
~~N COUNTY PUBLIC LIBRARY~~
LAKEWOOD, CO

FALCONGUIDES

GUILFORD, CONNECTICUT
HELENA, MONTANA

FALCONGUIDES®

An imprint of Rowman & Littlefield
Falcon, FalconGuides, and Outfit Your Mind are registered trademarks of Rowman & Littlefield.

Distributed by NATIONAL BOOK NETWORK

Copyright © 2016 by Rowman & Littlefield
A previous edition was published by Globe Pequot in 2006.

Maps by XNR Productions Inc. © Rowman & Littlefield
Photos by Jeffrey Probst, Brad Probst, Robert Morris, Robert Davidson, Matt McKell, Cordell Andersen, and the Utah Division of Wildlife Resources. Detailed help on hiking information from USDA Forest Service officials Kathy Jo Pollock, Ryan Buerkle, Bernard Asay, and Loyal Clark

All rights reserved. No part of this book may be reproduced in any form or by any electronic or mechanical means, including information storage and retrieval systems, without written permission from the publisher, except by a reviewer who may quote passages in a review.

British Library Cataloguing-in-Publication Information Available

Library of Congress Cataloging-in-Publication Data Available

ISBN 978-1-4930-0986-2 (paperback)
ISBN 978-1-4930-1512-2 (e-book)

∞™ The paper used in this publication meets the minimum requirements of American National Standard for Information Sciences—Permanence of Paper for Printed Library Materials, ANSI/NISO Z39.48-1992.

The authors and Globe Pequot assume no liability for accidents happening to, or injuries sustained by, readers who engage in the activities described in this book.

Contents

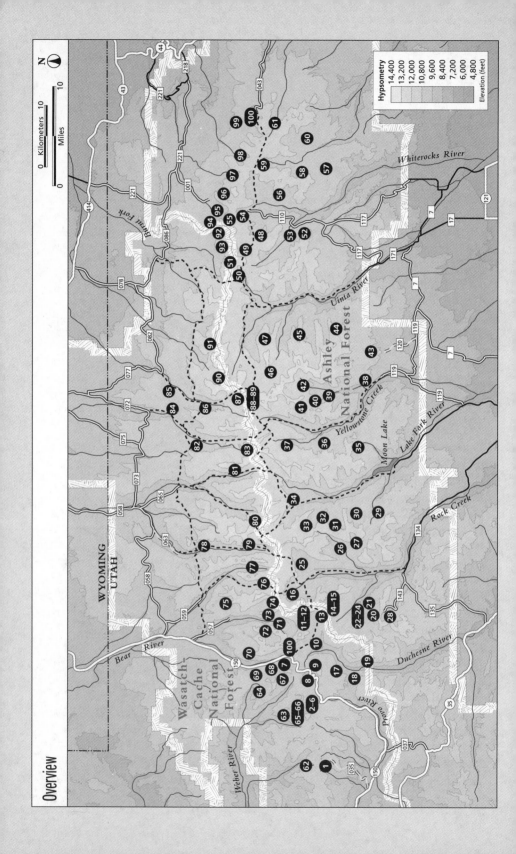

Overview

Introduction

The High Uintas backcountry has long been a favorite haunt for backpackers, anglers, and equestrians alike. Recreational use is heavy in some popular areas, while other remote spots may go years between visitors. Most lakes receive only light to moderate pressure. There is a lot of wilderness to go around, and you should have little trouble finding a lake that you can call your own for a few days. Maybe you'll discover your own special place—one that seems custom made just for you. This book can help you find such a place somewhere in the High Uintas.

We have detailed a substantial number of fantastic hikes and have compiled statistics on each lake. The usage, camping, and fishing have been noted. Elevation, miles, fish species, and spring water availability may be specified as well. This book is meant to be a trip planner. If you have an idea of what you are searching for in a backcountry experience, this guide can serve as an excellent tool in helping you find the best areas for your particular tastes.

As you might expect, fishing in the High Uintas is lightning fast at times for those willing to venture into the backcountry. Brook trout, cutthroat, rainbow, and even a few golden trout and arctic grayling inhabit the Uinta lakes and streams. There are more than 600 lakes in this alpine mountain range that are managed for fishing. Fishing is unpredictable but often great—there are no guarantees. A lake that was hot last year may be only marginal this year, or vice versa. That is why we haven't made an attempt to rate the fishing in each lake, but we will rate an area by how good the fishing prospects are in the general vicinity. Investigate several lakes. There are typically many in an area. If one lake doesn't produce, hike on to the next. That's part of the fun of alpine fishing. You get adventure mixed in with your fishing. And don't overlook the countless miles of streams. Most anglers do. The creeks are the most underutilized fisheries in the High Uintas.

In the section that describes specific hikes, we have tried to pinpoint the best camping spots, photo opportunities, and fishing holes. Sometimes we'll tell you exactly where we had the best angling and what lure we used. But try your own methods too. Chances are good that they will work just as well—maybe better.

The High Uinta Mountains offer more than fine fishing. Solitude and grand scenery are the real attractions. Peace and quiet abound—perhaps not in the roadside campgrounds, but certainly in the expanses of the backcountry. No motorized vehicles are allowed. You'll have to journey by foot or horseback. But if access were easily obtainable, then the area wouldn't be peaceful, would it? If you haven't done much hiking here, you may be amazed how little you need to travel to lose the crowds. Quite often only a half-mile of walking puts you in solitude. The wildflower season in the Uintas can provide an explosion of colors and aromas. Utah mushroom hunters make special forays into the range to find tasty morsels—but be careful, there are also some poisonous toadstools.

We hope you will seek out some of the hundreds of lakes and streams that we did not specifically highlight. Whether you wish to travel 2 miles, 10 miles, 20 miles, or more, the High Uintas has a wilderness adventure waiting for you. You could spend a lifetime exploring its many remote drainages. But be on guard. This mountain range has an almost spiritual addiction about it. Be prepared for a powerful craving to return for more.

Ibantik Lake

High Uintas Portfolio

The High Uinta Mountains, named for the Uint-At (Uintah and Uinta are other spellings) Indians, have the distinction of being the only mountain range in the lower forty-eight states that runs east to west. It is the birthplace of several major rivers that make up Utah's watersheds, including the Provo, Weber, Duchesne, and Bear Rivers. There are more than 400 miles of streams in these mountains, along with 1,000 ice-cold lakes and ponds. Over half of these lakes are managed to provide some of the best high-country fishing found anywhere.

Most of the destinations in this book lie within the official High Uintas Wilderness Area established by Congress in 1984. The High Uintas Wilderness Area is Utah's largest wilderness area.

The USDA Forest Service manages the Uinta Mountains with two forests: Uinta-Wasatch-Cache National Forest and Ashley National Forest. Ranger districts in Utah include Heber-Kamas, Duchesne-Roosevelt, Bear River Ranger Station, and Evanston-Mountain View (Wyoming).

Regulations have helped immensely in keeping a pristine environment. Livestock grazing still continues in some localized areas, but there is plenty of space where you can avoid their annoyances. Most cattle and sheep seem to be found around timberline, where they can feed on high grasses then retreat to the shelter of the pines.

Utah's tallest mountain is nestled deep in the center of the wilderness area. Kings Peak (elevation 13,528 feet) stands between the Yellowstone and Uinta River Drainages, but is probably best reached from the North Slope via Henrys Fork Drainage. Because it is Utah's highest point, it is extremely popular among "peak baggers" and can be conquered without the aid of climbing gear. It's a long hike though, no matter which approach you attempt.

Blue-ribbon backpacking is abundant throughout the High Uintas. Enjoy true wilderness experiences in rugged places with names such as Spread Eagle Peak, Highline Trail, Dead Horse Pass, Hells Kitchen, Lightning Lake, Yellowstone Creek, Buck Pasture, Amethyst Lake, and hundreds more.

The western half of the High Uintas is most popular, due simply to its proximity to Utah's main population centers of Salt Lake City, Provo, and Ogden. A 2-hour drive from any of these cities can put you at any one of a dozen Uinta trailheads. Generally, the farther east you travel by car, the more solitude you will find when traveling by foot or horseback.

The terrain is characterized by large stands of pines that lead into alpine basins and cirques. Small lakes generously dot the backcountry. They can be found almost anywhere: along a stream, at the foot of a talus slope, adjoining a lush meadow, or at the bottom of a towering cliff. Encase all of this within steep, rocky peaks that rise thousands of feet, and you'll have a pretty fair picture of what's in store for you.

Winter lasts a long time in the High Uintas. Much of the backcountry is not accessible until late June, and mountain passes may be snowbound until mid-July. Anytime after the middle of September, you risk being caught in a serious snowstorm. As you can quickly figure, the backpacking season lasts only three months, if we're fortunate. The best time to plan a trip into these mountains is during the second half of August. Then the days are warm, the snow is long gone, and those pesky mosquitoes have mostly died off. If you don't mind cooler temperatures, try these mountains after Labor Day.

Those familiar with mountain travel know that the weather can change rapidly. Regardless of the forecast, you should always be prepared for searing sun, pouring rain, lightning, and even snow. Wear and pack your clothes in layers. With a T-shirt, long-sleeved collared shirt, sweater, jacket, poncho, and brimmed hat, you can adjust your attire to match any weather condition.

The High Uintas vary in elevation from 8,000 to more than 13,000 feet. Most likely you will be camping somewhere between 10,000 and 10,800 feet. Going any higher puts you above timberline, where campsites are scarce and uncomfortable. At these elevations it is essential to know the effect elevation has on humans. Altitude sickness is dangerous. It can kill. If someone develops a hacking cough, spits up blood, or seems irrational or confused, then he or she may have altitude sickness. The only solution is to go down. If you have suffered from altitude sickness in the past, limit yourself to an altitude gain of 1,000 feet per day. Unfortunately, this may include elevation gained by your ride to the trailhead.

Bugs are a nuisance in the High Uintas backcountry. Mosquitoes can be terrible around moist meadows and ponds, so remember that when selecting a campsite. Bring your repellent or, as suggested earlier, wait until late in the season when the "skeeters" are gone. Deerflies and blackflies are pesky too. If bugs are bad, try camping in an open area where the wind can blow them down.

Giardia is a problem throughout the lakes, streams, and ponds of the Uintas. This tiny parasite can cause a severe flu-like disorder about two weeks after ingestion. Spring water is safe to drink without treatment, but all other water should be boiled, treated with iodine tablets, or filtered. If you choose to filter, be sure your filter will remove giardia. If you choose an iodine treatment, follow the instructions closely to ensure that giardia is destroyed.

Rules and regulations are minimal in the High Uintas, and if we all camp sensibly it will stay that way. No permits are needed. Registers exist at a few trailheads. Please use them. They are one of the few management tools that the forest service utilizes here. During dry spells, certain areas may have fire bans imposed. Check with the appropriate ranger district if the summer has been dry. In 2005 the forest service implemented a ban on campfires and wood stoves within ¼-mile of popular lakes within the High Uintas Wilderness Area. The ban was instigated due to a depletion of dead wood required for fires and a healthy ecosystem. Campers planning on fires will often attempt to unsuccessfully harvest live wood and kill remaining trees in the process.

Leave No Trace

Finally, let's talk about minimum-impact camping. There are a few rules that we all must follow to keep these mountains in their pristine state. This shouldn't sound like scolding or nagging, but rather a quick education in the basics of backcountry manners.

The national nonprofit Leave No Trace has provided a list of suggestions. Forest service officials encourage all visitors to wilderness areas to follow these simple but important tips.

PLAN AHEAD AND PREPARE

- Know the regulations and special concerns for the area you'll visit.
- Prepare for extreme weather, hazards, and emergencies.
- Schedule your trip to avoid times of high use.
- Visit in small groups when possible. Consider splitting larger groups into smaller groups.
- Repackage food to minimize waste.
- Use a map and compass to eliminate the use of marking paint, rock cairns, or flagging.

TRAVEL AND CAMP ON DURABLE SURFACES

- Durable surfaces include established trails and campsites, rock gravel, dry grasses, or snow.
- Protect riparian areas by camping at least 200 feet from lakes and streams.
- Good campsites are found, not made. Altering a site is not necessary.
- In popular areas: Concentrate use on existing trails and campsites; walk single file in the middle of the trail, even when wet or muddy; keep campsites small. Focus activity in areas where vegetation is absent.
- In pristine areas: Disperse use to prevent the creation of campsites and trails and avoid places where impacts are just beginning.

DISPOSE OF WASTE PROPERLY

- Pack it in, pack it out. Inspect your campsite and rest areas for trash or spilled foods. Pack out all trash, leftover food, and litter.
- Deposit solid human waste in shallow holes dug 6–8 inches deep at least 200 feet from water, camp, and trails. Cover and disguise the cathole when finished.
- Pack out toilet paper and hygiene products.
- To wash yourself or your dishes, carry water 200 feet away from streams or lakes and use small amounts of biodegradable soap. Scatter strained dishwater.

LEAVE WHAT YOU FIND

- Preserve the past: Examine, but do not touch, cultural or historic structures and artifacts.
- Leave rocks, plants, and other natural objects as you find them.
- Avoid introducing or transporting nonnative species.
- Do not build structures, furniture, or dig trenches.

MINIMIZE USE AND IMPACTS OF FIRE

- Campfires can cause lasting impacts to the backcountry. Use a lightweight stove for cooking, and enjoy a candle lantern for light.
- Where fires are permitted, use established fire rings, fire pans, or mound fires.
- Keep fires small and confined to a fire ring.
- Burn all wood and coals to ash, and extinguish campfires completely.

RESPECT WILDLIFE

- Observe wildlife from a distance. Do not follow or approach them.
- Never feed animals. Feeding wildlife damages their health, alters natural behaviors, and exposes them to predators and other dangers.
- Protect wildlife and your food by storing rations and trash securely.
- Control pets at all times, or leave them at home.
- Avoid encounters with wildlife during sensitive times: mating, nesting, raising young, or winter when they are experiencing physical stress to survive.

BE CONSIDERATE OF OTHER VISITORS

- Respect other visitors and protect the quality of their experience.
- Be courteous. Yield to other users on the trails.
- Step to the downhill side of the trail when encountering pack stock.
- Take breaks and camp away from trails and other visitors.
- Let nature's sounds prevail. Avoid loud voices and noises.

Fishing

Anglers should always review the fishing regulations. The trout limit when this book was published was four, but another four could be kept if the additional fish were all brook trout. There are some stream closures when salmon are spawning. A few lakes have restrictions on watercraft with motors.

Fishing is often superb in the High Uintas backcountry, but it is also unpredictable. A lake that provided fast fishing one year might be poor the next. Winterkill can take a toll, as does fishing pressure on popular lakes. If you're serious about catching lots of fish, then opt for an area with several lakes in the vicinity. If one doesn't produce, try another one nearby. Explore remote lakes, especially those that are off the trail or tough to reach. These are the real fishing gems of the High Uintas. You may find a lake where a pan-size cutthroat will spank your fly on every cast, or maybe you'll fool a chunky 2-pound-plus brook trout that has never before beheld an artificial lure.

Catch-and-release is commonly practiced by backcountry fishers and is often considered a good conservation ethic. Biologists now suggest that keeping some trout can help a fishery produce larger, healthier fish and prevent stunting (an overpopulation leads to fish not reaching their growth potential due to a lack of food). Releasing larger fish for other anglers to enjoy catching is a good thing to do, but don't hesitate to keep smaller fish for the frying pan.

Fishing nearly every lake in the Uintas was not something the first European travelers could do—at least not successfully. Colorado and Bonneville cutthroat trout were found in drainages of the Uintas below upstream obstacles like waterfalls when settlers started fishing, but the vast majority of the lakes and streams in the Uinta Mountains likely did not hold fish at that time, according to state fisheries biologists.

Early fisheries management of the Uintas involved introducing new trout and salmonoid species to the numerous lakes in an effort to provide food and opportunity for people visiting the range.

Brook trout made up the majority of the fish introduced into the Uintas. The aggressive trout are native to the eastern United States and Canada, but not in the West.

Through the years, the list of nonnative fish grew to include rainbow trout, Yellowstone cutthroat trout, kokanee salmon, brown trout, golden trout, arctic grayling, and two hybrid trout (tiger, a sterile mix between a brook and a brown trout, and splake, a mix between a brook and a lake trout).

Colorado and Bonneville cutthroat felt the squeeze and started to become more and more isolated. In more recent years biologists have turned their attention back to native species but are not giving up on the other fish.

Brook trout will likely always have a place in the Uintas. Rainbows and tiger trout will continue to be stocked in high-pressure put-and-take areas in the most easily accessed areas.

The first trout introduced into previously fish-free lakes of the Uintas arrived in milk cans carried into the backcountry on horseback. The state started using small planes to aerial stock the lakes in the mid-1950s. Horses are still used by biologists doing fish surveys in the backcountry. A plane can stock seven lakes on one trip and a total of forty to sixty lakes in a single day, depending on weather conditions. Aerial stocking is done in the spring. The fish—roughly 2,000 per drop—average 2½ to 3 inches. Larger fish are less likely to survive the free fall.

Approximately 150 Uinta Mountain backcountry lakes are stocked by aircraft each year. One key to fishing success, particularly those hoping to land larger fish, is to check the Division of Wildlife Resources fish stocking plans on the website wildlife .utah.gov. Fishing lakes that have just been stocked will not be as productive as hitting a water that was stocked three or four years previously.

Small flies are the most effective lure in these alpine lakes. That makes sense, since tiny bugs make up more than 80 percent of their diet. Give them what they are used to.

Moose, like this big bull, can be found throughout the range. Make sure to give them space, as they can be dangerous.
Photo provided by the Utah Division of Wildlife Resources

Good sizes are #18 and #16. Successful patterns include Renegade, Adams, black gnat, and an olive scud. Small spinners (sizes 0–2) are also effective, particularly on brook trout in deeper lakes. Streams are best fished with a flashy, lightweight spinner or a fly.

Wildlife

Fish are, of course, not the only wildlife that find a home in the Uintas.

Mule deer and elk are found scattered throughout the entire range and are the dominant big game species found on the Uinta Mountains. Visitors to the Uintas also commonly see mountain goats and moose. Bighorn sheep are often spotted on the North Slope of the range.

Mountain lion and black bears, Utah's two largest predators, also frequent the Uintas. They are rarely seen, but the presence of bears—and many other creatures that might find human food too tempting to resist—are a good reason to keep a bear-safe camp both in the backcountry and at developed campgrounds.

Numerous small mammals like pika, marten, and snowshoe hare are often sighted during excursions. Raptors, owls, and songbirds are also common in the Uintas. Attesting to the wildness of the Uintas, wolves and wolverines have been documented with sightings and trail camera photos.

Hunting is a popular activity in the Uintas, and hikers can expect to see hunters pursuing game from mid-August into November.

How to Use This Book

The High Uinta Mountains offer a variety of fishing and hiking opportunities, from brief day outings to extended overnight trips. This guidebook provides information on one hundred hikes to streams, ponds, and lakes in this wilderness area.

Each hike includes a short introduction to the area as well as the pertinent information you will need for a visit, such as hike distance, trail usage, nearest town, and trail contacts.

The difficulty rating is based on the average hiker's ability and may vary depending on a number of factors, including your physical condition and state of mind, the amount of gear you are carrying, and the weather conditions.

Approximate hiking times are based on the average hiker. Most hiking times listed are conservative estimates; you may make a trip in less time. It's best to plan your outing based on how long the hike will take rather than on the distance.

Waterfall near the east portal of the Duchesne Tunnel

Also included are detailed directions to the start of each hike, followed by an in-depth hike description that highlights key points along the route, campsites, and fishing opportunities.

Elevation Profiles

The elevation profiles show the general ups and downs of the route. You can see, at a glance, the general terrain of the route; however, the graphs are compressed (squeezed) to fit onto the page, so the actual slopes you will hike will not be as steep as the lines on the graphs (it may just feel that way). Also, many short dips and climbs are too small to show up on the graphs.

Maps

The maps in this book use elevation tints, called hypsometry, to portray relief. Each gray tone represents a range of equal elevation, as shown in the scale key with the map. These maps will give you a good idea of elevation gain and loss. The darker tones are lower elevations and the lighter grays are higher elevations. The lighter the tone, the higher the elevation. Narrow bands of different gray tones spaced closely together indicate steep terrain, whereas wider bands indicate areas of more gradual slope.

Map Legend

══150══	State Highway
──037──	Primary Road
──────	Other Road
══════	Unpaved Road
= = = = =	Unimproved Road
▰▰▰▰▰	Featured Unimproved Road
▬▬▬▬▬	Featured Trail
- - - - - -	Trail
··············	Faint Trail
～〰	River/Stream
＼ ～ ～	Intermittent Stream
⬤	Body of Water
≡≡≡	Wetland
▨▨▨	National Forest Boundary
─··─··─	State Boundary
)(	Bridge
⚠	Campground
🎴	Overlook
)(	Pass/Gap
▲	Peak/Spot Elevation
🏠	Ranger Station
⚲	Spring
58▷	Trail Locator
36	Trailhead
⊨═══⊣	Tunnel

South Slope

The South Slope is characterized by large, steep drainages that lead to high meadows above timberline. More than two-thirds of the High Uintas lie on the South Slope, so it's only natural that the majority of the lakes are on this side as well. The hikes can be long, if that's what you are looking for. There are many routes that can be combined to make up a 50-mile excursion.

X–86 of the Three Lakes

1 Big Elk Lake

You can pack extra gear into here. The hike is just a little over a mile one way, so bring the lawn chairs and float tube. There is a steep incline just before the dam, but otherwise it's an easy hike.

Start: Norway Flats
Distance: 2.2 miles out and back
Destination elevation: 10,020 feet
Approximate hiking time: 2 hours
Difficulty: Easy—one steep section
Usage: Heavy
Nearest town: Kamas, Utah
Drainage: Provo River

Maps: USGS Erickson Basin; USDA Forest Service High Uintas Wilderness; Trails Illustrated High Uintas Wilderness
Trail contacts: Wasatch National Forest, Forest Supervisor, 8226 Federal Building, 125 South State St., Salt Lake City, UT 84111; Kamas Ranger District, 50 East Center St., Kamas, UT 84036, (435) 783-4338

Finding the trailhead: The hardest part about this trek is finding the right road. From Kamas, go 15 miles west on Highway 150 to FR 035 and turn left. This road climbs onto Norway Flats. Norway Flats Road starts innocently enough as it turns off Highway 150, but it forks several times where there are no markers and the maps don't show. Stay with the road that shows the most wear until you are about 6 miles from Highway 150; turn right (east). If you stay on the road most traveled (to the left), you will end up at a beaver pond just below Hourglass Lake. This is the wrong starting place. Go back to the road that turned east and follow it down to the trailhead. You may need a four-wheel-drive vehicle to cover the last mile to the trailhead.

The Hike

From the end of Norway Flats Road, Little Elk Lake is about 0.3 mile to the west of the trail. Continue another 0.8 mile to a trail junction and Big Elk Lake.

At Big Elk Lake, fishing is generally good for stocked brook and cutthroat trout. A raft or canoe would be nice to escape the crowds and the bugs, but you can do just fine from shore. Fish with a small fly (#16) during the morning and evening, and you should have little trouble catching enough for a hearty meal.

Campsites are available on the south and east sides of this deep reservoir. There are no springs around, so plan on purifying your drinking water. Big Elk receives heavy pressure, especially on weekends. If you visit during the week, there might not be anybody else there. Pack out your litter and help keep Big Elk a clean and fun place to explore.

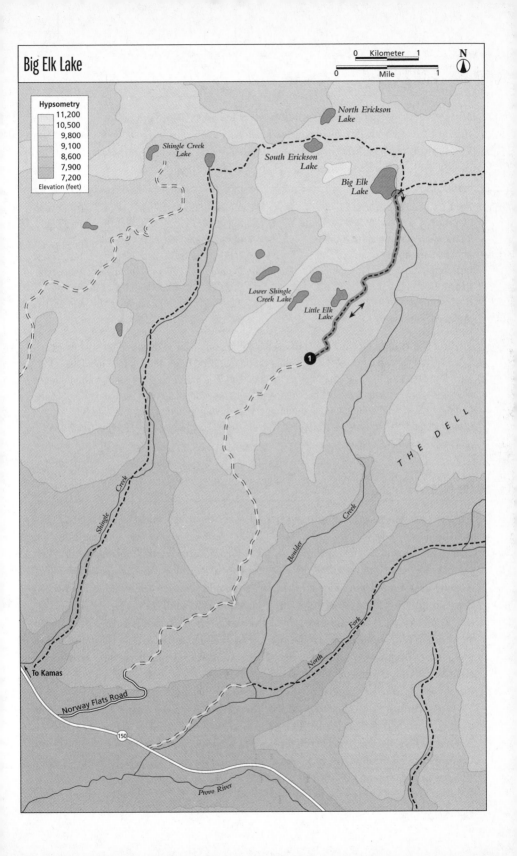

Big Elk Lake

Hypsometry

11,200
10,500
9,800
9,100
8,600
7,900
7,200

Elevation (feet)

0   Kilometer   1

0   Mile   1

N

North Erickson
Lake

Shingle Creek
Lake

South Erickson
Lake

Big Elk
Lake

Lower Shingle
Creek Lake

Little Elk
Lake

1

THE DELL

Shingle Creek

Boulder Creek

North Fork

To Kamas

Norway Flats Road

150

Provo River

2 Long Pond

Long Pond is just that—a long pond. It is immediately below the outlet of Long Lake. It is not a long hike, nor is there a long story to tell about why we've included Long Pond in this book. While the lake receives heavy usage, Long Pond is largely ignored, even though it has better fishing and more solitude than the lake.

Start: Crystal Lake trailhead
Distance: 4.0 miles out and back
Destination elevation: 10,100 feet
Approximate hiking time: 2.5 hours
Difficulty: Easy
Usage: Moderate
Nearest town: Kamas, Utah
Drainage: Provo River

Maps: USGS Mirror Lake; USDA Forest Service High Uintas Wilderness; Trails Illustrated High Uintas Wilderness
Trail contacts: Wasatch National Forest, Forest Supervisor, 8226 Federal Building, 125 South State St., Salt Lake City, UT 84111; Kamas Ranger District, 50 East Center St., Kamas, UT 84036, (435) 783-4338

Finding the trailhead: From Kamas, take the Mirror Lake Highway (Highway 150) 27 miles to Trial Lake Campground. Exit left (west) onto a paved road, and travel about a mile to a fork in the road. Turn right (north) for another mile to the trailhead. This is a popular trailhead, with room for fifty-seven vehicles and nice toilet facilities. Water and other amenities can be found at Trial Lake Campground. Crystal Lake trailhead is the main takeoff point to many lakes only 1 to 5 miles away, including Wall, Ibantik, Meadow, Cliff, Watson, Clyde, Long, Island, Big Elk, Fire, Duck, Weir, and the breathtaking Lovenia.

The Hike

This place is fun to fish. Long Pond has a variety of trout habitat to test your angling skills. Shallows, pools, rocks, and a few deadfalls combine to give you an array of fishing challenges. Expect the unexpected when exploring Long Pond. The trout you'll likely catch offer variety too. Count on a mixed bag of cutthroat and brook trout, which migrate from Long Lake. Since it has no water flow in winter, Long Pond is not stocked. But enough trout from Long Lake sneak into the pond to make fishing exciting.

From Crystal Lake trailhead, go 0.1 mile to a trail junction. This trail goes by the east end of Washington Lake to the turnoff of Trial Lake Road. Stay right and follow the Smith Morehouse Trail for 1.5 miles to another trail junction. The trail to the right drops down into the Middle Fork of the Weber River. Stay left for 0.3 mile to Long Lake. Cross the creek and continue another 0.1 mile to Long Pond.

Good campsites can be found along Long Pond. As noted earlier, you'll see fewer visitors here than at Long Lake. This is a good spot to camp for a small group (four or fewer). Usually it is a peaceful, serene place, sitting just down the hill from Long Lake—out of sight and out of earshot from the crowds at the lake. It is not a good area for horses to stop, so you can avoid them too.

Long Pond; Island Lake; Cliff Lake; Divide Lakes; Twin Lakes

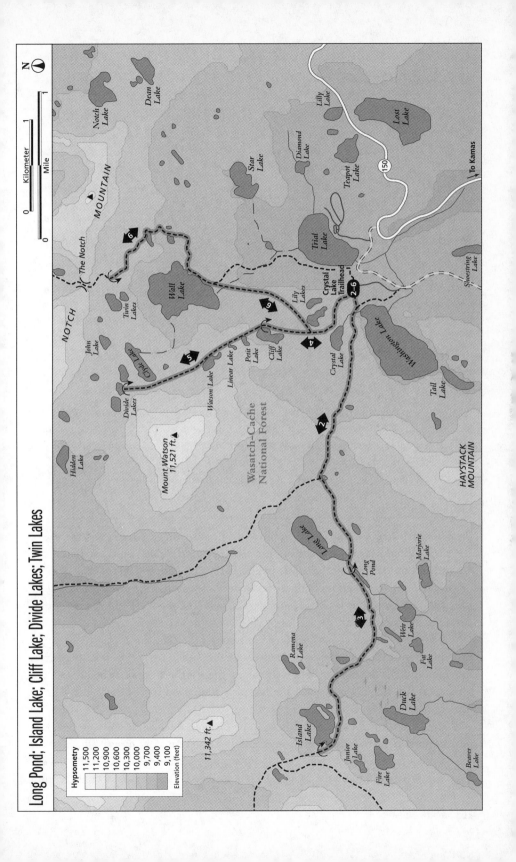

3 Island Lake

"Which Island Lake?" you may ask. Just as there are many Hidden Lakes and Lost Lakes, it seems that every other drainage has an Island Lake. This one sits high on the Provo River Drainage and can be reached fairly easily. The first mile is steep, and the last 0.5 mile is steep, but sandwiched between these sections is some easy and level hiking. The trail is quite popular among overnighters, so expect to see a few people, especially on weekends.

See map on page 15.
Start: Crystal Lake trailhead
Distance: 7.0 miles out and back
Destination elevation: 10,140 feet
Approximate hiking time: 4.5 hours
Difficulty: Moderate—some steep sections
Usage: Moderate
Nearest town: Kamas, Utah
Drainage: Provo River

Maps: USGS Erickson Basin; USDA Forest Service High Uintas Wilderness; Trails Illustrated High Uintas Wilderness
Trail contacts: Wasatch National Forest, Forest Supervisor, 8226 Federal Building, 125 South State St., Salt Lake City, UT 84111; Kamas Ranger District, 50 East Center St., Kamas, UT 84036, (435) 783-4338

Finding the trailhead: From Kamas, take the Mirror Lake Highway (Highway 150) 27 miles to Trial Lake Campground. Exit left (west) onto a paved road, and travel about a mile to a fork in the road. Then turn right (north) for another mile to the trailhead. This is a popular trailhead, with room for fifty-seven vehicles and nice toilet facilities. Water and other amenities can be found at Trial Lake Campground.

The Hike

From Crystal Lake trailhead, go 0.1 mile to a trail junction. This trail goes by the east end of Washington Lake to the turnoff of Trial Lake Road. Stay right and follow the Smith Morehouse Trail for 1.5 miles to another trail junction. The trail to the right drops down into the Middle Fork of the Weber River. Stay left for 0.3 mile to Long Lake. Cross the creek and continue another 0.1 mile to Long Pond. Continue another 1.5 miles to Island Lake.

There are sheltered campsites on the east side of the lake, and spring water might be available near the northeast corner. Island Lake is picturesque, with its high cliffs dropping straight down into deep water along the northern shore. Whether you are looking at these cliffs from across the lake or standing on top of them, you'll want your camera handy.

Large, wary cutthroat make fishing unpredictable. These fish are well fed by a healthy population of freshwater shrimp, and they don't hit a dry fly as readily as trout do on other backcountry lakes. Try a pink shrimp imitation. You will only need a couple of these trout to fill the frying pan. If you are looking for faster fishing, venture

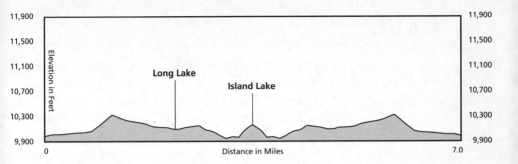

over the hill about 0.25 mile to Junior Lake. This tiny lake is often overlooked by anglers and usually provides very good fishing for smaller trout. Keep going a little farther and you'll descend to Fire Lake, where fishing can be fast at times. The lake doesn't get too much pressure, since it is situated in steep, rocky terrain; camping opportunities are virtually nonexistent. Other good fishing lakes in the immediate area are Duck and Beaver Lakes.

Back at Island Lake, enjoy a peaceful sunset, or stand atop the cliffs and peer into the depths of the lake for cruising trout. This lake will not satisfy true "solitude seekers," but it is a quick getaway.

4 Cliff Lake

You couldn't ask for a prettier setting. The stage is set with picture-perfect campsites that overlook a small lake dimpled by feeding fish. A stately cliff serves as a backdrop. Grassy campsites are just off the trail on the eastern shore, providing an ideal place to watch the sunset and reflect on the finer things of life. The whole scene mirrors off the clear water.

See map on page 15.
Start: Crystal Lake trailhead
Distance: 1.0 mile out and back
Destination elevation: 10,230 feet
Approximate hiking time: 1 hour
Difficulty: Easy
Usage: Heavy
Nearest town: Kamas, Utah
Drainage: Provo River

Maps: USGS Mirror Lake; USDA Forest Service High Uintas Wilderness; Trails Illustrated High Uintas Wilderness
Trail contacts: Wasatch National Forest, Forest Supervisor, 8226 Federal Building, 125 South State St., Salt Lake City, UT 84111; Kamas Ranger District, 50 East Center St., Kamas, UT 84036, (435) 783-4338

Finding the trailhead: From Kamas, take the Mirror Lake Highway (Highway 150) 27 miles to Trial Lake Campground. Exit left (west) onto a paved road, and travel about a mile to a fork in the road. Then turn right (north) for another mile to the trailhead. This is a popular trailhead, with room for fifty-seven vehicles and nice toilet facilities. Water and other amenities can be found at Trial Lake Campground.

The Hike

Cliff Lake is close enough to the trailhead that you should have plenty of time to watch the sunset and still make it back to the car before dark. It's also a great place to try out some new gear before taking on a more serious hike.

From Crystal Lake trailhead, go past the western Lily Lake 0.1 mile to a trail junction. The trail to the right goes to Wall Lake and the Notch. Stay left and go 0.4 mile to Cliff Lake.

Expect to see a fair amount of foot traffic pass this lake. Anglers and day hikers have to pass by to get to the many lakes above. Cliff Lake is obviously not for loners, but if you're the friendly type and enjoy a quaint little spot with a gorgeous view, then this may be for you.

A small population of cutthroat trout will keep you company. However, the fishing is likely to be only fair due to the easy access and the wary nature of these trout. Better fishing can be found by continuing up the trail another mile to Clyde Lake. Most hikers don't stop at Cliff Lake very long, but almost all remember the pleasant scenery. Try this trail on a weekday, and you might have it all to yourself.

5 Divide Lakes

Here's a campout to take the kids on. You'll see plenty of small lakes along the way, and the trail has a good mix of uphill and level slopes. Fairly easy to find, the trail is well marked except for the section just past Watson Lake. It looks like an avalanche wiped out a couple hundred yards of trail; just head due north to Clyde Lake, and you will easily pick up the trail again.

See map on page 15.
Start: Crystal Lake trailhead
Distance: 5.0 miles out and back
Destination elevation: 10,460 feet
Approximate hiking time: 3 hours
Difficulty: Moderate—some steep sections
Usage: Moderate
Nearest town: Kamas, Utah
Drainage: Provo River

Maps: USGS Mirror Lake; USDA Forest Service High Uintas Wilderness; Trails Illustrated High Uintas Wilderness
Trail contacts: Wasatch National Forest, Forest Supervisor, 8226 Federal Building, 125 South State St., Salt Lake City, UT 84111; Kamas Ranger District, 50 East Center St., Kamas, UT 84036, (435) 783-4338

Finding the trailhead: From Kamas, take the Mirror Lake Highway (Highway 150) 27 miles to Trial Lake Campground. Exit left (west) onto a paved road, and travel about a mile to a fork in the road. Then turn right (north) for another mile to the trailhead. This is a popular trailhead, with room for fifty-seven vehicles and nice toilet facilities. Water and other amenities can be found at Trial Lake Campground.

The Hike

This hike is a great overnighter for small groups—or a wonderful escape if you are camped at Trial Lake and want to get away from camp for a spell. You couldn't ask for a better nature trail; it offers a wide variety of scenery, complete with fishing holes.

From Crystal Lake trailhead, go past the western Lily Lake 0.1 mile to a trail junction. The trail to the right goes to Wall Lake and the Notch. Stay left and walk past Cliff, Petit, Linear, and Watson Lakes, all west of the trail. At about 2.1 miles from the trail junction, you will pass Clyde Lake on the right and Mount Watson on the left. It's another 0.3 mile to the Divide Lakes.

The best places to camp are at the west end of Divide Lake 2 and between Divide Lake 1 and Divide Lake 2. Choose the latter site if the weather looks to be fair; otherwise seek the safety of the pines at Divide Lake 2. Although these lakes are less than 100 yards apart, Divide Lake 1 is on the Provo River Drainage, and Divide Lake 2 is on the Weber River Drainage. There is a large rock between the two lakes—when rain falls on the rock, half the water heads toward the Provo River and half toward the Weber.

Several springs are located on the west end of Divide Lake 2. They are conveniently close to camp, and ice cold. Small lakes abound, and there is plenty to do and see without wandering too far. Nearby Booker Lake offers fair fishing, but you'll probably do better right at Divide Lake 1, which has a nice population of smallish brook trout. For best results, try the deeper southwest corner of the lake with a tiny fly.

If you're after bigger fish, try Little Hidden Lake on the Weber Drainage. You'll want a topographical map and a compass to find it. There is no trail, but stay close to the mountain to the east, and head north about half a mile. This lake has brookies ranging from half a pound to well over a pound. A #16 Renegade fly, cast in the northwest end of the lake, should put a few nicer trout in the creel. Be quiet here—the fish have learned to disappear when noisy visitors appear. As long as you're quiet, they'll keep biting. There is spring water to the northeast if you need to refill your canteen.

From Divide Lakes notice "The Notch" in the mountains to the northeast. This well-known pass is a thing of beauty, especially when you're on it. From the top of Notch Pass is a spectacular view right down into Lovenia Lake. It's worth the mile trip over; or you could go there on your way back to the trailhead. The Notch Pass Trail returns to Crystal Lake trailhead too.

Upper Twin Lake

6 Twin Lakes

Most people proceed unknowingly right past these lakes. It seems everyone makes the extra effort to hike over Notch Pass to see the beautiful scenery that Ibantic Lake offers. And rightly so. From Notch Pass, the country is amazing. On the other hand, Twin Lakes may make a good base camp that gives you the serenity no other lakes in this area can provide. Don't get us wrong; Twin Lakes get their fair share of attention, but they are often overlooked.

See map on page 15.
Start: Crystal Lake trailhead
Distance: 4.6 miles out and back
Destination elevation: 10,410 feet
Approximate hiking time: 3 hours
Difficulty: Easy—one steep section
Usage: Moderate
Nearest town: Kamas, Utah
Drainage: Provo River

Maps: USGS Mirror Lake; USDA Forest Service High Uintas Wilderness; Trails Illustrated High Uintas Wilderness
Trail contacts: Wasatch National Forest, Forest Supervisor, 8226 Federal Building, 125 South State St., Salt Lake City, UT 84111; Kamas Ranger District, 50 East Center St., Kamas, UT 84036, (435) 783-4338

Finding the trailhead: From Kamas, take the Mirror Lake Highway (Highway 150) 27 miles to Trial Lake Campground. Exit left (west) onto a paved road, and travel about a mile to a fork in the road. Then turn right (north) for another mile to the trailhead. This is a popular trailhead, with room for fifty-seven vehicles and nice toilet facilities. Water and other amenities can be found at Trial Lake Campground.

The Hike

It's rather easy to find Twin Lakes. Even though these lakes lie off the beaten path, rock piles are displayed to show the way. Begin your journey at the Crystal Lake trailhead. Follow the trail 1.0 mile to Wall Lake. Here the trail takes off to the east, then up some steep rocky switchbacks. Just past the top of all the switchbacks, rock cairns mark the turnoff. A faint trail then makes its way west to Lower Twin Lake.

Twin Lakes offer a number of amenities. The vista is pretty and only a short distance from the trailhead. Fishing is good for 9- to 15-inch brook trout, and other exciting excursions lie just beyond the immediate. Spring water is only found in the early summer months, and camping areas are only fair due to rocky terrain. However, there is one excellent campsite near the northwest end of Upper Twin. This site sits on a bench overlooking the lakes.

7 Castle Lake

This hike is for the roadside camper looking for a short diversion. Castle Lake is less than half a mile west of Butterfly Lake. Butterfly Lake has excellent campground facilities, as well as a parking area for day-use anglers. There is no trail to Castle Lake, but just head due west, stay close to the base of the cliffs, and you can't miss it. There are several small ponds on the way. Don't mistake one of them for Castle Lake.

Start: Butterfly Lake
Distance: 0.8 mile out and back
Destination elevation: 10,300 feet
Approximate hiking time: 1 hour
Difficulty: Moderate—cross-country hiking
Usage: Moderate
Nearest town: Kamas, Utah
Drainage: Duchesne River

Maps: USGS Hayden Peak; USDA Forest Service High Uintas Wilderness; Trails Illustrated High Uintas Wilderness
Trail contacts: Wasatch National Forest, Forest Supervisor, 8226 Federal Building, 125 South State St., Salt Lake City, UT 84111; Kamas Ranger District, 50 East Center St., Kamas, UT 84036, (435) 783-4338

Finding the trailhead: Start at Butterfly Lake. From Kamas, take the Mirror Lake Highway (Highway 150) about 33 miles. The trailhead is on the west side of the road.

The Hike

Cliffs parallel Castle Lake just beyond its northern shore. This is a quiet little place (1 acre) that can be a welcome reprieve from the public campground scene. A round-trip from Butterfly Lake to beautiful Castle Lake makes a wonderful evening stroll that should only take an hour, unless you stop to sit awhile or try the fishing. There is no trail to Castle Lake from Butterfly Lake, but it's easy to reach by going west from the inlet of Butterfly Lake near the campground.

Open shorelines make casting easy, but also make for wary trout; Castle Lake has both. Cutthroat trout are the fish of the day at Castle. This is a good second option if the shores at Butterfly are crowded, which is usually the case. There are a few moist areas around the lake, so mosquitoes can be a nuisance. Give yourself a good dose of insect repellent, and you'll breathe easier while enjoying this secluded spot. It seems farther away than it is from the crowded campgrounds and the highway.

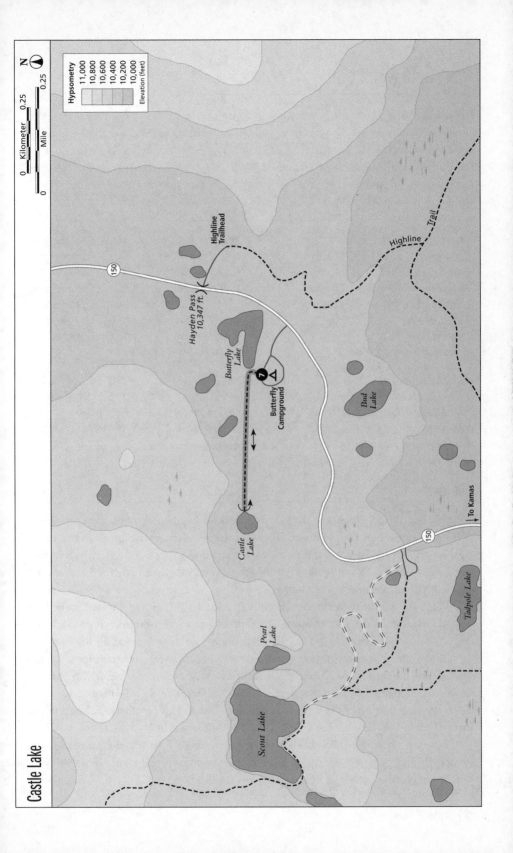

Castle Lake

Hayden Pass
10,347 ft.

Highline
Trailhead

150

Butterfly
Lake

7

Butterfly
Campground

Castle
Lake

Highline   Trail

Bud
Lake

Pearl
Lake

Scout Lake

150

To Kamas

Tadpole Lake

N

0   Kilometer   0.25

0   Mile   0.25

Hypsometry
11,000
10,800
10,600
10,400
10,200
10,000
Elevation (feet)

8 Bald Mountain

Bald Mountain—the best time investment you can make in the High Uintas. If you only have a few hours to spend and want to experience some grand vistas, then this is the place. Just 2.5 miles of steep hiking puts you atop this well-known peak, where you'll have a bird's-eye view of four of Utah's major watersheds. Scan the cliffs and debris fields of Bald Mountain for moving white spots; there is a high chance of spotting mountain goats.

Start: Bald Mountain trailhead
Distance: 5.0 miles out and back
Destination elevation: 11,943 feet
Approximate hiking time: 3.5 hours
Difficulty: Moderate—steady climbing
Usage: Heavy
Nearest town: Kamas, Utah
Drainage: Duchesne River

Maps: USGS Mirror Lake; USDA Forest Service High Uintas Wilderness; Trails Illustrated High Uintas Wilderness
Trail contacts: Wasatch National Forest, Forest Supervisor, 8226 Federal Building, 125 South State St., Salt Lake City, UT 84111; Kamas Ranger District, 50 East Center St., Kamas, UT 84036, (435) 783-4338

Finding the trailhead: From Kamas, take the Mirror Lake Highway (Highway 150) 30 miles to Bald Mountain overlook. About 0.5 mile north of the overlook is the left turn to Bald Mountain. Bald Mountain has space for twenty-five cars and offers picnic tables and toilets. No water is available. Bald Mountain trailhead is heavily used by hikers making the 2.5-mile trek to the top of Bald Mountain, where you can peer into four major drainages.

The Hike

The Weber, Provo, Duchesne, and Bear Rivers all begin near here. Looking to the west, you can spot a couple dozen lakes that speckle the upper regions of the Provo and Weber Rivers. Turn around to the east, and enjoy a spectacular view of the Mirror Lake Highway winding its way through heavy timber, past Mirror Lake, and on toward Mount Agassiz and Hayden Peak.

This hike begins at the well-marked Bald Mountain trailhead, located at the base of Bald Mountain. You start climbing immediately and will soon find yourself traversing a series of switchbacks on the western slope. The view is great all the way, and it somehow manages to improve with every step. Listen for and then look for the unique small mammals known as pikas along the way. Near the summit, the trail follows a thin ridge with steep drops off either side. There's really no danger if you stick with the trail, but a person with acrophobia might feel uncomfortable. Then take a natural rock stairway to what feels like the top of the world.

Take your time on this hike. It is steep. Allow about four hours for a round-trip, which should give you plenty of time at the top to appreciate the views in every direction. Heed a couple of safety reminders on this hike:

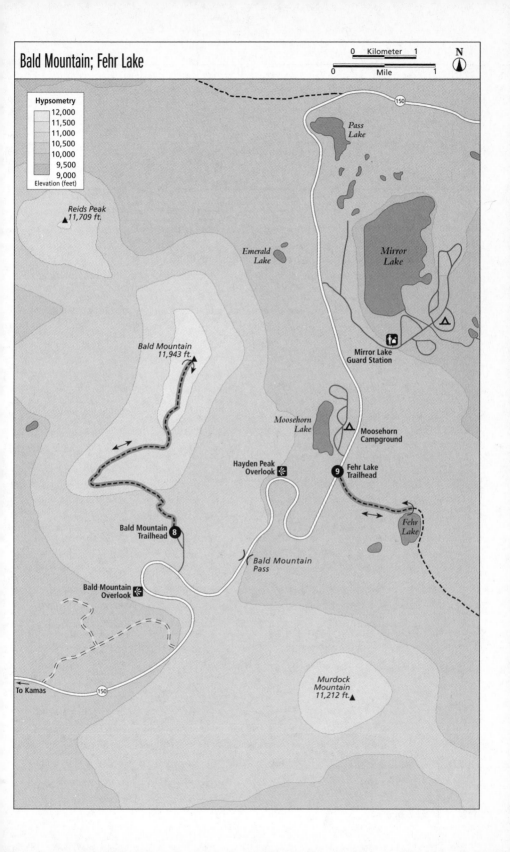

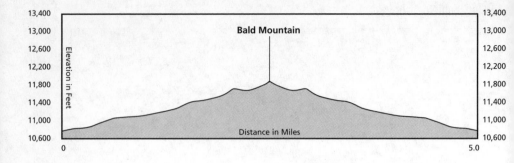

1. Stay off Bald Mountain when lightning is possible.
2. Don't get too close to the cliff edges on the east side—they can break away.

Follow these rules and your name won't be added to Bald Mountain's casualty list. OK, now don't let us scare you away. This hike is time well spent.

9 Fehr Lake

Even small kids can enjoy this hike. You don't have to be in good shape either. This is a mini-hike. If you only have a couple of hours to spend, you could take a leisurely stroll down to Fehr Lake, fish a bit, and still make it back in time for lunch.

See map on page 25.
Start: Fehr Lake trailhead
Distance: 0.6 mile out and back
Destination elevation: 10,260 feet
Approximate hiking time: 1 hour
Difficulty: Easy
Usage: Heavy
Nearest town: Kamas, Utah
Drainage: Duchesne River

Maps: USGS Mirror Lake; USDA Forest Service High Uintas Wilderness; Trails Illustrated High Uintas Wilderness
Trail contacts: Wasatch National Forest, Forest Supervisor, 8226 Federal Building, 125 South State St., Salt Lake City, UT 84111; Kamas Ranger District, 50 East Center St., Kamas, UT 84036, (435) 783-4338

Finding the trailhead: From Kamas, take the Mirror Lake Highway (Highway 150) 31 miles to the trailhead parking lot. If you pass Moosehorn Lake or Mirror Lake, you've gone a little too far.

The Hike

The only thing difficult about this hike is spotting the trailhead. There is a nice large sign indicating where to begin the trail, but some people drive right past it while looking for a place to park. Look for the trailhead immediately after turning off Highway 150. When you spot it, turn left to the parking area.

The hike to Fehr is gentle and provides a variety of scenery in its short distance. You'll pass through cool groves of pines and mountain meadows and stroll past a small waterfall or two. It's a great place to get away from busy campgrounds. You'll feel more removed than you really are. Notice the quiet. Fehr is a natural lake (6 acres) in a picture-book setting. It is surrounded on three sides by pines and bounded by a meadow on the south. Beyond the meadow are more pines, backed by a stately mountain.

Fishing at Fehr is only fair, which is probably as good as you'll find at any of the roadside lakes. But you won't be crowded here. Move around and try various lures and flies, or just sit on the bank and drown a worm. The odds are you will catch a few fat brook trout—maybe even a nap. Here's a great little body of water to portage a canoe into and then try fishing the middle of the lake, where nobody ever does.

The trail continues past Fehr Lake, going down to Shepard, Maba, Hoover, and Marshall Lakes. People using this trail are just out for a hike, because you could drive to these lakes on the Murdock Basin Road. Try it for a relaxing day hike. It may seem a little steep on the return trip though.

10 Packard and Wyman Lakes

Packard Lake makes a great day hike for kids and adults alike. Most people begin their adventure from Mirror Lake rather than the Highline trailhead, which is about 1 mile shorter, because better accommodations are found at Mirror Lake.

Start: Highline trailhead
Distance: 7.0 miles out and back
Destination elevation: 9,980 feet
Approximate hiking time: 4 hours
Difficulty: Easy to moderate—some steep sections
Usage: Moderate
Nearest town: Kamas, Utah
Drainage: Duchesne River

Maps: USGS Hayden Peak; USDA Forest Service High Uintas Wilderness; Trails Illustrated High Uintas Wilderness
Trail contacts: Wasatch National Forest, Forest Supervisor, 8226 Federal Building, 125 South State St., Salt Lake City, UT 84111; Kamas Ranger District, 50 East Center St., Kamas, UT 84036, (435) 783-4338

Finding the trailhead: The Highline is the most popular trailhead of the High Uintas. From Kamas, take the Mirror Lake Highway (Highway 150) 34 miles to a large sign on the east side of the road that says "Highline Trail." You can't get lost finding this one.

This trailhead has a listed capacity of twenty-four vehicles, but there are often considerably more parked here on busy weekends. The overcrowded trailhead is equipped with toilets, water, stock ramp, and nearby campsites. This is the main takeoff point for popular treks ranging from 5 to 50 miles in length.

The Hike

Wyman Lake features heavy timber and pretty lily pads clinging to the shore. Campsites are plentiful, but Wyman and Packard Lakes are located in a fire restriction area; fuel wood may not be burned. Bring a stove if you want to cook any meals. Wyman receives heavy camping and angling use and frequently experiences winterkill, which usually means only fair fishing. This lake is stocked yearly.

From the Highline trailhead, the trail descends about 300 feet to the Mirror Lake Trail junction. Access from Mirror Lake begins near the east side of the lake at the north end of the campgrounds. The trail makes its way 2 miles northeast, then connects with the Highline Trail. From this junction, follow the Highline Trail 2 miles southeast to a posted sign on the eastern top of a ravine. Follow the Packard Lake trail 1 mile south down a steep and rocky slope, past Wilder Lake, then up and down a hill to Wyman Lake. Packard Lake is another 0.25 mile southeast of Wyman Lake.

Packard is a pretty lake located on a high ledge with a view of the East Fork of the Duchesne River Drainage. Good campsites are available, but horse pasture and spring water are limited. This lake receives heavy fishing pressure, but a good supply of brook

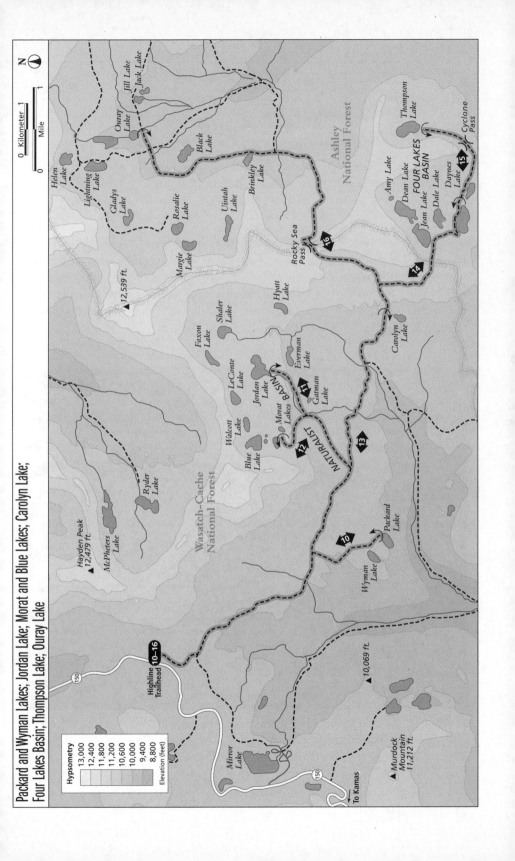

Packard and Wyman Lakes; Jordan Lake; Morat and Blue Lakes; Carolyn Lake; Four Lakes Basin; Thompson Lake; Ouray Lake

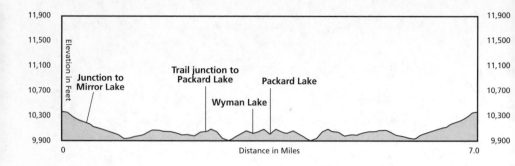

trout inhabits the lake. All lakes in this area receive heavy usage and are prone to litter. Help keep them clean.

If there's too much company at Packard and Wyman Lakes, try going back to Wilder Lake. Surrounded by heavy timber, this small lake has nice camping, horse pasture, and willing brook trout. Heck, maybe you should just stop here to begin with and make camp.

Packard Lake is a popular Uinta Mountains destination accessed from either the Highline trailhead or Mirror Lake.

PHOTO BY MATT MCKELL/UTAH DIVISION OF WILDLIFE RESOURCES

11 Jordan Lake

Considering the heavy usage thrown upon this area, Naturalist Basin remains remarkably clean. Thoughtful hikers and the forest service deserve kudos for keeping this beautiful wilderness free of debris and litter. To ensure that this mountain range remains unscarred, fire restrictions are in effect throughout Naturalist Basin.

See map on page 29.
Start: Highline trailhead
Distance: 13.0 miles out and back
Destination elevation: 10,660 feet
Approximate hiking time: 8 hours
Difficulty: Moderate—some steep sections
Usage: Heavy
Nearest town: Kamas, Utah
Drainage: Duchesne River

Maps: USGS Hayden Peak; USDA Forest Service High Uintas Wilderness; Trails Illustrated High Uintas Wilderness
Trail contacts: Wasatch National Forest, Forest Supervisor, 8226 Federal Building, 125 South State St., Salt Lake City, UT 84111; Kamas Ranger District, 50 East Center St., Kamas, UT 84036, (435) 783-4338

Finding the trailhead: The Highline is the most popular trailhead of the High Uintas. From Kamas, take the Mirror Lake Highway (Highway 150) 34 miles to a large sign on the east side of the road that says "Highline Trail." You can't get lost finding this one.

This trailhead has a listed capacity of twenty-four vehicles, but there are often considerably more parked here on busy weekends. The overcrowded trailhead is equipped with toilets, water, stock ramp, and nearby campsites. This is the main takeoff point for popular treks ranging from 5 to 50 miles in length.

The Hike

In scenic timbered terrain, a steep boulder slope, pickled with pine trees on the northwest side, identifies Jordan Lake. Excellent posted campsites are located west of the lake. Other camping areas can be found along the east side of the outlet. This wide outlet is composed of several small ponds connected by a meandering stream. A small source of spring water can be found trickling into the northwest side of the lake. Be prepared though. During dry years, the lake will be the only water source.

A large population of brook trout inhabits the outlet, making fly fishing a pleasure. The lake is stocked regularly. Angling can be kind of slow until dusk. Then they're jumping like popcorn.

The only lakes that have campsites in the Jordan Lake vicinity are Jordan, Hyatt, and Everman. Shaler Lake can be found on the Naturalist Basin Trail 0.75 mile northeast of Jordan Lake. Hyatt is located on a scenic rocky shelf 0.5 mile east of Everman. Everman is in a small meadow 0.75 mile east of the Blue-Jordan Trail junction and just 200 yards east of the Naturalist Basin Trail. LeConte is situated above timberline

Jordan Lake is a good place to camp while exploring the Naturalist Basin.
PHOTO BY MATT MCKELL/UTAH DIVISION OF WILDLIFE RESOURCES

0.5 mile northwest of Jordan, over steep and rocky terrain. Faxon and Gatman Lakes do not sustain fish life.

From the Highline trailhead, the trail descends about 300 feet to the Mirror Lake Trail junction. Then follow the Highline Trail 4.0 miles southeast across several gentle ravines to a posted sign at the Naturalist Basin turnoff. Proceed 1.8 miles northeast

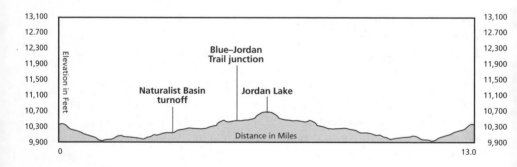

Cutthroat trout can be caught at LeConte Lake.
PHOTO BY MATT MCKELL/UTAH DIVISION OF WILDLIFE RESOURCES

to the Blue-Jordan Trail junction. At this point the Jordan Lake Trail crosses the river and heads east through a scenic meadow. Then it turns north up a couple of rocky switchbacks, leveling out at the lake.

12 Morat and Blue Lakes

The Morat Lakes receive heavy usage from both backpackers and day hikers. Fishing pressure remains somewhat moderate at these lakes because many anglers bypass the Morat Lakes and begin to fish at Blue Lake. However, large cutthroat trout can often be netted at Morat #1. Try the west end in the early morning with a small fly, and practice your stealth. The big ones are extremely wary.

See map on page 29.
Start: Highline trailhead
Distance: 11.0 miles out and back
Destination elevation: 10,740 feet
Approximate hiking time: 8.5 hours
Difficulty: Moderate—some steep sections
Usage: Moderate
Nearest town: Kamas, Utah
Drainage: Duchesne River

Maps: USGS Hayden Peak; USDA Forest Service High Uintas Wilderness; Trails Illustrated High Uintas Wilderness
Trail contacts: Wasatch National Forest, Forest Supervisor, 8226 Federal Building, 125 South State St., Salt Lake City, UT 84111; Kamas Ranger District, 50 East Center St., Kamas, UT 84036, (435) 783-4338

Finding the trailhead: The Highline is the most popular trailhead of the High Uintas. From Kamas, take the Mirror Lake Highway (Highway 150) 34 miles to a large sign on the east side of the road that says "Highline Trail."

This trailhead has a listed capacity of twenty-four vehicles, but there are often considerably more parked here on busy weekends. The overcrowded trailhead is equipped with toilets, water, stock ramp, and nearby campsites. This is the main takeoff point for popular treks ranging from 5 to 50 miles in length.

The Hike

From the Highline trailhead, the trail descends about 300 feet to the Mirror Lake Trail junction. Then follow the Highline Trail 4.0 miles southeast across several gentle ravines to a posted sign at the Naturalist Basin turnoff. Proceed 1.8 miles northeast to the Blue-Jordan Trail junction.

From the Blue-Jordan Trail junction, follow the Blue Lake Trail 0.5 mile west then north to Morat Lakes. The last 0.125 mile is excessively rocky and almost vertical.

Morat #1 is at the base of Blue Lake Ridge next to a talus slope interspersed with conifers. Morat #2 is located just east of Morat #1. Even though these lakes sit in rocky, timbered terrain, several good camping areas can be found. But remember, a fire restriction is often in effect at Naturalist Basin, and campfires can only be built at posted campsites. If your horse can make it up the hill that is encountered just before Morat Lakes, bring along some oats. Only limited feed is available. The only dependable source of spring water in the Morat or Blue Lake area is at Morat #2.

The Morat Lakes in the Naturalist Basin hold cutthroat trout and are a good place to set up a camp.
PHOTO BY MATT MCKELL/UTAH DIVISION OF WILDLIFE RESOURCES

Blue Lake is located over a ridge 0.25 mile north of Morat #1. A steep, rocky basin at the east base of Mount Agassiz characterizes this pretty lake. There are no campsites, and spring water can only be found in early summer. Fishing is usually fast for small brook trout. Blue and Morat Lakes sit in the cooler part of Naturalist Basin and are usually not free of ice until mid-July.

Near the Blue-Jordan Trail junction, there are a couple of nice campsites near the main stream. This might be a good place to stay if you wanted to fish deep, slow waters flowing through open meadows.

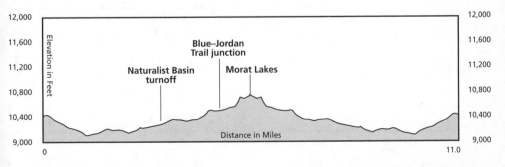

13 Carolyn Lake

Although Carolyn Lake is in a popular area, it is most often passed by. This small lake is in timbered country characterized by boggy shorelines and a small, wet meadow. Spring water is somewhat limited, but good running water can be found on the southeast side of the lake.

See map on page 29.
Start: Highline trailhead
Distance: 13.0 miles out and back
Destination elevation: 10,460 feet
Approximate hiking time: 9 hours
Difficulty: Moderate—some steep sections
Usage: Moderate
Nearest town: Kamas, Utah
Drainage: Duchesne River

Maps: USGS Hayden Peak; USDA Forest Service High Uintas Wilderness; Trails Illustrated High Uintas Wilderness
Trail contacts: Wasatch National Forest, Forest Supervisor, 8226 Federal Building, 125 South State St., Salt Lake City, UT 84111; Kamas Ranger District, 50 East Center St., Kamas, UT 84036, (435) 783-4338

Finding the trailhead: The Highline is the most popular trailhead of the High Uintas. From Kamas, take the Mirror Lake Highway (Highway 150) 34 miles to a large sign on the east side of the road that says "Highline Trail."

This trailhead has a listed capacity of twenty-four vehicles, but there are often considerably more parked here on busy weekends. The overcrowded trailhead is equipped with toilets, water, stock ramp, and nearby campsites. This is the main takeoff point for popular treks ranging from 5 to 50 miles in length.

The Hike

One reason we think this lake is so often overlooked is because Carolyn contains a large population of arctic grayling. This is no problem if you know how to prepare the little suckers, but most anglers prefer high-mountain trout. If grayling are on your menu, you should have no problem limiting out. The fish seem to be jumping all day long and will smack a small, colorful fly or flashy spinner.

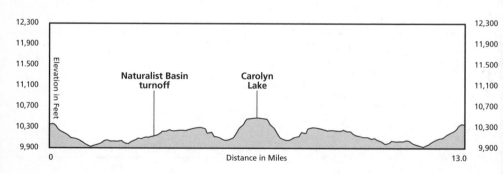

There are plenty of good camping areas at Carolyn Lake. However, a fire restriction is in effect in this area, and only posted campsites may be used. These designated sites are located on the west side of the lake, 50 yards from shore. Unposted camping areas exist near the south end of the lake on a little plateau. About 100 feet south of these campsites is an awesome view of the West Fork Rock Creek Drainage.

Access is 6.5 miles south then east on the Highline Trail. From the Highline Trail, look for a deeply rutted trail that takes off to the south and across an open meadow. About 200 yards down this trail lies Carolyn Lake. No posted signs point the direction to the lake, but the trail can be clearly seen if you're watching for it.

This is a great place for an overnighter that will seem more remote than it is.

Arctic grayling are one of the various species of fish anglers pursue in the Uintas.
PHOTO BY CORDELL ANDERSEN

14 Four Lakes Basin

Jean, Dean, Dale, and Daynes Lakes make up Four Lakes Basin. The best places to stay are at Dale or Daynes Lake. Campsites, horse pasture, and spring water are plentiful at both lakes, and there is plenty of space for horses. Backpackers might opt for a little more solitude at Dean Lake, which is not as suitable for horses. There is spring water at Dean Lake, but it is on the extreme northern shore (a long walk from the campsites).

See map on page 29.
Start: Highline trailhead
Distance: 18.0 miles out and back
Destination elevation: 10,700 feet
Approximate hiking time: 12 hours
Difficulty: Moderate
Usage: Heavy
Nearest town: Kamas, Utah
Drainage: Rock Creek

Maps: USGS Hayden Peak; USDA Forest Service High Uintas Wilderness; Trails Illustrated High Uintas Wilderness
Trail contacts: Ashley National Forest, Forest Supervisor, 355 North Vernal Ave., Vernal, UT 84078, (435) 781-1181; Duchesne Ranger District, 85 West Main, Duchesne, UT 84021, (435) 738-2482

Finding the trailhead: The Highline is the most popular trailhead of the High Uintas. From Kamas, take the Mirror Lake Highway (Highway 150) 34 miles to a large sign on the east side of the road that says "Highline Trail." You can't get lost finding this one.

This trailhead has a listed capacity of twenty-four vehicles, but there are often considerably more parked here on busy weekends. The overcrowded trailhead is equipped with toilets, water, stock ramp, and nearby campsites. This is the main takeoff point for popular treks ranging from 5 to 50 miles in length.

The Hike

Four Lakes Basin is 9.0 miles from either the Highline or Grandview trailhead. We suggest using the Highline trailhead, since the hike has less than half the elevation gain as the hike from the Grandview trailhead does. The Highline trailhead is also closer and easier to reach if you are coming from the population centers of Utah (Salt Lake City, Provo, and Ogden).

From the Highline trailhead, descend 300 feet over a mile to the Mirror Lake Trail junction. Stay left and follow the Highline Trail 4.0 miles southeast across several gentle ravines to a posted sign at the Naturalist Basin turnoff. Stay right (east) at this junction, continuing on the Highline Trail. Go about 1.0 mile to another junction with the trail heading into the East Fork of the Duchesne River. Stay right (south then east) at another junction about 1.0 mile farther with the trail heading over the high pass to the Four Lakes Basin.

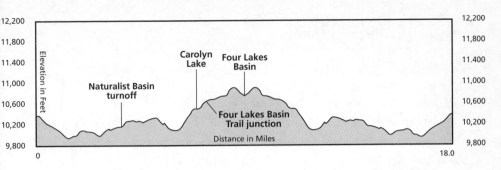

Fishing pressure is heavy at all four lakes except Dean Lake, which receives moderate pressure. If you take the time to walk to the back side of Dean Lake, you'll find that hardly anyone else has been there. You might have your best success there. The predominant species in these lakes is brook trout. An occasional cutthroat may be caught, and Daynes Lake has a few arctic grayling to spice up your fishing. Fly fishing works best, but a surprising number of anglers use worms here. You don't find many lakes in the High Uintas where bait anglers are as successful as they are in the Four Lakes Basin.

Photographers can find plenty of subject matter in this basin. Jean and Dean Lakes provide spectacular alpine scenery. Keep your camera handy as you ride or hike around. For a breathtaking view, hike to the top of Cyclone Pass, where you can see the vast regions of the Rock Creek Drainage on either side of the pass. Daynes Lake is especially pretty from Cyclone Pass.

Daynes Lake from Cyclone Pass

15 Thompson Lake

One word can describe Thompson Lake—inaccessible. In fact, some call Thompson Lake the most inaccessible lake in the High Uintas. Because of this distinction, we have included it in this book, though we don't recommend it for everyone. If you're up for some serious mountaineering and some truly remote fishing, you might like it.

See map on page 29.
Start: Highline trailhead
Distance: 22.5 miles out and back
Destination elevation: 10,690 feet
Approximate hiking time: 17 hours
Difficulty: Difficult—mountain passes and boulder field
Usage: Very light
Nearest town: Kamas, Utah

Drainage: Rock Creek
Maps: USGS Hayden Peak and USGS Explorer Peak; USDA Forest Service High Uintas Wilderness; Trails Illustrated High Uintas Wilderness
Trail contacts: Ashley National Forest, Forest Supervisor, 355 North Vernal Ave., Vernal, UT 84078, (435) 781-1181; Duchesne Ranger District, 85 West Main, Duchesne, UT 84021, (435) 738-2482

Finding the trailhead: The Highline is the most popular trailhead of the High Uintas. From Kamas, take the Mirror Lake Highway (Highway 150) 34 miles to a large sign on the east side of the road that says "Highline Trail." You can't get lost finding this one.

This trailhead has a listed capacity of twenty-four vehicles, but there are often considerably more parked here on busy weekends. The overcrowded trailhead is equipped with toilets, water, stock ramp, and nearby campsites. This is the main takeoff point for popular treks ranging from 5 to 50 miles in length.

The Hike

From the Highline trailhead, descend 300 feet over a mile to the Mirror Lake Trail junction. Stay left and follow the Highline Trail 4.0 miles southeast across several gentle ravines to a posted sign at the Naturalist Basin turnoff. Stay right (east) at this junction, continuing on the Highline Trail. Go about 1.0 mile to another junction with the trail heading into the East Fork of the Duchesne River. Stay right (south then east) at another junction about 1.0 mile farther with the trail heading over the high pass to Four Lakes Basin. From here, a steep trail goes another 1.0 mile to Cyclone Pass and ends in a massive boulder field on the other side. The boulders continue all the way to Thompson Lake. You can avoid some of the boulder field by leaving the trail about halfway down the eastern slope and traversing the mountainside on an obscure game trail. It is easier walking than stumbling on the brutal boulders. Eventually you will still have to cross the rocks—and a lot of them. Plan on about an hour of tricky boulder hopping. Do not attempt this hike with full packs on. It is treacherous without packs—and downright foolish with them.

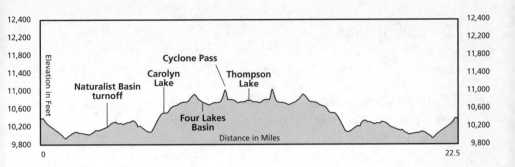

Literally thousands of GIANT SPIDERS can reside throughout the boulders that must be crossed to reach Thompson Lake. These arachnids sit virtually still in the middle of their radial web, waiting for prey. Upon human arrival, a most peculiar display attracts your attention. When moves are made toward the spiders' domain, a skittish shake of the web mimics a vicious assault. We think this action is not to strike out at intruders, but rather is a plea of "please don't destroy my web."

Boulders surround Thompson Lake too. There are no suitable campsites or spring water in this glacial cirque. It would be mighty uncomfortable to spend the night here, so leave yourself plenty of time to get back out. If a storm approaches, get out fast. Wet boulders are much more dangerous than dry ones, and Cyclone Pass is no place to be when lightning is brewing.

Crazed anglers might try to reach Thompson Lake. Big brook trout roam these waters and will savagely attack a fly or lure. You'll have a fight on your hands when one of these brookies slams your lure. Average size is well over a pound, and who knows how big some of the old monarchs are. This is a true wilderness experience that should only be attempted by the hardy, or the foolhardy.

16 Ouray Lake

It doesn't look like much at first glance, but give it a chance. This is a good place to establish a base camp, or just hide out. At the north end of the lake is a great little campsite, complete with rock tables; nearby, a couple of springs enter the small streams that feed Ouray Lake. Equestrians particularly like this spot because it is situated in a box canyon with plenty of horse pasture.

See map on page 29.
Start: Highline trailhead
Distance: 23.0 miles out and back
Destination elevation: 10,380 feet
Approximate hiking time: 15 hours
Difficulty: Moderate—mountain pass
Usage: Light
Nearest town: Kamas, Utah
Drainage: Rock Creek

Maps: USGS Hayden Peak and USGS Explorer Peak; USDA Forest Service High Uintas Wilderness; Trails Illustrated High Uintas Wilderness
Trail contacts: Ashley National Forest, Forest Supervisor, 355 North Vernal Ave., Vernal, UT 84078, (435) 781-1181; Duchesne Ranger District, 85 West Main, Duchesne, UT 84021, (435) 738-2482

Finding the trailhead: The Highline is the most popular trailhead of the High Uintas. From Kamas, take the Mirror Lake Highway (Highway 150) 34 miles to a large sign on the east side of the road that says "Highline Trail." You can't get lost finding this one.

This trailhead has a listed capacity of twenty-four vehicles, but there are often considerably more parked here on busy weekends. The overcrowded trailhead is equipped with toilets, water, stock ramp, and nearby campsites. This is the main takeoff point for popular treks ranging from 5 to 50 miles in length.

The Hike

The quickest way to reach this area is via Rocky Sea Pass. From the Highline trailhead, descend 300 feet over a mile to the Mirror Lake Trail junction. Stay left and follow the Highline Trail 4.0 miles southeast across several gentle ravines to a posted sign at the Naturalist Basin turnoff. Stay right (east) at this junction, continuing on the Highline Trail. Go about 1.0 mile to another junction with the trail heading into the East Fork of the Duchesne River. Stay left (east). At another junction about 1.0 mile farther on with the trail heading south toward Four Lakes Basin, stay left (east) on the trail going over Rocky Sea Pass. The view of the Rock Creek Drainage is awesome from atop the pass. Descend the trail to Rock Creek and another trail junction. Stay left. It's another mile to Black Lake. About 0.5 mile from Black Lake, turn right onto a cutoff trail toward Ouray Lake. The lake is about 0.5 mile from the turnoff.

Fishing at Ouray is excellent at times and good most any time. The east side of the lake is the deepest and harbors most of the fish. Flies or a small spinner will take a

Many visitors to the Uinta Mountains use horses to cover more ground while exploring the country. This pack train was spotted on the Highline Trail.

PHOTO BY MATT McKELL/UTAH DIVISION OF WILDLIFE RESOURCES

limit of brookies and cutthroat in short time. Don't forget to fish the main stream that flows into Ouray. The fish are there if you're cautious and lucky enough.

If you are up to some hearty day hikes, there are plenty of other fishing opportunities in the area. Lightning Lake to the northwest is fun. It's not lightning fast, but there are enough feisty fish to keep you interested for quite a while. If it's fast fishing you want, try Doug Lake to the northeast. Small brook trout will smack a fly on just about every cast. Next to Doug Lake is Boot Lake. It is much larger and deeper and is a good place to experiment with various lures and flies.

If you like the area but have a large group, try camping at Black Lake. It is popular with Boy Scouts and has nice camping. Both Black and Ouray Lakes are down from the trail and sheltered by pines—an important factor in this windswept region of upper Rock Creek.

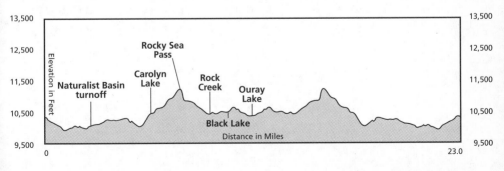

17 Joan Lake

It's only 0.3 mile to Joan Lake, as the crow flies, from Echo Lake. Unfortunately we can't fly. If you want to check out Joan Lake, you will have to pick your way up an extremely steep hill through loose rock, sand, and deadfall timber. There is no trail, and you'll have to choose your route carefully to avoid several sizable cliffs. It can be done, but don't try it on a horse.

Start: Echo Lake
Distance: 0.6 mile out and back
Destination elevation: 10,050 feet
Approximate hiking time: 1 hour
Difficulty: Moderate—very steep
Usage: Moderate
Nearest town: Kamas, Utah
Drainage: Duchesne River

Maps: USGS Mirror Lake; USDA Forest Service High Uintas Wilderness; Trails Illustrated High Uintas Wilderness
Trail contacts: Ashley National Forest, Forest Supervisor, 355 North Vernal Ave., Vernal, UT 84078, (435) 781-1181; Duchesne Ranger District, 85 West Main, Duchesne, UT 84021, (435) 738-2482

Finding the trailhead: From Kamas, take the Mirror Lake Highway (Highway 150) about 22 miles to the Murdock Basin Road. Turn right and follow the dirt road for about 5 miles to the Echo Lake turnoff, then left (north) another 0.5 mile. The last 0.5 mile may require high-clearance four-wheel drive.

The Hike

You can start hiking from Echo Lake. You may wish to try fishing at Echo Lake for a while before you hike. It receives heavy pressure but is one of the few lakes in the High Uintas containing golden trout. Joan Lake can be found by heading west up an extremely steep hill via a "chute" of loose rocks, sand, and deadfall timber. It's a nasty hill that seems longer than it really is.

Once you reach Joan Lake, there are four good fishing prospects to check out: Joan Lake, Gem Lake, Lake D–26, and the stream connecting Gem and Joan. Take a full day and explore the possibilities. This could be a fun-filled fishing trip for brook and cutthroat trout. Joan Lake receives moderate angling pressure, but the other locations get only light use. Don't worry if you don't see Gem Lake on your USGS topo map. Somehow they missed it. It seems a lot of other people miss it too.

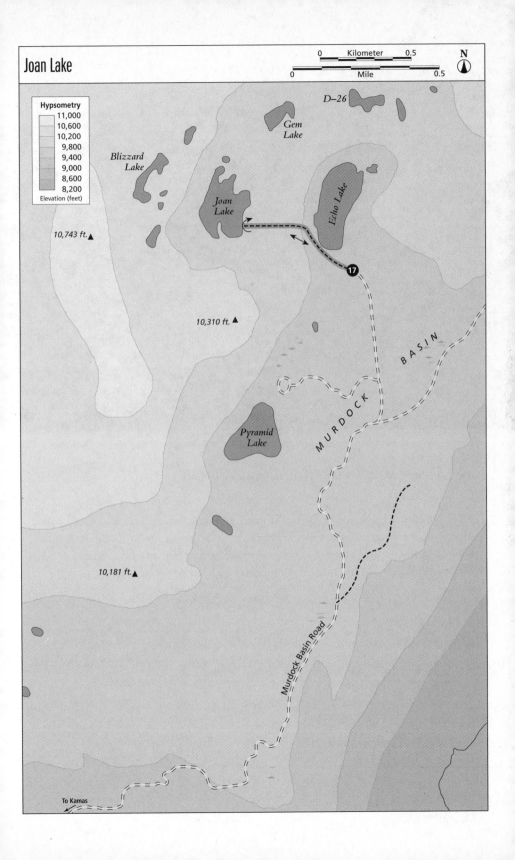

Joan Lake

Hypsometry

11,000
10,600
10,200
9,800
9,400
9,000
8,600
8,200

Elevation (feet)

0   Kilometer   0.5

0   Mile   0.5

N

D–26

Gem Lake

Blizzard Lake

Joan Lake

Echo Lake

10,743 ft. ▲

17

10,310 ft. ▲

B A S I N

Pyramid Lake

M U R D O C K

10,181 ft. ▲

Murdock Basin Road

To Kamas

Every lake in the Uinta Mountains could be considered a gem, but this one on the Duchesne River drainage actually earned the name.
PHOTO BY MATT McKELL/UTAH DIVISION OF WILDLIFE RESOURCES

A good place to camp is along the small stream between Joan and Gem Lakes. There are good campsites and spring water along the stream, and you will have quick access to most of the fishing. Litter is sometimes a problem around the lake, so how about pitching in and packing out some extra garbage when you leave?

18 Broadhead Lake

Depending on your priorities, you may want to leave the backpack behind. Access is somewhat steep, and large rocks with deadfall literally litter the way. On the other hand, many people avoid difficult obstructions. Which means you should have this lake all to yourself. Broadhead Lake remains remarkably untouched, as fire rings have promptly perished. (Let's keep it that way.) There is no need for the daytime explorer to make a fire.

Start: Murdock Basin
Distance: 1.6 miles out and back
Destination elevation: 9,960 feet
Approximate hiking time: 3 hours
Difficulty: Difficult—steep and cross-country
Usage: Light
Nearest town: Kamas, Utah
Drainage: Duchesne River

Maps: USGS Iron Mine Mountain; USDA Forest Service High Uintas Wilderness; Trails Illustrated High Uintas Wilderness
Trail contacts: Ashley National Forest, Forest Supervisor, 355 North Vernal Ave., Vernal, UT 84078, (435) 781-1181; Duchesne Ranger District, 85 West Main, Duchesne, UT 84021, (435) 738-2482

Finding the trailhead: From Kamas, take the Mirror Lake Highway (Highway 150) about 22 miles to the Murdock Basin Road. The shortest route begins from the Mirror Lake Highway, about 2 miles up Murdock Basin Road. Look for an ATV road that turns right by a group of campsites. This ATV road has been named Buckeye Road. Follow it 0.5 mile to Greenhorn Road. From here, take Greenhorn Road almost to its end.

The Hike

The hike begins at the end of Greenhorn Road. Then pick your way up the left side of a steep and rocky ravine to Broadhead Lake. According to the stats, Broadhead Lake is only just under a mile in distance. This may be true if you could walk straight from point A to point B. However, by the time you maneuver around deadfall and hop some rocks, you can add another 0.5 mile to your adventure.

Broadhead Lake

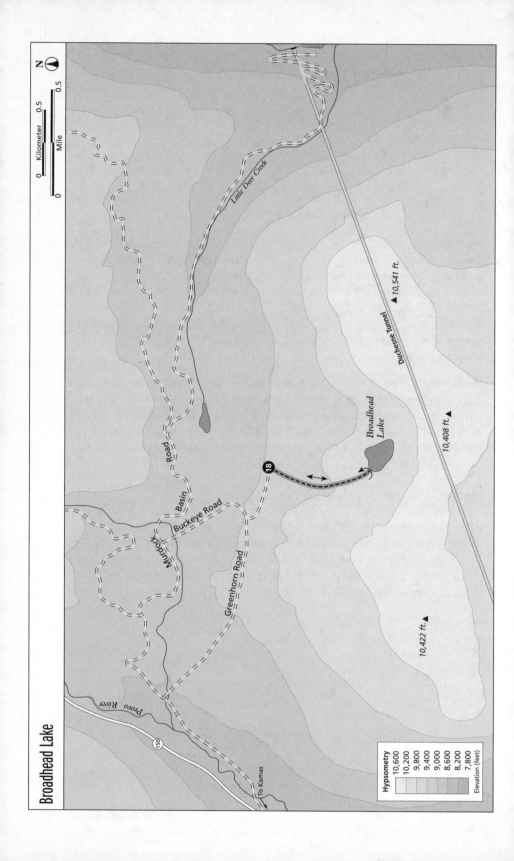

The view from above Broadhead Lake will stick in your memory for future use.
PHOTO BY MATT McKELL/UTAH DIVISION OF WILDLIFE RESOURCES

Broadhead is a scenic alpine lake, nestled within a small rocky basin. Spring water flows into the lake from the west, while the outlet displays a unique waterfall. Angling is unpredictable. Broadhead has been stocked with brook trout. If you're an avid angler, take a pole along. You may be in for a rewarding surprise.

19 Meadow Muffin Trail (Duchesne River)

Most people use the Mirror Lake entryway instead of Mill Flat, solely because the trail loses elevation starting from Mirror Lake. Usually two vehicles are used to support this trip. One vehicle transports the trekkers to Mirror Lake, while the other is left behind at Mill Flat. Another alternate route can be made via a branch off the Murdock Basin Road. This four-wheel-drive road takes you to the east portal of the Duchesne Tunnel.

Start: Mirror Lake trailhead
Distance: 11.0-mile one-way shuttle
Destination elevation: 7,520 feet
Approximate hiking time: 6 hours
Difficulty: Moderate—some steep sections
Usage: Moderate
Nearest town: Kamas, Utah
Drainage: Duchesne River

Maps: USGS Iron Mine Mountain; USDA Forest Service High Uintas Wilderness; Trails Illustrated High Uintas Wilderness
Trail contacts: Ashley National Forest, Forest Supervisor, 355 North Vernal Ave., Vernal, UT 84078, (435) 781-1181; Duchesne Ranger District, 85 West Main, Duchesne, UT 84021, (435) 738-2482

Finding the trailhead: From Kamas, take the Mirror Lake Highway (Highway 150) 31 miles to Mirror Lake. You will find the trailhead about 0.5 mile east of the Mirror Lake entrance. This trailhead has eighteen parking places and offers a very popular and well-maintained campground with water, toilets, and a stock-unloading ramp.

The Hike

Start your adventure at Mirror Lake, on the West Fork Trail of the Duchesne River Drainage. After a slight incline, the trail descends rapidly to the Pinto Lake–Mill Flat junction 2.5 miles from the trailhead. Following the trail to Mill Flat, a deep river gorge begins to emerge. Spectacular views of plummeting cliffs soon appear, as mystic scenery stimulates the soul.

Six miles from the trailhead, near the east portal of the Duchesne Tunnel, the gorge widens to a ford. This is also where the trail crosses the river. Due to high water, it is not feasible—or safe—to cross the river until after the month of July. The gate of the east portal remains closed until water is needed downstream in the Provo River. Water is then diverted through the Duchesne Tunnel, dropping the Duchesne River to expose a makeshift trail, which runs along the top of a dike.

Excellent campsites can be found before and after the ford, and spring water is available all along the trail. However, the presence of cows makes drinking water hard to find. Angling is best upstream from the portal. The fish are small, but they can prove to be exciting. (That's if you don't mind stepping in a cow pie or two.) The trail upstream from the portal is plagued with cow-tainted mud holes. If you're not careful, one of these stench-pots can suck your boot right off.

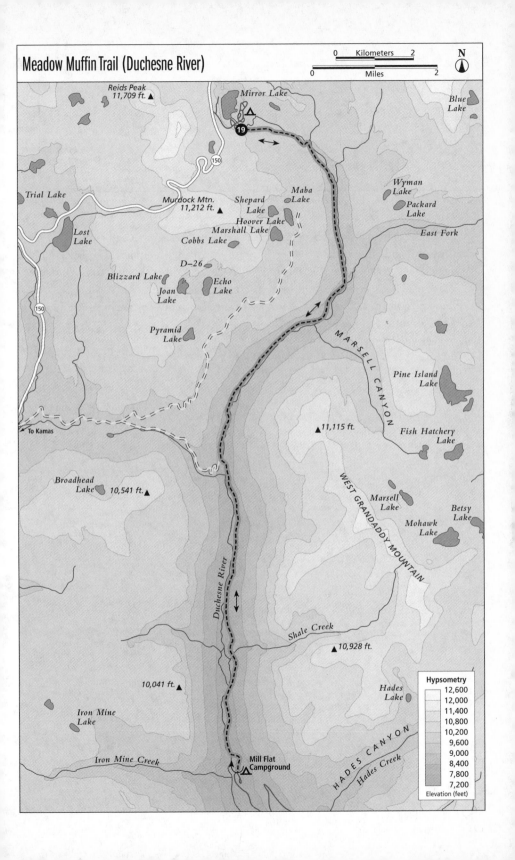

Meadow Muffin Trail (Duchesne River)

N

0 — Kilometers — 2
0 — Miles — 2

Reids Peak 11,709 ft. ▲

Mirror Lake

Blue Lake

19

150

Trial Lake

Murdock Mtn. 11,212 ft. ▲

Shepard Lake

Maba Lake

Wyman Lake

Packard Lake

Hoover Lake
Marshall Lake

Lost Lake

Cobbs Lake

East Fork

150

D–26

Blizzard Lake

Echo Lake

Joan Lake

Pyramid Lake

MARSELL CANYON

Pine Island Lake

To Kamas

▲11,115 ft.

Fish Hatchery Lake

Broadhead Lake 10,541 ft. ▲

WEST GRANDADDY MOUNTAIN

Marsell Lake

Betsy Lake

Mohawk Lake

Duchesne River

Shale Creek

▲10,928 ft.

10,041 ft. ▲

Hades Lake

Iron Mine Lake

HADES CANYON

Iron Mine Creek

Mill Flat Campground

Hades Creek

Hypsometry	
	12,600
	12,000
	11,400
	10,800
	10,200
	9,600
	9,000
	8,400
	7,800
	7,200

Elevation (feet)

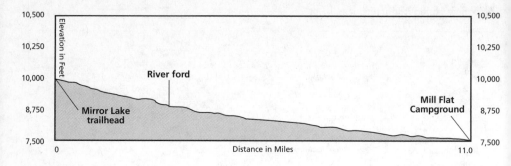

After the portal, the trail becomes rather relaxing. Vistas of a deep river gorge are seen nearby, and an excellent trail reclines on down the mountain. The last couple of miles of this trek can be a little confusing. A hit-or-miss trail winds through dense vegetation as it crosses lots of tiny streams. In any case, you'll soon know when you are on the right track. The friendly service of our courteous cows will leave a trail of meadow muffins for you to follow.

20 Grandaddy Lake

Grandaddy Lake—the name implies that it is the largest and best of all the lakes. Is it the largest? Yes, it is easily the largest natural lake in the High Uintas. Is it the best? Judging solely by the number of backcountry visitors, the answer to that question also is yes. Usage is very heavy at this well-known lake that can be extremely busy in July, August, and early September. If you are looking for solitude a different wilderness destination should be considered. Litter can be a problem, so clean up your mess, leaving a spotless campsite for the next guests.

Start: Grandview trailhead
Distance: 6.4 miles out and back
Destination elevation: 10,310 feet
Approximate hiking time: 4.5 hours
Difficulty: Moderate—some steep sections
Usage: Heavy
Nearest town: Hanna, Utah
Drainage: Rock Creek

Maps: USGS Grandaddy Lake; USDA Forest Service High Uintas Wilderness; Trails Illustrated High Uintas Wilderness
Trail contacts: Ashley National Forest, Forest Supervisor, 355 North Vernal Ave., Vernal, UT 84078, (435) 781-1181; Duchesne Ranger District, 85 West Main, Duchesne, UT 84021, (435) 738-2482

Finding the trailhead: From Heber City, take US 40 east to SR 208, which is about 6 miles east of Fruitland. Head north on SR 208 for 10 miles to SR 35. Follow SR 35 northwest 10 miles to Hanna. From Hanna, follow a dirt road, FR 144, 11 miles northwest to Hades Campground. Stay on the same road another 0.5 mile to a junction. One road takes off to Mill Flat; the other road ventures right (northeast) about 5 steep miles to Grandview trailhead.

Grandview trailhead has fifty parking places; the amenities here include toilets and a stock-unloading ramp. Sorry, there's no drinking water here. Grandview is the starting point for lakes in the West Fork of the Rock Creek Drainage.

The Hike

It's not a long hike to Grandaddy Lake, but it is a strenuous one. A well-traveled trail climbs more than 800 feet in just 2.0 miles to the top of Hades Pass. There you'll have a "grand view" of Heart Lake, Grandaddy Lake, and countless acres of the pine-covered hills of the Rock Creek Drainage. Walk another 1.0 mile to a trail junction in the narrow piece of land between Betsy and Grandaddy Lakes. Stay right and go another 0.2 mile to a peninsula on the north side of Grandaddy Lake.

When selecting a campsite at Grandaddy, use one of the existing sites. There are lots of them, and building new camps will only further burden the fragile environment. It may be a long walk to a spring from your camp, so it would be wise to bring along something to purify your drinking water. There is a campfire and firewood gathering restriction in the Grandaddy Basin, making it illegal to have a campfire or gather firewood within 0.25 mile of all the larger lakes in the basin.

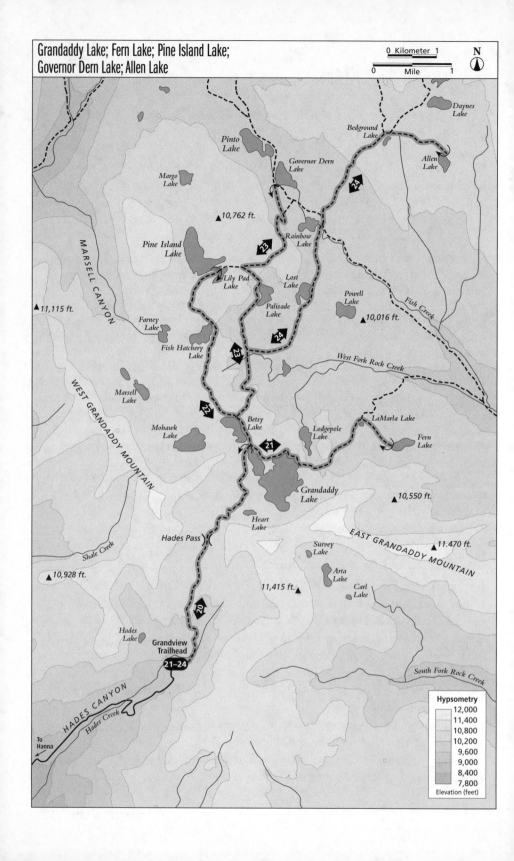

Grandaddy Lake; Fern Lake; Pine Island Lake; Governor Dern Lake; Allen Lake

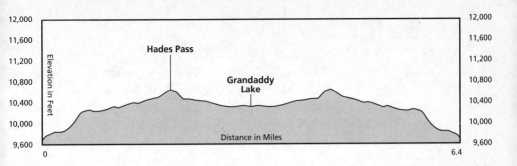

Cutthroat and brook trout provide fair to good fishing. These trout are not stocked; replenishment is by natural reproduction only. Catch-and-release angling is encouraged here, especially for larger fish. Many other angling and camping opportunities are nearby. Betsy and Mohawk Lakes are practically right next door, and Lodgepole Lake is just a few hundred yards northeast of Grandaddy. Heart Lake is up a steep hill, just south of Grandaddy. You'll pass it if you hike to Grandaddy Lake via Hades Pass.

There's a lot happening in this basin. Any fan of the High Uintas will enjoy this area, whether you are camping here or just passing through—even if it's just to be able to say that you visited the largest and most popular backcountry lake in the High Uintas.

21 Fern Lake

This hike is a pretty one, but it seems like it's uphill both ways. You'll rise more than 800 feet traversing Hades Pass, and then you'll give almost all that elevation back as you descend to Fern Lake. Even though the elevation gain is a mere 100 feet in less than 6 miles, level ground is unheard of. If you're not forging up, you're dropping down.

See map on page 54.
Start: Grandview trailhead
Distance: 11.4 miles out and back
Destination elevation: 9,890 feet
Approximate hiking time: 8 hours
Difficulty: Moderate
Usage: Moderate
Nearest town: Hanna, Utah
Drainage: Rock Creek

Maps: USGS Grandaddy Lake; USDA Forest Service High Uintas Wilderness; Trails Illustrated High Uintas Wilderness
Trail contacts: Ashley National Forest, Forest Supervisor, 355 North Vernal Ave., Vernal, UT 84078, (435) 781-1181; Duchesne Ranger District, 85 West Main, Duchesne, UT 84021, (435) 738-2482

Finding the trailhead: From Heber City, take US 40 east to SR 208, which is about 6 miles east of Fruitland. Head north on SR 208 for 10 miles to SR 35. Follow SR 35 northeast 10 miles to Hanna. From Hanna, follow a dirt road, FR 144, 11 miles northwest to Hades Campground. Stay on the same road another 0.5 mile to a junction. One road takes off to Mill Flat; the other road ventures northeast about 5 steep miles to Grandview trailhead.

Grandview trailhead has fifty parking places; amenities include toilets and a stock-unloading ramp. Sorry, there's no drinking water here. Grandview is the starting point for lakes in the West Fork of the Rock Creek Drainage.

The Hike

It's not a long hike to Fern Lake, but it is a strenuous one. A well-traveled trail climbs more than 800 feet in just 2.0 miles to the top of Hades Pass. There you'll have a "grand view" of Heart Lake, Grandaddy Lake, and countless acres of the pine-covered hills of the Rock Creek Drainage. Walk another 1.0 mile to a trail junction in the narrow piece of land between Betsy and Grandaddy Lakes.

Take a right at Betsy Lake. Follow the West Fork Rock Creek Trail past Lodgepole Lake a couple of miles to LaMarla Lake, then cut cross-country southeast another 0.5 mile. Fern Lake is nestled at the base of East Grandaddy Mountain below a steep, boulder-strewn slope. The terrain is rough. Rocks and deadfall timber are prevalent, making travel a little slow around the immediate area.

The main attractions at Fern Lake are solitude and fishing. It can be hard to find an unoccupied lake in this basin. Fern may be your best bet if you are searching for a quiet, secluded spot. There are a few comfortable campsites for setting up your

Betsy Lake near Fern Lake

wilderness abode. Ice-cold spring water is located on the west side of the lake. There is a campfire and firewood gathering restriction within 0.25 mile of the lake. In all, it's a pretty good place to just settle back and let the world pass you by.

Fern Lake has been known for some darn good fishing in the past too. And they might be big ones. Fat brookies up to 2 pounds have been known to succumb to a well-presented fly or lure. Don't plan solely on fish for your meals though. If they are not biting here, there are no other lakes nearby to count on. Of course you could plan a trout dinner—but bring some extra beef jerky, just in case.

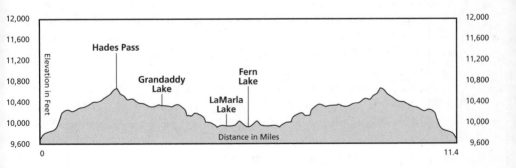

22 Pine Island Lake

It's no wonder this lake is popular among Scout groups—it is gorgeous. If aesthetics and a nice campsite are important to you, then check out Pine Island Lake. It is the gem of the West Fork of Rock Creek. Small, pine-covered islands rise peacefully out of the clear blue waters of this large natural lake. There is something especially appealing about islands on a wilderness lake. In the background, a steep talus slope adds to the alpine atmosphere. You can easily just sit in camp, munch granola bars, and enjoy the view.

See map on page 54.
Start: Grandview trailhead
Distance: 12.0 miles out and back
Destination elevation: 10,300 feet
Approximate hiking time: 8 hours
Difficulty: Moderate
Usage: Heavy
Nearest town: Hanna, Utah
Drainage: Rock Creek

Maps: USGS Grandaddy Lake and USGS Hayden Peak; USDA Forest Service High Uintas Wilderness; Trails Illustrated High Uintas Wilderness
Trail contacts: Ashley National Forest, Forest Supervisor, 355 North Vernal Ave., Vernal, UT 84078, (435) 781-1181; Duchesne Ranger District, 85 West Main, Duchesne, UT 84021, (435) 738-2482

Finding the trailhead: From Heber City, take US 40 east to SR 208, which is about 6 miles east of Fruitland. Head north on SR 208 for 10 miles to SR 35. Follow SR 35 northeast 10 miles to Hanna. From Hanna, follow a dirt road, FR 144, 11 miles northwest to Hades Campground. Stay on the same road another 0.5 mile to a junction. One road takes off to Mill Flat; the other road ventures northeast about 5 steep miles to Grandview trailhead.

Grandview trailhead has fifty parking places; amenities include toilets and a stock-unloading ramp.

The Hike

From Grandview trailhead, it's a steep 2.0-mile climb to Hades Pass. From the top of the pass, walk another 1.0 mile to a trail junction in the narrow piece of land between Betsy and Grandaddy Lakes. Turn left (north) and go 0.1 mile to another trail junction on the north end of Betsy Lake. Turn left (northwest) again. It's about 2.0 miles to Fish Hatchery Lake and another 0.9 mile to Pine Island Lake.

A few spacious campsites are located along the southeast shoreline, just off the main trail. There is plenty of level ground for a large group to set up several tents, and large flat boulders are conveniently located to serve as tables or benches. There is a campfire and firewood gathering restriction within 0.25 mile of the lake. Spring water is nonexistent. Be prepared to purify all your drinking water.

Fishing pressure is moderate to heavy—and unpredictable. You may have good luck, but you should have a backup plan if you are planning on fish for dinner. Brook

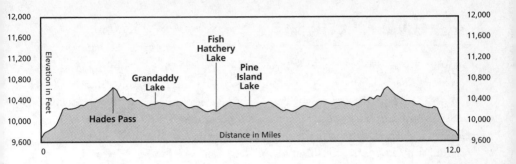

trout are stocked on a regular basis, and a few cutthroat still remain. Lily Pad Lake offers similar angling and is just 200 yards southeast. Give it a try if Pine Island doesn't yield the fishing you want.

If you have horses to carry your load, a rubber raft could be a lot of fun at Pine Island Lake. Paddle out to the islands and fish around them. Remember the life jackets. These icy waters are as dangerous as they are beautiful.

23 Governor Dern Lake

A lot of equestrians use this area. Between Governor Dern Lake and the Pinto Lake area there are lots of places to graze your horses and plenty of roomy campsites. Once you get past Hades Pass, the journey is a gentle ride through the pine forests of the West Fork of the Rock Creek Drainage. Or you can avoid the steep pass and reach Governor Dern Lake from the Highline trailhead. It is a couple of miles longer this way, but it may be easier on the animals. There is a campfire and firewood gathering restriction within 0.25 mile of Governor Dern, Pinto, and Rainbow Lakes.

See map on page 54.
Start: Grandview trailhead
Distance: 15.6 miles out and back
Destination elevation: 9,990 feet
Approximate hiking time: 10 hours
Difficulty: Moderate
Usage: Moderate
Nearest town: Hanna, Utah
Drainage: Rock Creek

Maps: USGS Grandaddy Lake and USGS Hayden Peak; USDA Forest Service High Uintas Wilderness; Trails Illustrated High Uintas Wilderness

Trail contacts: Ashley National Forest, Forest Supervisor, 355 North Vernal Ave., Vernal, UT 84078, (435) 781-1181; Duchesne Ranger District, 85 West Main, Duchesne, UT 84021, (435) 738-2482

Finding the trailhead: From Heber City, take US 40 east to SR 208, which is about 6 miles east of Fruitland. Head north on SR 208 for 10 miles to SR 35. Follow SR 35 northeast 10 miles to Hanna. From Hanna, follow a dirt road, FR 144, 11 miles northwest to Hades Campground. Stay on the same road another 0.5 mile to a junction. One road takes off to Mill Flat; the other road ventures northeast about 5 steep miles to Grandview trailhead.

Grandview trailhead has fifty parking places; amenities include toilets and a stock-unloading ramp.

The Hike

From Grandview trailhead it's a steep 2.0-mile climb to Hades Pass. From the top of the pass, walk another 1.0 mile to a trail junction in the narrow piece of land between Betsy and Grandaddy Lakes. Turn left (north) and go 0.1 mile to another trail junction on the north end of Betsy Lake. Turn right (northwest) and go about 1.3 miles to the junction with the trail that goes to Powell Lake. Stay left (north) and go past a lake on the right about 0.8 mile from the junction. It's another 0.5 mile to the junction with the trail going to Pine Island Lake. Stay right at this fork and go 2.1 miles to Governor Dern Lake.

Spring water is present on either the north or east shore of Governor Dern Lake. The lake is shallow for its size but is still very pretty and easily fished. It is stocked periodically with brook trout, and a cutthroat may show up in the creel from time to time. Try a small fly in the morning and late evening for best results.

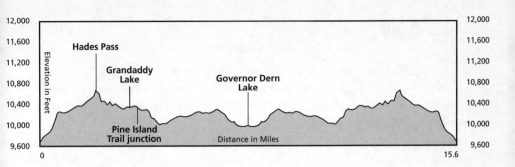

Nearby Pinto Lake is more popular, but it doesn't have any more to offer than Governor Dern Lake. In fact, Governor Dern is more scenic. Given that Pinto Lake is more crowded, Governor Dern seems to be the better choice. Rainbow Lake is less than a mile away (south). It is also worth a look, whether you're looking for a camping spot or a different fishing hole or you're just taking a horse ride.

24 Allen Lake

Anglers seeking large arctic grayling must visit Allen Lake. Grayling over a pound are reported. A few big brook trout inhabit this lake too. You won't catch a lot of fish at Allen Lake, but what you do catch will be sizable. Fishing pressure is light here, so the fish have a chance to grow large.

See map on page 54.
Start: Grandview trailhead
Distance: 18.6 miles out and back
Destination elevation: 10,390 feet
Approximate hiking time: 12 hours
Difficulty: Moderate
Usage: Light
Nearest town: Hanna, Utah
Drainage: Rock Creek

Maps: USGS Grandaddy Lake and Hayden Peak; USDA Forest Service High Uintas Wilderness; Trails Illustrated High Uintas Wilderness
Trail contacts: Ashley National Forest, Forest Supervisor, 355 North Vernal Ave., Vernal, UT 84078, (435) 781-1181; Duchesne Ranger District, 85 West Main, Duchesne, UT 84021, (435) 738-2482

Finding the trailhead: From Heber City, take US 40 east to SR 208, which is about 6 miles east of Fruitland. Head north on SR 208 for 10 miles to SR 35. Follow SR 35 northeast 10 miles to Hanna. From Hanna, follow a dirt road, FR 144, 11 miles northwest to Hades Campground. Stay on the same road another 0.5 mile to a junction. One road takes off to Mill Flat; the other road ventures northeast about 5 steep miles to Grandview trailhead.

Grandview trailhead has fifty parking places; amenities include toilets and a stock-unloading ramp. Sorry, there's no drinking water here. Grandview is the starting point for lakes in the West Fork of the Rock Creek Drainage.

The Hike

Allen Lake was named in honor of Floyd Allen, a ranger who was killed by lightning while on duty. A wooden monument still stands as a solemn reminder of the man and the awesome powers of nature. We arrived at Allen Lake on August 26—the same day of the year that Mr. Allen met his fate in 1938. The coincidence left us wondering how he might have looked, and how isolated the High Uintas were back in 1938. We checked the sky for storm clouds.

From Grandview trailhead, it's a steep 2.0-mile climb to Hades Pass. From the top of the pass, walk another 1.0 mile to a trail junction in the narrow piece of land between Betsy and Grandaddy Lakes. Turn left (north) and go 0.1 mile to another trail junction on the north end of Betsy Lake. Turn right (northwest) about 1.3 miles to the junction with the trail that goes past Powell Lake. Stay right and go 1.0 mile to Lost Lake. The Fish Creek Trail junction is another 1.0 mile after you cross the creek. Go a short distance and turn right (north), then travel another 1.3 miles to Bedground Lake. Situated in a large, grassy meadow, Allen Lake can be located by

Allen Lake

traveling due east from Bedground Lake about 0.75 mile. A hit-or-miss game trail takes off from the northeast side of Bedground Lake, so get your compass out and follow it religiously. It is easy to get turned around in this heavily timbered terrain.

Allen Lake is ideal for horses. Horse pasture and water are plentiful, and there are places to picket or hobble the horses. Spacious campsites make it easy to watch your stock from camp while still receiving shelter from large pines. The best camps dot the western side of the lake. There is a campfire and firewood gathering restriction within 0.25 mile of the lake. A small campsite on the eastern side of the lake can accommodate one tent. Good drinking water can be found along the eastern shore, where several springs emerge.

Watch out for lightning.

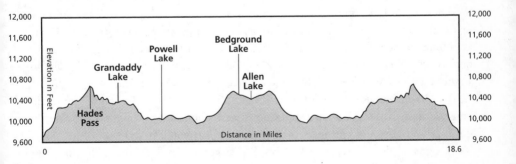

25 Ledge Lake

Geologically, this area is the oldest in the High Uintas. Some refer to it as the backbone of the Uintas, while others call it the heart. After all, the upper basins of Rock Creek are shaped somewhat like a heart. Ledge Lake is a haven in this vast heart, providing everything one could want in a camp. Spring water is abundant, as is horse pasture, but so are mosquitoes around the waterlogged outlet. The fishing may be surprising. Brook trout weigh in at well over a pound and seem to prefer an olive-green scud fly for dinner. The problem is finding out what time dinner is served.

Start: Rock Creek trailhead
Distance: 29.0 miles out and back
Destination elevation: 10,845 feet
Approximate hiking time: 17 hours
Difficulty: Difficult—long and steep
Usage: Moderate
Nearest town: Duchesne, Utah
Drainage: Rock Creek

Maps: USGS Explorer Peak; USDA Forest Service High Uintas Wilderness; Trails Illustrated High Uintas Wilderness

Trail contacts: Ashley National Forest, Forest Supervisor, 355 North Vernal Ave., Vernal, UT 84078, (435) 781-1181; Duchesne Ranger District, 85 West Main, Duchesne, UT 84021, (435) 738-2482

Finding the trailhead: From Heber City, take US 40 east 69 miles to Duchesne. Then take SR 87 north 14 miles to Mountain Home. Rock Creek trailhead is 22 miles northwest of Mountain Home on FR 134. Turn west (left) on FR 135 for 0.25 mile. The trailhead is on the right (north). There are no campsites, but the Upper Stillwater Campground is just 0.25 mile away. There are toilets, water, a stock ramp, and a stock corral at the trailhead. This is a popular takeoff point for equestrians heading into the Fall Creek or Squaw Basin areas. It's a long, steep hike to any lakes from here. Some lakes at the head of the Rock Creek Drainage are more easily reached via the Highline Trail over Rocky Sea Pass.

The Hike

From Rock Creek trailhead the trail climbs up the hill to the west and the passes by the Upper Stillwater Dam approximately 0.3 mile from the trailhead. The trail then parallels the Upper Stillwater Reservoir for 1.7 miles. The trail then follows Rock Creek for 0.8 mile until meeting the junction of the West Fork Rock Creek Trail. Continue up the Rock Creek Drainage. After 1.0 mile, the trail meets the trail from Squaw Basin. Continue up the valley for another 5.5 miles to another trail junction. The valley splits here. Rock Creek goes to the left; stay right, following Fall Creek another 5.0 miles to a trail junction. Continue straight for another 1.5 miles to Ledge Lake.

This basin houses some of the best-quality fishing holes in the whole mountain range. Continent Lake, about 2 miles northwest, commonly surrenders brookies in the 2-pound class and cutthroat over 16 inches. But you'll have to work for them. Work a green spinner deep, or a #14 Black Gnat just under the surface. The northeast

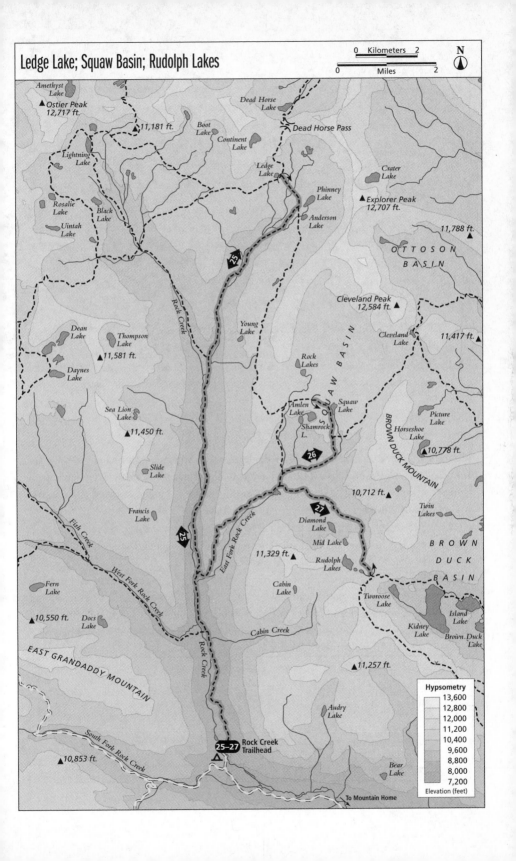

Ledge Lake; Squaw Basin; Rudolph Lakes

Kilometers

Miles

N

Amethyst Lake
▲ Ostier Peak 12,717 ft.

Dead Horse Lake

11,181 ft.

Boot Lake

Continent Lake

Dead Horse Pass

Lightning Lake

Ledge Lake

Crater Lake

Rosalie Lake

Black Lake

Phinney Lake

▲ Explorer Peak 12,707 ft.

Uintah Lake

Anderson Lake

11,788 ft. ▲

OTTOSON BASIN

Rock Creek

25

Young Lake

Cleveland Peak 12,584 ft. ▲

Cleveland Lake

11,417 ft. ▲

Dean Lake

Thompson Lake

▲ 11,581 ft.

Rock Lakes

SQUAW BASIN

Daynes Lake

Sea Lion Lake

▲ 11,450 ft.

Amlen Lake

Squaw Lake

Picture Lake

Shamrock L.

Horseshoe Lake

BROWN DUCK MOUNTAIN

10,778 ft. ▲

26

Slide Lake

10,712 ft. ▲

Twin Lakes

Francis Lake

East Fork Rock Creek

Diamond Lake

27

BROWN

Fish Creek

25

Mid Lake

DUCK

West Fork Rock Creek

11,329 ft. ▲

Rudolph Lakes

BASIN

Fern Lake

Cabin Lake

Tworoose Lake

Island Lake

10,550 ft. ▲

Docs Lake

Cabin Creek

Kidney Lake

Brown Duck Lake

EAST GRANDADDY MOUNTAIN

Rock Creek

11,257 ft. ▲

South Fork Rock Creek

Audry Lake

10,853 ft. ▲

25–27 Rock Creek Trailhead

Bear Lake

To Mountain Home

Hypsometry
13,600
12,800
12,000
11,200
10,400
9,600
8,800
8,000
7,200
Elevation (feet)

Fishing in the Uintas is not only fun. Many anglers augment their backcountry meal plans with fresh trout like these cutthroat.

PHOTO BY CORDELL ANDERSEN

segment of the lake may be the best place to start. Southeast from Ledge Lake are Phinney and Anderson Lakes. They offer fast fishing for smaller trout. They'll hit anything that moves. One guy in our party caught a fish on a piece of dried apricot, but I'm sure you will have even better success on flies.

Ledge Lake gets its name from the tall ledges behind its northern shore. It is easy to find, but there is no easy way to it. It's almost 15 miles from the Stillwater Dam trailhead and seems twice that long with the tremendous elevation gain. There are two other trails that may prove less taxing on the body. Both trails start at a higher elevation, but both also require traversing a steep mountain pass. It's about 12 miles to Ledge Lake coming from Blacks Fork over Dead Horse Pass and about 14 hilly miles via the Highline Trail over Rocky Sea Pass. Use Dead Horse if you're traveling by foot, Rocky Sea if by horse.

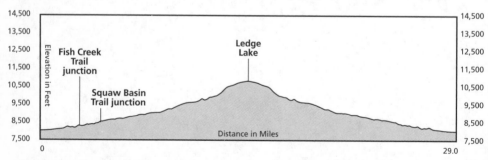

26 Squaw Basin

A compass is a must in this heavily timbered area. It's easy to get headed in the wrong direction as the trails twist, turn, intersect, and sometimes disappear in Squaw Basin. Getting into the area is not a problem, but finding your way around Squaw Basin can be confusing. Keep your map and compass handy, and keep your group together.

See map on page 65.
Start: Rock Creek trailhead
Distance: 18.0 miles out and back
Destination elevation: 10,400 feet
Approximate hiking time: 10.5 hours
Difficulty: Moderate—some steep sections
Usage: Moderate
Nearest town: Duchesne, Utah
Drainage: Rock Creek

Maps: USGS Explorer Peak; USDA Forest Service High Uintas Wilderness; Trails Illustrated High Uintas Wilderness
Trail contacts: Ashley National Forest, Forest Supervisor, 355 North Vernal Ave., Vernal, UT 84078, (435) 781-1181; Duchesne Ranger District, 85 West Main, Duchesne, UT 84021, (435) 738-2482

Finding the trailhead: From Heber City, take US 40 east 69 miles to Duchesne. Then take SR 87 north 14 miles to Mountain Home. Rock Creek trailhead is 22 miles northwest of Mountain Home on FR 134, mostly a good dirt road.

Rock Creek trailhead has space for twenty-five vehicles and offers campsites, toilets, water, and a stock ramp. This is a popular takeoff point for equestrians heading into the Fall Creek or Squaw Basin areas. It's a long, steep hike to any lakes from here. Some lakes at the head of the Rock Creek Drainage are more easily reached via the Highline Trail over Rocky Sea Pass.

The Hike

From Rock Creek trailhead the trail climbs up the hill to the west and then passes by the Upper Stillwater Dam approximately 0.3 mile from the trailhead. The trail then parallels the Upper Stillwater Reservoir for 1.7 miles. The trail then follows Rock Creek for 0.8 mile until meeting the junction of the West Fork Rock Creek Trail. Continue up the Rock Creek Drainage. After 1.0 mile, the trail meets the trail from Squaw Basin. It's 3.5 miles to the junction with the trail from Rudolph Lake. Stay left (north). There will be another junction with the trail coming down East Fork. Stay right (east) here. It's 3.0 miles to Squaw Lake in the middle of Squaw Basin.

Squaw Lake is a popular camping location, featuring plenty of spring water and horse pasture. Backpackers using the Highline Trail find this a convenient spot to spend the night before hiking over Cleveland or Tworoose Pass into the Lake Fork Drainage. If you are one of these long-trekkers, we suggest Cleveland Pass if you have the time. It offers an unsurpassed view of the upper regions of the Lake Fork Drainage and is well worth the extra effort.

If you are looking for a little more solitude, pitch your tent at Amlen or Shamrock Lake. These lakes are only a few hundred yards apart, and between the two you should find excellent campsites and spring water but only fair horse pasture. There is no trail to these lakes for the last 0.5 mile. Cross-country access is easiest from the southwest.

Fishing prospects are good to excellent throughout this large basin. Take a short hike up to Rock Lakes. These lakes see few visitors and house large populations of brook trout. The southern section of Squaw Basin could have some real fishing holes too. Diamond, Mid, and Rudolph Lakes are just far enough off the beaten path to sustain good fisheries, with only light to moderate pressure.

Squaw Basin is a good area for equestrians. The elevation gain is huge if you're starting at the Rock Creek trailhead and can quickly turn legs into rubber. Letting a horse do the heavy work is a great idea. Once into Squaw Basin, there is lots of room to roam and explore, and a good steed can be a real leg and time saver. Horse pasture is abundant near most suitable campsites, and of course water is everywhere.

There is a campfire and firewood gathering restriction within 0.25 mile of Rock Lakes, Shamrock Lake, and Squaw Lake.

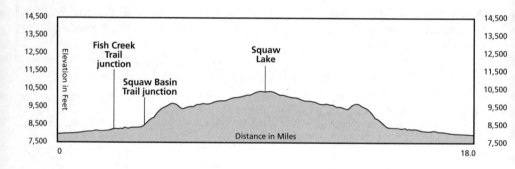

27 Rudolph Lakes

There are three different routes to Rudolph Lakes 1–3. One trail begins at Moon Lake via Brown Duck Trail; total distance 11.5 miles. Another starts at the Bear Wallow–Dry Ridge Road; total distance is 10 miles. The most popular of the three begins at the Upper Stillwater–Rock Creek trailhead.

See map on page 65.
Start: Rock Creek trailhead
Distance: 24.0 miles out and back
Destination elevation: 10,470 feet
Approximate hiking time: 14 hours
Difficulty: Moderate–some steep sections
Usage: Moderate
Nearest town: Duchesne, Utah
Drainage: Rock Creek

Maps: USGS Kidney Lake and USGS Tworoose Pass; USDA Forest Service High Uintas Wilderness; Trails Illustrated High Uintas Wilderness
Trail contacts: Ashley National Forest, Forest Supervisor, 355 North Vernal Ave., Vernal, UT 84078, (435) 781-1181; Duchesne Ranger District, 85 West Main, Duchesne, UT 84021, (435) 738-2482

Finding the trailhead: From Heber City, take US 40 east 69 miles to Duchesne. Then take SR 87 north 14 miles to Mountain Home. Rock Creek trailhead is 22 miles northwest of Mountain Home on FR 134, mostly a good dirt road. Rock Creek trailhead has space for twenty-five vehicles and offers campsites, toilets, water, and a stock ramp. This is a popular takeoff point for equestrians heading into the Fall Creek or Squaw Basin areas. It's a long, steep hike to any lakes from here.

The Hike

From Rock Creek trailhead the trail climbs up the hill to the west and then passes by the Upper Stillwater Dam approximately 0.3 mile from the trailhead. The trail then parallels the Upper Stillwater Reservoir for 1.7 miles. The trail then follows Rock Creek for 0.8 mile until meeting the junction of the West Fork Rock Creek Trail. Continue up the Rock Creek Drainage. After 1.0 mile, the trail meets the trail from Squaw Basin. It's 3.5 miles to the junction with the trail from Rudolph Lakes. Stay right and travel 6.0 miles to Rudolph Lakes.

Rudolph Lakes lie in an alpine ravine at the base of several talus slopes. No permanent trail exists to the lakes, but a posted sign clearly points the way. Campsites can be found on the east side of Rudolph Lakes #2 and #3, while spring water is located on the south side of Rudolph #1. There is a campfire and firewood gathering restriction within 0.25 mile of the lakes. These lakes receive light to moderate usage, and anglers should have no problem limiting. If by chance Rudolph Lakes don't produce, try Mid or Diamond. These small lakes sit in heavy timber and are off the beaten path. Angling pressure is almost nil, and fishing should be fast for brook and cutthroat trout.

Another angling trip worth checking out is Cabin Lake. It is located 1.0 mile southwest of Rudolph #1. Follow an old sheep trail over the saddle of Rudolph Mountain, then on through several boulder fields. The saddle creates no difficult problems, but afterward, rugged boulder fields make travel tiring and time-consuming.

Cabin Lake gets very little usage. This isolated lake sits all by its lonesome in its own little basin. Campsites are undesirable due to rocky and heavily timbered terrain. However, camping areas can be found near the open meadows to the north. If angling is what you're after, you're in luck. Tall tales of this lake speculate that big brook trout are healthy and not too smart—our kind of lake!

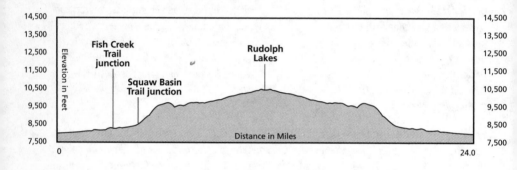

28 Arta Lake

Long drive, short hike, and solitude pretty well sum up this day trip. No matter which way you come from, you will probably be in for a long drive before you start hiking. But if you would rather spend more time driving through scenic country than hiking it, then this hike may interest you, especially if you're looking to get away from other people.

Start: End of the road
Distance: 1.0 mile out and back
Destination elevation: 10,450 feet
Approximate hiking time: 1.5 hours
Difficulty: Moderate—cross-country
Usage: Light
Nearest town: Duchesne, Utah
Drainage: Rock Creek

Maps: USGS Grandaddy Lake; USDA Forest Service High Uintas Wilderness; Trails Illustrated High Uintas Wilderness
Trail contacts: Ashley National Forest, Forest Supervisor, 355 North Vernal Ave., Vernal, UT 84078, (435) 781-1181; Duchesne Ranger District, 85 West Main, Duchesne, UT 84021, (435) 738-2482

Finding the trailhead: From Heber City, take US 40 east 69 miles to Duchesne. Then take SR 87 north 14 miles to Mountain Home. Rock Creek trailhead is 22 miles northwest of Mountain Home on FR 134; the road is paved to Upper Stillwater Reservoir. Turn west on FR 135 and continue past the Rock Creek trailhead. At the junction of FR 135 and FR 143 turn right and continue to the end of the road.

The Hike

It is only a 0.5-mile trek to Arta Lake from the end of FR 143, but it seems longer. A faint trail begins where the road ends but disappears after a couple hundred yards. Then you are left to pick your own route around lots of deadfall timber. Just keep heading due west and you will soon run into Arta Lake. Although attractive and quiet, this lake doesn't offer much in the way of good overnight campsites. The ground is strewn with boulders and pines. Water can be found on the northwest side, where it drains down a steep hill from Survey Lake, but you will need to purify it.

If you've come as far as Arta Lake, we suggest that you make the extra effort to hike the short, steep hill up to Survey Lake. The vista from the top of the hill overlooking Arta is magnificent, and on the other side of the hill Survey Lake lies in a great little alpine cirque (more pristine solitude). If you're really feeling ambitious, trek up the mountain behind Survey Lake and look down on Grandaddy Lake— what a view!

Fishing was lousy when we visited these lakes, as they probably experienced winterkill. We didn't catch anything, and the only sign of life was large schools of tiny minnows at Arta Lake. You never know, though—fishing could improve after

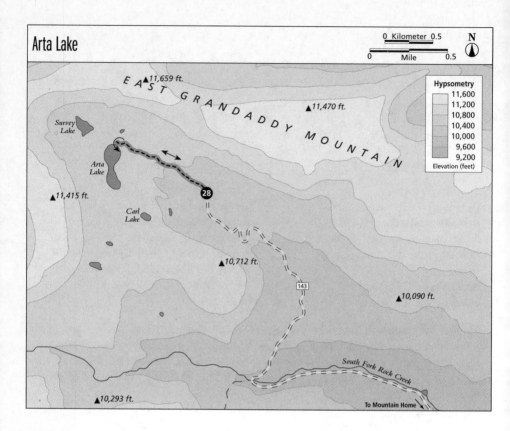

periodic stocking, or maybe the thousands of minnows that we saw will grow up (maybe we will too, someday). It would at least be worth a try if you were making the trip anyway.

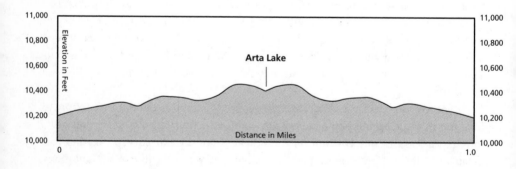

29 Kidney Lake

Topping out at 190 acres, Kidney Lake is one of the largest reservoirs in the High Uintas backcountry. Just try walking around it, and you'll become a believer. Because of its "kidney" shape, you don't really see all of it at any one time, so it is even bigger than it looks.

Start: Lake Fork trailhead before Moon Lake Campground
Distance: 18.0 miles out and back
Destination elevation: 10,267 feet
Approximate hiking time: 11 hours
Difficulty: Moderate
Usage: Heavy
Nearest town: Duchesne, Utah
Drainage: Lake Fork

Maps: USGS Kidney Lake; USDA Forest Service High Uintas Wilderness; Trails Illustrated High Uintas Wilderness
Trail contacts: Ashley National Forest, Forest Supervisor, 355 North Vernal Ave., Vernal, UT 84078, (435) 781-1181; Duchesne Ranger District, 85 West Main, Duchesne, UT 84021, (435) 738-2482

Finding the trailhead: From Heber City, take US 40 east 69 miles to Duchesne. Turn north onto SR 87 and travel 14 miles to Mountain Home. Take the Moon Lake Road north about 15 miles to the Lake Fork trailhead.

The trailhead has forty vehicle parking places with water and toilets. The Moon Lake Campground is 0.25 mile past the Lake Fork trailhead. Lake Fork is the main takeoff point for Brown Duck, East, and Ottoson Basins and is an optional trailhead for Squaw Basin.

The Hike

From Lake Fork trailhead, the trail is wide and clear for the first few miles, following Brown Duck Creek on the west side of Round Mountain. After about 7.0 miles, there is a trail junction with the trail going to Clements Reservoir. Shortly after this junction, the trail passes Brown Duck Lake and in 1.0 mile, Island Lake (yes, another one). Kidney Lake is 1.0 mile from the first glimpse of Island Lake.

There's a lot of room to spread out, so despite heavy pressure you should still find some solitude. This area is attractive to equestrians because of the large campsites that are available and a good supply of horse pasture. The eastern shoreline has the best accommodations, including a limited supply of spring water. The area is popular with backpackers too, but they might be happier at more isolated nearby lakes, like Tworoose Lake. Tworoose is another mile up the trail from Kidney, but it doesn't see many campers.

The streams linking Kidney, Island, and Brown Duck Lakes have good flow and should provide an opportunity for some good stream fishing. Try a flashy spinner in the ripples and pools. These lakes and streams are fun to fish because of the variety of opportunities that exist. Fish the lakes for a while, then check out one of the streams

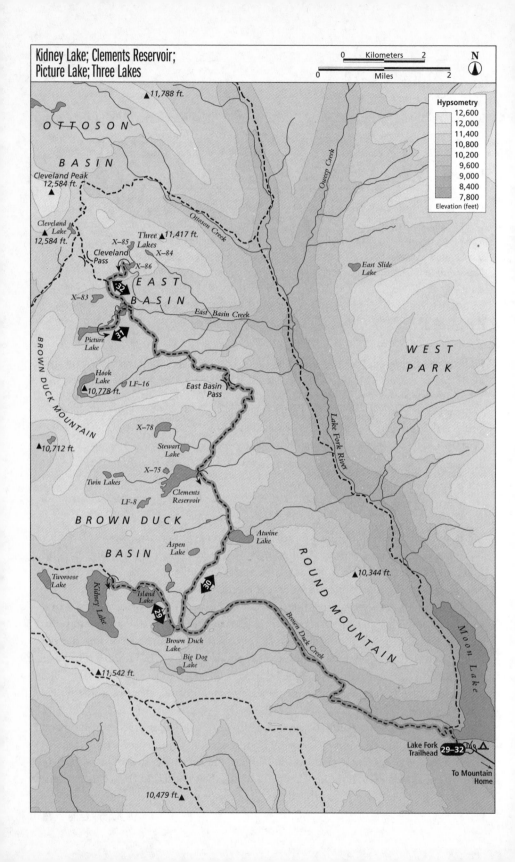

Kidney Lake; Clements Reservoir;
Picture Lake; Three Lakes

Kilometers

Miles

N

Hypsometry
12,600
12,000
11,400
10,800
10,200
9,600
9,000
8,400
7,800
Elevation (feet)

▲11,788 ft.

OTTOSON

BASIN

Cleveland Peak
12,584 ft. ▲

Owep Creek

Cleveland
Lake
12,584 ft. ▲

Cleveland
Pass

Three ▲11,417 ft.
Lakes

X–85
X–84
X–86

EAST

BASIN

Ottoson Creek

East Slide
Lake

X–83

32

WEST

PARK

Picture
Lake

37

East Basin Creek

Hook
Lake
10,778 ft. ▲

LF–16

East Basin
Pass

BROWN DUCK MOUNTAIN

▲10,712 ft.

X–78

Lake Fork River

Stewart
Lake

X–75

Twin Lakes

LF-8

Clements
Reservoir

BROWN DUCK

Atwine
Lake

ROUND MOUNTAIN

▲10,344 ft.

BASIN

Aspen
Lake

Tworoose
Lake

30

Kidney Lake

Island
Lake

29

Brown Duck
Lake

Big Dog
Lake

Brown Duck Creek

Moon Lake

▲11,542 ft.

Lake Fork
Trailhead

29–32

To Mountain
Home

10,479 ft. ▲

for a change of pace. Cutthroat trout are stocked throughout the region, but an occasional brook trout may show up.

Kidney Lake is also a convenient stopover for hikers continuing on into the Rock Creek Drainage. Spend a night near the trail at Kidney Lake, then you'll be fresh the next day to tackle Tworoose Pass (about 2.0 miles west).

There is a campfire and firewood gathering restriction within 0.25 mile of Kidney, Island, Tworoose, Brown Duck, Big Dog, and Dog Lakes.

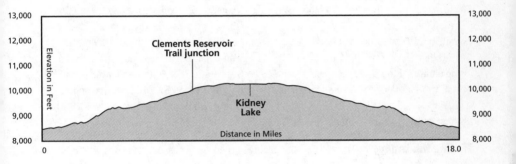

30 Clements Reservoir

After a long, steep climb, Clements Reservoir will look mighty good. Sheltered campsites are abundant along the northern shoreline, and you can easily imagine what it would be like to have a cabin overlooking the lake. The setting is rustic and peaceful.

See map on page 74.
Start: Lake Fork trailhead before Moon Lake Campground
Distance: 21.0 miles out and back
Destination elevation: 10,444 feet
Approximate hiking time: 12 hours
Difficulty: Moderate—some steep sections
Usage: Heavy
Nearest town: Duchesne, Utah

Drainage: Lake Fork
Maps: USGS Kidney Lake and Oweep Creek; USDA Forest Service High Uintas Wilderness; Trails Illustrated High Uintas Wilderness
Trail contacts: Ashley National Forest, Forest Supervisor, 355 North Vernal Ave., Vernal, UT 84078, (435) 781-1181; Duchesne Ranger District, 85 West Main, Duchesne, UT 84021, (435) 738-2482

Finding the trailhead: From Heber City, take US 40 east 69 miles to Duchesne. Turn north on SR 87 and travel 14 miles to Mountain Home. Take the Moon Lake Road north about 15 miles to the Lake Fork trailhead.

The trailhead has forty vehicle parking places with water and toilets. The Moon Lake Campground is 0.25 mile past the Lake Fork trailhead. Lake Fork is the main takeoff point for Brown Duck, East, and Ottoson Basins and is an optional trailhead for Squaw Basin.

The Hike

The trail from Moon Lake starts out easy. An old road is now a wide, clear trail for the first few miles. Then the going gets tough as the trail rears its ugly head, and you find yourself picking your way through the steep and rocky path. After 7.0 miles, there is a junction with the trail that goes to Kidney Lake, just before reaching Brown Duck Lake. Stay to the right here. The cursed rocks are relentless and don't give you a break until you reach Clements Reservoir. Level ground never looked so good as it does here.

Spring water is available, but it's a long walk to the back side of the lake to get any. It would probably be easier to purify some water from the lake or its outlet. Because of heavy use, firewood is scarce near the campsites. You'll have to walk a little for this commodity as well.

Fishing might be excellent at Clements. This relatively large lake can withstand heavy pressure and frequently provides fast fishing for fat cutthroat from 13 to 17 inches. Fly-fish right off the dam about an hour before sunset, and you'll likely catch all you want. If you want to get away from the people at Clements, there are three other small lakes nearby that offer fishing. Who knows what you'll find. Southwest of Clements is LF–8. Head west to X–75 or another mile to Twin Lakes. A short journey

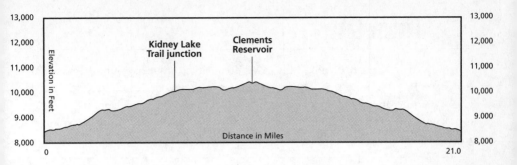

north to Stewart Lake may prove rewarding. Any of these lakes might produce the "mother lode" of fish you're looking for. There are no trails to any of these lakes, so be prepared for some rough cross-country travel that includes hopping over a lot of deadfall and boulders.

For spectacular scenery, hike up the trail 1.0 mile to East Basin Pass. From there you can view the entire upper region of the Lake Fork Drainage, including such sights as Mount Lovenia and Squaw Pass. Although East Basin Pass isn't as high as most other passes, it provides one of the most panoramic vistas in the High Uintas.

There is a campfire and firewood gathering restriction within 0.25 mile of Clements, Mud, Stewart, Atwine, and Aspen Lakes.

31 Picture Lake

"Thar's gold in them thar hills." This may be your first impression upon arriving at East Basin Pass. From here you'll have an inspirational view of the whole Upper Lake Fork Drainage. It leads you to believe that no one has ever been here before. That may have been the case a couple hundred years ago, but now a variety of explorers and Scout troops make East Basin a popular place.

See map on page 74.
Start: Lake Fork trailhead before Moon Lake Campground
Distance: 34.0 miles out and back
Destination elevation: 10,731 feet
Approximate hiking time: 22 hours
Difficulty: Moderate—some steep sections
Usage: Moderate
Nearest town: Duchesne, Utah

Drainage: Lake Fork
Maps: USGS Oweep Creek; USDA Forest Service High Uintas Wilderness; Trails Illustrated High Uintas Wilderness
Trail contacts: Ashley National Forest, Forest Supervisor, 1680 West US 40, Vernal, UT 84078; Duchesne Ranger District, 85 West Main, Duchesne, UT 84021, (435) 738-2482

Finding the trailhead: From Heber City, take US 40 east 69 miles to Duchesne. Turn north on SR 87 and travel 14 miles to Mountain Home. Take Moon Lake Road north about 15 miles to the Lake Fork trailhead. The trailhead has forty vehicle parking places with water and toilets. The Moon Lake Campground is 0.25 mile past the Lake Fork trailhead. Lake Fork is the main takeoff point for Brown Duck, East, and Ottoson Basins and is an optional trailhead for Squaw Basin.

The Hike

From Lake Fork trailhead, the trail is wide and clear for the first few miles, following Brown Duck Creek on the west side of Round Mountain. After about 7.0 miles, there is a junction with the trail going to Clements Reservoir. Stay to the right here and go 3.5 miles to Clements Reservoir. The trail continues another 6.0 miles to two small lakes, then follow the creek southwest another 0.5 mile to the lake.

Most groups make their base camp at the three small lakes that lie below Picture Lake. Several good camping areas exist near these lakes, and others can be found along the inlet streams. These lakes receive moderate to heavy angling pressure but can still be hot at times. Try a small spinner or fly. With a little skill, brook trout can be hooked throughout the deepwater channels. Two major inlets feed these lakes. By following the southwest inlet 0.5 mile up a timbered slope, you'll find a beautiful lake called Picture.

Picture Lake fits its name perfectly. This lake has a pretty talus slope as a backdrop, with timber-mirrored waters and a large outlet cascading down the mountainside. Rocky, timbered terrain surrounds the lake on three sides, adding to its artistic value. Due to this same fact, campsites are poorly defined.

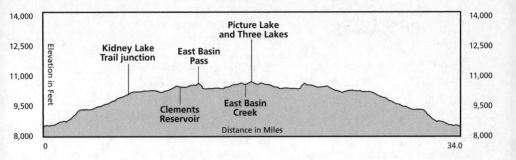

Hook Lake is located 1.0 mile south of Picture. There is no trail from Picture to Hook, and the terrain is consistently rough, rocky, and filled with deadfalls. A horse will not make it through here. However, an alternate route starting from LF–16 is much easier. From LF–16, follow the inlet stream 0.5 mile west along the base of a ridge to the lake. Hook is situated in the southwest corner of East Basin next to a glacial talus slope. Huge boulders interspersed with heavy timber make camping poor, but spring water can be found near the outlet.

32 Three Lakes

Three Lakes are not to be confused with the three lakes that lie just below Picture Lake. Three Lakes are located in a remote area 1 mile north of the three smaller lakes next to the East Basin Trail.

See map on page 74.
Start: Lake Fork trailhead before Moon Lake Campground
Distance: 34.0 miles out and back
Destination elevation: 10,860 feet
Approximate hiking time: 22 hours
Difficulty: Moderate—some steep sections
Usage: Very light
Nearest town: Duchesne, Utah

Drainage: Lake Fork
Maps: USGS Oweep Creek; USDA Forest Service High Uintas Wilderness; Trails Illustrated High Uintas Wilderness
Trail contacts: Ashley National Forest, Forest Supervisor, 355 North Vernal Ave., Vernal, UT 84078, (435) 781-1181; Duchesne Ranger District, 85 West Main, Duchesne, UT 84021, (435) 738-2482

Finding the trailhead: From Heber City, take US 40 east 69 miles to Duchesne. Turn north on SR 87 and travel 14 miles to Mountain Home. Take the Moon Lake Road north about 15 miles to the Lake Fork trailhead.

The trailhead has forty vehicle parking places with water and toilets. The Moon Lake Campground is 0.25 mile past the Lake Fork Trailhead. Lake Fork is the main takeoff point for Brown Duck, East, and Ottoson Basins and is an optional trailhead for Squaw Basin.

The Hike

From Lake Fork trailhead, the trail is wide and clear for the first few miles, following Brown Duck Creek on the west side of Round Mountain. After about 7.0 miles, there is a junction with the trail going to Clements Reservoir. Stay to the right here and go 3.5 miles to Clements Reservoir. The trail continues another 6.0 miles to two small lakes. From here follow the East Basin Trail north about 200 yards to where the trail levels out a bit. At this point, cut cross-country 1.0 mile northeast to the outlet of X–86.

Lake X–86 is the first of the Three Lakes you'll reach. Due to the rocky nature of this terrain, only one decent campsite exists. This campsite is found near the outlet, where you'll find good running water as well.

X–85 is the place to stay. This lake plays host to several good camping areas on the southwest side. It is also equipped with a superb spring that flows into the lake from the north. X–85 should produce some fairly good fishing for fat brook trout. Access the lake by following the inlet of X–86 0.25 mile to the north.

Like the other lakes, X–84 is in a rough alpine setting that may remind you of a desolate and faraway place. Hmmm, maybe it is. Campsites and spring water are not available. Angling usage is quite light, which means fishing prospects may be worthwhile. Reach X–84 by following a couple of ponds that lie northeast of X–86.

33 Ottoson Basin

Ottoson Basin offers one of the grandest views in the High Uintas, especially when viewed from the top of Cleveland Pass. Shutterbugs will want to be on the pass in early morning when the sun illuminates the peaks. Mornings are also very good for fishing, but you can always find fast fishing in the evening. If you want superb photos, choose the early hike up Cleveland Pass.

Start: Lake Fork trailhead before Moon Lake Campground
Distance: 30.4 miles out and back
Destination elevation: 11,075 feet
Approximate hiking time: 18 hours
Difficulty: Moderate
Usage: Light
Nearest town: Duchesne, Utah
Drainage: Lake Fork

Maps: USGS Oweep Creek; USDA Forest Service High Uintas Wilderness; Trails Illustrated High Uintas Wilderness
Trail contacts: Ashley National Forest, Forest Supervisor, 355 North Vernal Ave., Vernal, UT 84078, (435) 781-1181; Duchesne Ranger District, 85 West Main, Duchesne, UT 84021, (435) 738-2482

Finding the trailhead: From Heber City, take US 40 east 69 miles to Duchesne. Turn north on SR 87 and travel 14 miles to Mountain Home. Take the Moon Lake Road north about 15 miles to the Lake Fork trailhead.

The trailhead has forty vehicle parking places with water and toilets. The Moon Lake Campground is 0.25 mile past the Lake Fork trailhead. Lake Fork is the main takeoff point for Brown Duck, East, and Ottoson Basins and is an optional trailhead for Squaw Basin.

The Hike

The easiest access to Ottoson Basin is the Lake Fork River Trail. (The most scenic route, however, is via the Brown Duck Trail, then through East Basin and over Cleveland Pass.) From Moon Lake, follow the Lake Fork River trail 11.0 miles north to the Ottoson Basin Trail junction. From here go 3.0 miles northwest up a 1,200-foot incline to the base of Cleveland Peak. Then cut across rugged country 1.2 miles northwest to Lower Ottoson Lake.

Upper and Lower Ottoson Lakes are in open terrain in the upper west portion of Ottoson Basin. These lakes lie at the base of a talus ridge that connects Explorer and Squaw Peaks. There are no decent campsites at these lakes, but good camping areas and horse pasture can be found 0.5 mile southeast of Lower Ottoson. Both lakes contain healthy populations of cutthroat trout, and fishing pressure remains mostly light. During the late summer months, sheep grazing takes place in the whole upper part of Ottoson Basin. This activity depreciates the glamour of this beautiful basin and adds the need for extra caution where drinking water is concerned.

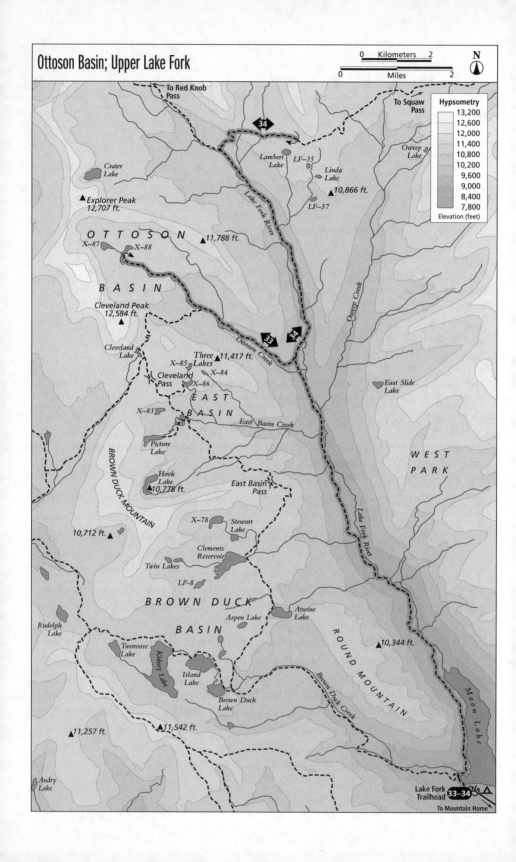

Ottoson Basin; Upper Lake Fork

Hypsometry
13,200
12,600
12,000
11,400
10,800
10,200
9,600
9,000
8,400
7,800
Elevation (feet)

To Red Knob Pass

To Squaw Pass

Oweep Lake

Lambert Lake

LF-35

Linda Lake

▲ 10,866 ft.

LF-37

Crater Lake

Lake Fork River

▲ Explorer Peak
12,707 ft.

O T T O S O N

X-87   X-88

▲ 11,788 ft.

B A S I N

Cleveland Peak
12,584 ft.
▲

Queey Creek

Ottoson Creek

33   34

Cleveland Lake

Three Lakes
X-85   ▲ 11,417 ft.
X-84
Cleveland Pass
X-86

East Slide Lake

X-83

E A S T

B A S I N

East Basin Creek

BROWN DUCK MOUNTAIN

Picture Lake

W E S T
P A R K

Hook Lake
▲ 10,778 ft.

East Basin Pass

Lake Fork River

10,712 ft. ▲

X-78   Stewart Lake

Clements Reservoir

Twin Lakes

LF-8

B R O W N   D U C K

Rudolph Lake

B A S I N

Aspen Lake   Atwine Lake

Twooroose Lake

Kidney Lake

Island Lake

Brown Duck Creek

R O U N D   M O U N T A I N

▲ 10,344 ft.

Moon Lake

Brown Duck Lake

▲ 11,257 ft.   ▲ 11,542 ft.

Audry Lake

Lake Fork Trailhead
33-34

To Mountain Home

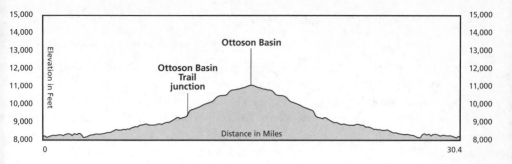

The best place to make base camp is at Ameoba Lake, just 0.5 mile north of the trail once you reach the base of Cleveland Peak. Ameoba is situated in a meadow near timberline, 14.0 miles from Moon Lake. This lake provides good campsites, horse pasture, and hot fishing for cutthroat trout.

Ottoson Basin from Cleveland Pass

34 Upper Lake Fork

The upper regions of the Lake Fork Drainage display some of the finest scenery in the High Uintas. From one pass to another, grand panoramas seem to enchant the mind. Red Knob Pass grants access to two other beautiful drainages, while Squaw and Porcupine Passes branch into others. To say the least, this area is a gold mine for photographers. However, the Lake Fork Trail from Moon Lake is not as seductive as it winds through a 14-mile corridor of tall standing pines. Not much else can be seen until you get to the upper basins.

See map on page 82.

Start: Lake Fork trailhead before Moon Lake Campground
Distance: 30.0 miles out and back
Destination elevation: 11,200 feet
Approximate hiking time: 19 hours
Difficulty: Moderate to difficult
Usage: Light
Nearest town: Duchesne, Utah

Drainage: Lake Fork
Maps: USGS Oweep Creek and USGS Explorer Peak; USDA Forest Service High Uintas Wilderness; Trails Illustrated High Uintas Wilderness
Trail contacts: Ashley National Forest, Forest Supervisor, 355 North Vernal Ave., Vernal, UT 84078, (435) 781-1181; Duchesne Ranger District, 85 West Main, Duchesne, UT 84021, (435) 738-2482

Finding the trailhead: From Heber City, take US 40 east 69 miles to Duchesne. Turn north onto SR 87 and travel 14 miles to Mountain Home. Take the Moon Lake Road north about 15 miles to the Lake Fork trailhead.

The trailhead has forty vehicle parking places with water and toilets. The Moon Lake Campground is 0.25 mile past the Lake Fork trailhead. Lake Fork is the main takeoff point for Brown Duck, East, and Ottoson Basins and is an optional trailhead for Squaw Basin.

The Hike

Although Crater, Lambert, and Oweep Lakes are located in the Lake Fork River Drainage, they are easier reached from East Fork Blacks Fork by way of Red Knob or Squaw Pass—if the passes are free of snow. Not only is this route a mile or two shorter, it is more scenic and supports a loop trail. Be prepared for some hard work going over Red Knob Pass.

In the middle of the upper Lake Fork Drainage lies Lambert Lake. Find this alpine water by following the Highline Trail. If you're coming from the west, keep to the trail until you get above timberline. Once you exit the pines, the lake should be south of the trail just a few hundred yards. Lambert offers good campsites and horse pasture, but spring water is limited. It receives moderate usage from those hiking the Highline Trail. Fly fishing is often great for feisty, fat brook trout. The best campsite at Lambert Lake is located just above the cliffs overlooking the lake. It includes a small spring that emerges from the rocks and rolls down to the lake.

Nearby Linda Lake sits in a boggy meadow 0.5 mile east on the Highline Trail from Lambert, then 0.25 mile south from the trail. Campsites and spring water are limited, but a wary population of brook trout await your offerings. LF–35 is right next to Linda Lake and may provide faster fishing. For some reason, the brookies at LF–35 preferred a flashy lure the day we stopped by.

In the eastern portion of the upper Lake Fork Drainage lies Oweep Lake. This scenic lake is at the base of a long talus slope bordering the Lake Fork and Yellowstone Drainages. Surrounded by rocky terrain, camping areas are limited. Spring water is abundant, and usage by anglers is considered light. In late summer, sheep grazing occurs in the whole upper Lake Fork Drainage. Oweep Lake receives the least amount of this activity.

Crater Lake lies at the northeast base of Explorer Peak and is encased by a spectacular cirque basin. Steep cliffs and talus slopes abut the water from the north, west, and south. Crater is known to be a mystifying lake. Some say that brook trout rise to the surface all at once, then mysteriously disappear for the rest of the day. "Where do they go?" we ask. Who knows? This lake has a depth of at least 150 feet, and no one really knows if anybody has found the bottom yet.

If you are planning to stay at Crater Lake to see if these stories are true, good luck. Due to open, rocky terrain, campsites are poorly defined. Camping areas and spring water can be found 1.0 mile to the east. Access to Crater is 16.0 miles north on the Lake Fork River Trail, then cross-country 2.0 miles west.

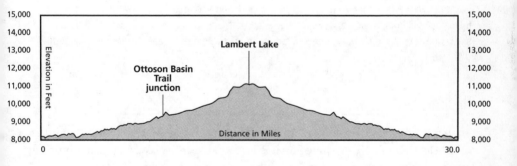

35 Toquer Lake

This is one of those places where you go to be alone. Toquer Lake is the only body of water in the area deserving of the designation "lake." It's not on the way to anywhere else, so very few hikers bother checking it out. But if you're looking for a short, mild hike that leads to serene scenery and a great chance for some genuine solitude, then look no further.

Start: Center Park trailhead
Distance: 6.0 miles out and back
Destination elevation: 10,470 feet
Approximate hiking time: 4 hours
Difficulty: Easy
Usage: Light
Nearest town: Duchesne, Utah
Drainage: Lake Fork

Maps: USGS Garfield Basin; USDA Forest Service High Uintas Wilderness; Trails Illustrated High Uintas Wilderness
Trail contacts: Ashley National Forest, Forest Supervisor, 355 North Vernal Ave., Vernal, UT 84078, (435) 781-1181; Duchesne Ranger District, 85 West Main, Duchesne, UT 84021, (435) 738-2482

Finding the trailhead: From Heber City, take US 40 east 69 miles to Duchesne. Turn north on SR 87 and travel 14 miles to Mountain Home. Follow Moon Lake Road north 4 miles to where Yellowstone River Road intersects on the east side. From this point, follow Yellowstone River Road another 4 miles to Hell's Canyon Road. Center Park trailhead is 7 miles northwest up Hell's Canyon Road.

Center Park has room for fifteen vehicles to park and has an information board and a vault toilet. Hell's Canyon Road fits its name perfectly—it is a road from hell. It is well defined but steep and very rocky. A truck/jeep is recommended, and the road may require four-wheel drive when wet.

The Hike

Toquer Lake offers an exquisite setting, but better campsites can be found about 0.25 mile below the lake. Everything you need is found near the lake. A cold, free-flowing spring on the north side provides drinking water, and firewood is virtually everywhere throughout the heavily timbered terrain. If you're lucky, the lake will even yield a few of its brook trout for your evening meal. But don't expect great fishing. An avid angler would probably be happier somewhere else, and that's OK. That means there will be even fewer visitors here.

The trail from the Center Park trailhead is a tough one to follow. It frequently disappears, and you may find yourself picking through the many fallen trees. Keep your map handy while hiking, and keep bearing northwest. You can always just find Fish Creek and then follow it up to Toquer Lake.

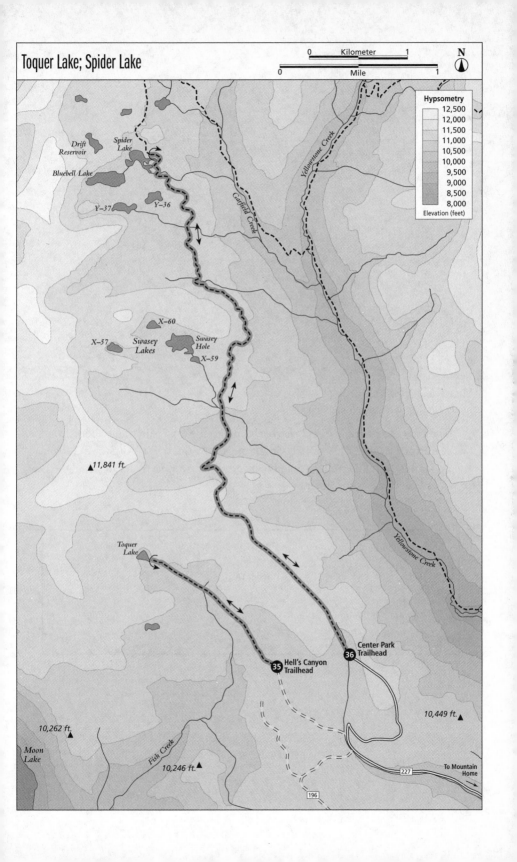

Toquer Lake; Spider Lake

0   Kilometer   1
0   Mile   1

N

Drift Reservoir

Spider Lake

Bluebell Lake

Y-37   Y-36

Garfield Creek

Yellowstone Creek

Hypsometry
12,500
12,000
11,500
11,000
10,500
10,000
9,500
9,000
8,500
8,000
Elevation (feet)

X-60
X-57   Swasey   Swasey
Lakes   Hole
X-59

▲11,841 ft.

Toquer Lake

Yellowstone Creek

Center Park
Trailhead

35 Hell's Canyon
Trailhead

36

Moon Lake

10,262 ft.
▲

Fish Creek

10,246 ft. ▲

10,449 ft. ▲

227

To Mountain
Home

196

An elk near Toquer Lake

If you are camped at Toquer Lake, try hiking to the top of the ridge about 1.0 mile to the northeast. From there you'll witness one of the finest vistas of Swasey Hole and the upper regions of the Yellowstone Drainage. On a clear day you can see all the way to Kings Peak. Take your camera.

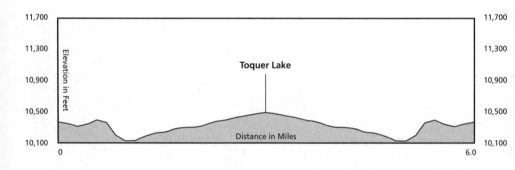

36 Spider Lake

Spider is named for its many elongated bays that offer interesting, but not particularly good, fishing. However, we rate this area as very good fishing because of the many opportunities nearby.

See map on page 87.
Start: Hell's Canyon trailhead
Distance: 15.5 miles out and back
Destination elevation: 10,876 feet
Approximate hiking time: 12 hours
Difficulty: Difficult—up and down many times
Usage: Heavy
Nearest town: Duchesne, Utah
Drainage: Yellowstone River

Maps: USGS Garfield Basin; USDA Forest Service High Uintas Wilderness; Trails Illustrated High Uintas Wilderness
Trail contacts: Ashley National Forest, Forest Supervisor, 355 North Vernal Ave., Vernal, UT 84078, (435) 781-1181; Duchesne Ranger District, 85 West Main, Duchesne, UT 84021, (435) 738-2482

Finding the trailhead: From Heber City, take US 40 east 69 miles to Duchesne. Turn north onto SR 87 and travel 14 miles to Mountain Home. Follow Moon Lake Road north 4 miles to where Yellowstone River Road intersects on the east side. From this point, follow Yellowstone River Road another 4 miles to Hell's Canyon Road. Hell's Canyon trailhead is west of the Center Park trailhead. There is an information board and vault toilet at the trailhead.

Hell's Canyon Road fits its name perfectly—it is a road from hell. It is well defined but steep and very rocky. A truck/jeep is recommended, and the road may require four-wheel drive when wet.

The Hike

Don't let the elevation gain fool you. This is a tiring hike; although, for the most part, it's a straight shot without any forks. On paper the terrain doesn't look that bad, but you'll feel like a yo-yo upon arrival. The trail seems to go up and down endlessly. Allow yourself extra hiking time to make up for the rest stops you're bound to need. Take your time and enjoy the scenery. It is a pretty hike. You may have a tough time remembering any level ground until you reach Spider Lake. Then things get much better. The camping sites are plentiful all around the lake, and that's good, because this aesthetic lake sees lots of pressure on the weekends. Be sure to clean up your mess and practice low-impact camping.

Bluebell Lake has some nice-size brooks and cutthroat. A small fly should yield fish. Or try Y–36 and Y–37 just to the south. These lakes are stocked with brook trout and receive little attention. Head northwest from Spider Lake about 0.5 mile, and you'll run into Drift Reservoir. Who knows what you will find here. It is out of the way just enough to keep a few secrets.

Take plenty of mosquito repellent if you are traveling during bug season. There are several moist areas that produce some fair-size clouds of mosquitoes. Take that into consideration when selecting your campsite, and you'll breathe easier.

The 0.25 mile campfire restriction applies to Spider, Bluebell, Drift, Gem, Five Point, Doll, Superior, and Little Superior Lakes.

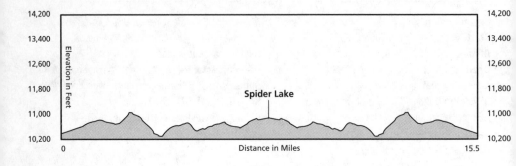

37 North Star Lake

Of all the lakes in the High Uintas, North Star is considered to be closest to the exact center of this mountain range. Due to this fact, access is possible from several locations.

Start: Swift Creek trailhead
Distance: 31.0 miles out and back
Destination elevation: 11,395 feet
Approximate hiking time: 18 hours
Difficulty: Moderate—some steep sections
Usage: Light
Nearest town: Duchesne, Utah
Drainage: Yellowstone River

Maps: USGS Garfield Basin and USGS Mount Powell; USDA Forest Service High Uintas Wilderness; Trails Illustrated High Uintas Wilderness
Trail contacts: Ashley National Forest, Forest Supervisor, 355 North Vernal Ave., Vernal, UT 84078, (435) 781-1181; Duchesne Ranger District, 85 West Main, Duchesne, UT 84021, (435) 738-2482

Finding the trailhead: From Heber City, take US 40 east 69 miles to Duchesne. Turn north onto SR 87 and travel 14 miles to Mountain Home. Follow Moon Lake Road north 4 miles to where Yellowstone River Road intersects on the east side. Follow Yellowstone River Road another 4 miles past the rough-and-tumble Hell's Canyon Road. Stay on Yellowstone River Road another 6 miles to the Swift Creek trailhead.

The Swift Creek trailhead can handle parking for twenty-five vehicles and is equipped with campsites, toilets, water, and a stock ramp. Many of the high lakes are 10 to 15 miles away, up steep and rocky terrain. Swift Creek also serves as an optional trailhead for the Yellowstone River Drainage.

The Hike

The shortest routes are found at either Center Park or the Swift Creek trailhead. From Swift Creek follow the Yellowstone Creek Trail 8.0 miles to the Garfield Basin junction, then proceed 4.0 miles northwest up a 1,600-foot incline to Five Point Lake. Past Five Point, keep following the Garfield Basin Trail 3.0 miles north then northeast to the Highline Trail. Then follow the Highline Trail another 0.75 mile north to North Star Lake. Other starting points are at China Meadows, East Fork Blacks Fork, and the Highline trailhead.

North Star is a popular stopping point for backpackers making the Highline trek. Although only a few mediocre campsites exist, it is the only decent place to make camp in the area. If you are traveling via the Garfield Basin route, you may want to pitch your tent at Five Point Lake and save North Star Lake as an exciting day hike. The upper portion of Garfield Basin is characterized by rocky, windswept tundra. There is little or no horse pasture, and firewood is extremely scarce.

North Star and Tungsten Lakes receive moderate angling pressure for brook and cutthroat trout. If you are looking for more solitude and more remote fishing

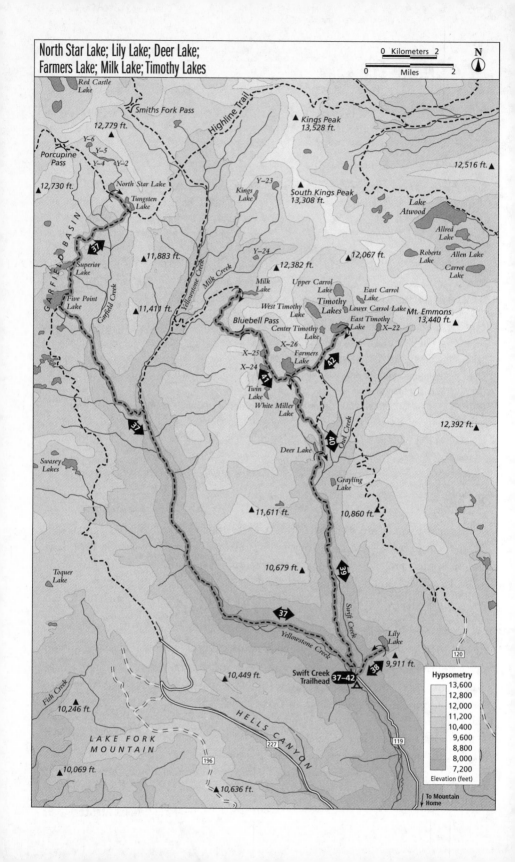

North Star Lake; Lily Lake; Deer Lake;
Farmers Lake; Milk Lake; Timothy Lakes

Red Castle
Lake

Smiths Fork Pass

Highline Trail

12,779 ft.

Kings Peak
13,528 ft.

12,516 ft.

Y–6

Porcupine
Pass

Y–5

Y–4 Y–2

North Star Lake

Y–23

Kings
Lake

South Kings Peak
13,308 ft.

Lake
Atwood

12,730 ft.

Tungsten
Lake

Allred
Lake

37

11,883 ft.

Y–24

12,382 ft.

12,067 ft.

Roberts
Lake

Allen Lake

Carrot
Lake

Superior
Lake

Milk
Lake

Upper Carrol
Lake

East Carrol
Lake

Five Point
Lake

11,411 ft.

West Timothy
Lake

Timothy
Lakes

Lower Carrol Lake

Mt. Emmons
13,440 ft.

Bluebell Pass

Center Timothy
Lake

East Timothy
Lake

X–22

GARFIELD BASIN

Garfield Creek

Yellowstone Creek

Milk Creek

X–25

X–26

Farmers
Lake

X–24

42

37

41

Twin
Lake

White Miller
Lake

12,392 ft.

Swasey
Lakes

40

Owl Creek

Deer Lake

Grayling
Lake

11,611 ft.

10,860 ft.

Toquer
Lake

10,679 ft.

39

37

Swift Creek

Lily
Lake

Yellowstone Creek

120

10,449 ft.

Swift Creek
Trailhead

38

9,911 ft.

37–42

Fish Creek

10,246 ft.

HELLS CANYON

LAKE FORK
MOUNTAIN

227

119

196

10,069 ft.

10,636 ft.

Hypsometry

	Elevation (feet)
	13,600
	12,800
	12,000
	11,200
	10,400
	9,600
	8,800
	8,000
	7,200

To Mountain
Home

possibilities, try lakes Y–2, Y–4, and Y–5. These lakes receive little attention and harbor an excellent supply of pan-size brook trout. Find these lakes by following the inlet of North Star Lake 1.0 mile north to Y–2. Then just follow a string of lakes to Y– 4, 5, and 6. Sorry, there are no fish at Y–6.

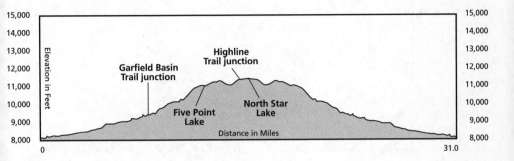

38 Lily Lake

A short but strenuous day hike can put you at beautiful Lily Lake, surrounded by pines and quaking aspens that hiss in the breeze. The lake is clear and deep except for the southern end, where numerous aquatic plants grow in the shallows. If Swift Creek Campground is your base camp, Lily Lake is an excellent place to escape the crowds and find some peace and quiet.

See map on page 92.
Start: Swift Creek trailhead
Distance: 2.0 miles out and back
Destination elevation: 9,346 feet
Approximate hiking time: 2 hours
Difficulty: Moderate—some steep sections
Usage: Moderate
Nearest town: Duchesne, Utah
Drainage: Swift Creek

Maps: USGS Burnt Mill Spring; USDA Forest Service High Uintas Wilderness; Trails Illustrated High Uintas Wilderness
Trail contacts: Ashley National Forest, Forest Supervisor, 355 North Vernal Ave., Vernal, UT 84078, (435) 781-1181; Duchesne Ranger District, 85 West Main, Duchesne, UT 84021, (435) 738-2482

Finding the trailhead: From Heber City, take US 40 east 69 miles to Duchesne. Turn north onto SR 87 and travel 14 miles to Mountain Home. Follow Moon Lake Road north 4 miles to where Yellowstone River Road intersects on the east side. Follow Yellowstone River Road another 4 rough miles past Hell's Canyon Road. Stay on Yellowstone River Road another 6 miles to the Swift Creek trailhead.

The Swift Creek trailhead can handle parking for twenty-five vehicles and is equipped with campsites, toilets, water, and a stock ramp. Many of the high lakes are 10 to 15 miles away, up steep and rocky terrain. Swift Creek also serves as an optional trailhead for the Yellowstone River Drainage.

The Hike

From Swift Creek trailhead, go back down Yellowstone River Road about 0.5 mile to Grant Springs. From there, a good trail will lead you safely up the mountainside northeast to Lily Lake. It is quite steep—you'll pick up more than 1,200 feet of elevation in just 1.0 mile. It may seem farther than a mile. Mountain miles usually do. But don't give up; you should complete the trek in about 30 to 45 minutes. The walk back down should be a lot quicker.

Anglers like to venture to Lily Lake in hopes of finding faster fishing than near the campgrounds. This may or may not happen. Lily Lake is stocked with brook trout, but stocking schedules, angling pressure, and the mood of the fish will determine your fishing luck. Try to be at the lake in early morning or late evening. This should be feasible because of the short hike. Try a small fly (#16) around the inlet and outlet, and don't overlook the lily pads. Brook trout like to hang around these looking for bugs. Lily Lake is just close enough to camp that you won't mind toting a few fish back for dinner.

Lily Lake doesn't sport good camping facilities. It is not a good place to spend the night. Don't make any new camping areas or fire pits. This area is more suitable for day use and probably should remain that way.

An old-growth tree near Lily Lake

39 Deer Lake

Early in the summer season, before the higher country opens up, you may find your-self wanting some alpine adventure. Here's a lake that just might provide some early relief from cabin fever; that is, if you call mid-June early. Pack some warm clothes. The temperatures can still be pretty brisk during June. Much of the hike is steep, but it's not very far. Deer Lake makes an excellent primer hike that can easily fit into a weekend.

See map on page 92.
Start: Swift Creek trailhead
Distance: 11.0 miles out and back
Destination elevation: 10,240 feet
Approximate hiking time: 6.5 hours
Difficulty: Moderate
Usage: Moderate
Nearest town: Duchesne, Utah
Drainage: Swift Creek

Maps: USGS Mt. Emmons; USDA Forest Service High Uintas Wilderness; Trails Illustrated High Uintas Wilderness
Trail contacts: Ashley National Forest, Forest Supervisor, 355 North Vernal Ave., Vernal, UT 84078, (435) 781-1181; Duchesne Ranger District, 85 West Main, Duchesne, UT 84021, (435) 738-2482

Finding the trailhead: From Heber City, take US 40 east 69 miles to Duchesne. Turn north onto SR 87 and travel 14 miles to Mountain Home. Follow Moon Lake Road north 4 miles to where Yellowstone River Road intersects on the east side. Follow the rough Yellowstone River Road another 4 miles past Hell's Canyon Road. Stay on Yellowstone River Road another 6 miles to the Swift Creek trailhead.

The Swift Creek trailhead can handle parking for twenty-five vehicles and is equipped with campsites, toilets, water, and a stock ramp. Many of the high lakes are 10 to 15 miles away, up steep and rocky terrain. Swift Creek also serves as an optional trailhead for the Yellowstone River Drainage.

The Hike

From Swift Creek trailhead, it's a short distance to where the trail forks left to Yellowstone River or right to Swift Creek. Stay right and climb 5.5 miles to Deer Lake.

Deer Lake is probably at its best early in the season. Later on, the lake becomes less attractive as the water level drops, leaving a muddy, rocky shoreline. If you can get there just after "ice-off," you could experience some fast fishing for pan-size brook and cutthroat trout. Other fishing opportunities include Grayling Lake (about 1.0 mile southeast) and Swift Creek. The outlet from Deer Lake joins Swift Creek about 0.5 mile below. Hardly anyone fishes the creek. Try it with a small spinner and you might be pleasantly surprised.

Fair campsites can be found near the outlet. They are not top-quality camping spots, but they will suffice. Spring water is available at the inlet, as is a small amount of horse pasture. There is a campfire restriction within 0.25 mile of Deer Lake. Most travelers only stop for lunch on their way to more popular lakes. You should have it all to yourself during the evening hours.

Shutterbugs will enjoy the view back down Swift Creek Drainage, as well as the setting around Deer Lake. Deer Lake lies in a narrow valley, surrounded by pines on its long sides, with a picturesque cliff sealing off the back end.

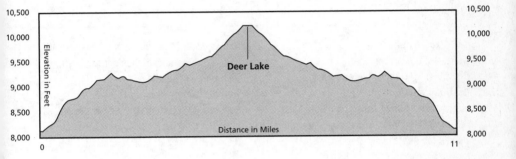

40 Farmers Lake

If you like to get a lot of elevation gain out of the way early, then this hike is for you. Right from the start, you'll traverse a long series of switchbacks that pick up 1,000 feet in 1.5 miles. Then the trail levels off for a few miles before another steep ascent to Deer Lake. Deer Lake is a great place to stop for lunch, and maybe catch a few neglected brook trout.

See map on page 92.
Start: Swift Creek trailhead
Distance: 15.0 miles out and back
Destination elevation: 10,990 feet
Approximate hiking time: 10 hours
Difficulty: Moderate—some steep sections
Usage: Moderate
Nearest town: Duchesne, Utah
Drainage: Swift Creek

Maps: USGS Mt. Emmons; USDA Forest Service High Uintas Wilderness; Trails Illustrated High Uintas Wilderness
Trail contacts: Ashley National Forest, Forest Supervisor, 355 North Vernal Ave., Vernal, UT 84078, (435) 781-1181; Duchesne Ranger District, 85 West Main, Duchesne, UT 84021, (435) 738-2482

Finding the trailhead: From Heber City, take US 40 east 69 miles to Duchesne. Turn north onto SR 87 and travel 14 miles to Mountain Home. Follow Moon Lake Road north 4 miles to where Yellowstone River Road intersects on the east side. Follow Yellowstone River Road another 4 miles past Hell's Canyon Road. Stay on Yellowstone River Road another 6 miles to the Swift Creek trailhead.

The Swift Creek trailhead can handle parking for twenty-five vehicles and is equipped with campsites, toilets, water, and a stock ramp. Many of the high lakes are 10 to 15 miles away, up steep and rocky terrain. Swift Creek also serves as an optional trailhead for the Yellowstone River Drainage.

The Hike

From Swift Creek trailhead, it's a short distance to where the trail forks left to Yellowstone River or right to Swift Creek. Stay right and climb 5.5 miles to Deer Lake. Farmers Lake is another 2.0 miles up the valley.

You will pass White Miller Lake on the way. This is a tempting place to camp and fish, but push on another mile to Farmers Lake. Farmers is a better base camp. It sits in the middle of several good fishing lakes and has excellent horse pasture nearby to the west. The best campsite is about 0.25 mile below Farmers Lake. Just follow the outlet stream and you can't miss it.

Fishing at Farmers Lake varies greatly from year to year. Some years you can catch eager brook trout on every other cast. At other times, the lake seems empty. If it doesn't produce for you, then head north over the hill to X–26. It frequently has fast fishing for pan-size brookies. The lakes west of Farmers hold a few surprises too.

Large cutthroat roam these lakes. Try the inlets with a salmon-egg fly, and look out. You won't catch too many, but you'll only need a couple to make a hearty meal.

Timothy and Carrol Lakes are not far from Farmers. A short day hike of 2.0 to 4.0 miles northeast will put you right in the middle of this open basin. Cattle graze up here, which detracts from the aesthetics of the vast tundra, but it's still worth seeing—and definitely worth fishing. Plenty of open shoreline exists for the fly fisher.

Campfires are not allowed within 0.25 mile of Farmers, White Miller, West Timothy, Upper Carrol, Lower Carrol, East Timothy, and East Carrol Lakes.

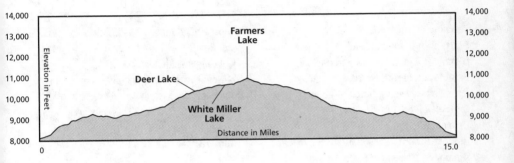

41 Milk Lake

Milk Lake is for loners. In fact, Milk Lake is a loner itself. Situated high on the east side of the Yellowstone Drainage, there are no other lakes for miles in any direction. It's a long, steep hike whether you're following Yellowstone Creek or coming over Bluebell Pass from the Swift Creek Drainage. The Swift Creek route is shorter by 3.0 miles and is the suggested route. You'll need to traverse Bluebell Pass, but it is not bad as mountain passes go, even by horseback.

See map on page 92.
Start: Swift Creek trailhead
Distance: 22.0 miles out and back
Destination elevation: 10,983 feet
Approximate hiking time: 14 hours
Difficulty: Moderate to difficult
Usage: Light
Nearest town: Duchesne, Utah
Drainage: Yellowstone River

Maps: USGS Garfield Basin; USDA Forest Service High Uintas Wilderness; Trails Illustrated High Uintas Wilderness
Trail contacts: Ashley National Forest, Forest Supervisor, 355 North Vernal Ave., Vernal, UT 84078, (435) 781-1181; Duchesne Ranger District, 85 West Main, Duchesne, UT 84021, (435) 738-2482

Finding the trailhead: From Heber City, take US 40 east 69 miles to Duchesne. Turn north onto SR 87 and travel 14 miles to Mountain Home. Follow Moon Lake Road north 4 miles to where Yellowstone River Road intersects on the east side. Follow Yellowstone River Road another 4 miles past Hell's Canyon Road. Stay on Yellowstone River Road another 6 miles to the Swift Creek trailhead.

The Swift Creek trailhead can handle parking for twenty-five vehicles and is equipped with campsites, toilets, water, and a stock ramp. Many of the high lakes are 10 to 15 miles away, up steep and rocky terrain. Swift Creek also serves as an optional trailhead for the Yellowstone River Drainage.

The Hike

If you feel alone and remote at Milk Lake, it's because, well, you are. It's a great feeling. You might feel almost like an explorer in this vast country that rarely sees visitors of the human kind. This is a true wilderness experience. You should be in great physical shape and confident of your skills before coming out here.

From Swift Creek trailhead, it's a short distance to where the trail forks left to Yellowstone River or right to Swift Creek. Stay right and climb 5.5 miles to Deer Lake. Farmers Lake is another 2.0 miles up the valley. At Farmers Lake turn left (west) past a few small lakes and over Bluebell Pass. The trail descends then turns to the right (north) and follows the small creek up to Milk Lake.

The best camping and horse pastures are located just west or south of the lake. Spring water is hard to come by, so bring along a water purification method. Giardia can be found anywhere in the High Uintas, even in high, remote alpine lakes.

As for fishing, who knows what to expect. This is the type of water that could produce some quality fishing time. Stocked brook trout can live many seasons without seeing an artificial lure and may have the chance to reach large proportions. If the fish aren't cooperating at Milk, you are out of luck. There's no place else nearby.

Perhaps here it is better to just relax and enjoy the quiet space. You will most certainly have earned it.

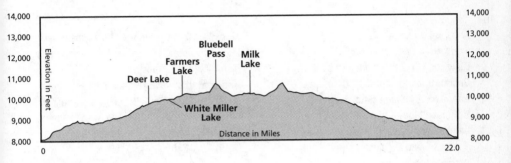

42 Timothy Lakes

Timothy Lakes offer an excellent chance for an "above timberline" experience. A grueling 8.5-mile hike places you in an open basin where Swift Creek originates. Equestrians and fly fishers adore this area because of the wide-open tundra. Horses have plenty of room to roam, and anglers have plenty of room for back casting. Fishing is a primary reason for coming here. Combine the three Timothy Lakes with the three Carrol Lakes, and you have some of the finest fishing you can find packed into 2 miles.

See map on page 92.
Start: Swift Creek trailhead
Distance: 17.0 miles out and back
Destination elevation: 11,000 feet
Approximate hiking time: 12 hours
Difficulty: Moderate
Usage: Moderate
Nearest town: Duchesne, Utah
Drainage: Swift Creek

Maps: USGS Mt. Emmons; USDA Forest Service High Uintas Wilderness; Trails Illustrated High Uintas Wilderness
Trail contacts: Ashley National Forest, Forest Supervisor, 355 North Vernal Ave., Vernal, UT 84078, (435) 781-1181; Duchesne Ranger District, 85 West Main, Duchesne, UT 84021, (435) 738-2482

Finding the trailhead: From Heber City, take US 40 east 69 miles to Duchesne. Turn north onto SR 87 and travel 14 miles to Mountain Home. Follow Moon Lake Road north 4 miles to where Yellowstone River Road intersects on the east side. Follow Yellowstone River Road another 4 miles past Hell's Canyon Road. This is a rough road. Stay on Yellowstone River Road another 6 miles to the Swift Creek trailhead.

The Swift Creek trailhead can handle parking for twenty-five vehicles and is equipped with campsites, toilets, water, and a stock ramp. Many of the high lakes are 10 to 15 miles away, up steep and rocky terrain. Swift Creek also serves as an optional trailhead for the Yellowstone River Drainage.

The Hike

From Swift Creek trailhead, it's a short distance to where the trail forks left to Yellowstone River or right to Swift Creek. Stay right and climb 5.5 miles to Deer Lake. Farmers Lake is another 2.0 miles up the valley. From Farmers Lake turn right (east) and go 1.0 mile to the lower Timothy Lake.

Good camps can be set up at East Timothy or Center Timothy. At the latter you'll probably see fewer people and will also stand a better chance of locating some spring water. But either place is a good choice. Sometimes cattle range up here, so don't be surprised if you wake up in the morning to the sound of mooing. The 0.25 mile campfire restriction applies to West Timothy, Upper Carrol, Lower Carrol, East

Timothy, and East Carrol Lakes. A gas stove is a worthwhile investment if you are planning on cooking up some trout.

The trout should cooperate here. Brook trout are in all of these lakes, and cutthroat will appear from time to time. It's hard to recommend the best fishing hole. Try them all. If one lake doesn't produce, scoot over to the next one. You're bound to find at least one lake that will yield some lightning-fast fishing. Check the connecting streams too. Many trout migrate from lake to lake or simply prefer to spend their summer in the creeks. A small spinner can produce some fun action on the streams when your arms tire of fly-casting on the lakes.

Farmers Lake is not too far from here, especially if you have horses. It's a nice change of scenery and may offer some better sheltered camping.

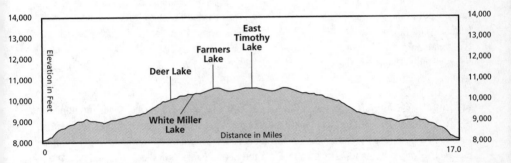

43 Crow Basin

This is good horse country. The Dry Gulch Drainage is the smallest in the Uintas Mountains, and Crow Basin forms a natural box canyon at the top of the drainage. These factors, along with abundant pasture and water, make it well suited for horses. Recreational use is generally quite light, but it appears to be more heavily used than it is. Litter and well-worn horse camps take away from the aesthetics.

Start: Jackson Park trailhead
Distance: 6.0 miles out and back
Destination elevation: 10,320 feet
Approximate hiking time: 4 hours
Difficulty: Moderate
Usage: Moderate
Nearest town: Duchesne, Utah
Drainage: Dry Gulch

Maps: USGS Mt. Emmons; USDA Forest Service High Uintas Wilderness; Trails Illustrated High Uintas Wilderness
Trail contacts: Ashley National Forest, Forest Supervisor, 355 North Vernal Ave., Vernal, UT 84078, (435) 781-1181; Duchesne Ranger District, 85 West Main, Duchesne, UT 84021, (435) 738-2482

Finding the trailhead: From Heber City, take US 40 east 69 miles to Duchesne. Turn north onto SR 87 and travel 14 miles to Mountain Home. Follow Moon Lake Road north 4 miles to where Yellowstone River Road intersects on the east side. Follow Yellowstone River Road another 4 miles past Hell's Canyon Road. It's a rough ride. From the Center Park–Swift Creek junction, follow Yellowstone River Road northeast about 3 miles to a four-wheel-drive road (#119) that winds southeast then east about 5 miles to Jackson Park Road (#120). About 3 miles northwest up Jackson Park Road, it turns into a rough jeep road. It is really quite inaccessible, even with four-wheel drive. This is Jackson Park trailhead.

There are no facilities at this trailhead.

The Hike

From where you park your car, continue up the jeep trail. At its end, turn east and climb about 0.5 mile to Crow Lake.

Crow Lake probably offers the best base camp in the basin. It features good campsites, spring water, and plenty of horse pasture. Again, trash is often a problem, so it may be worth a few minutes of your time to pick up garbage. It may improve your camping experience and will certainly enhance the natural appearance of the lake.

Fishing at Crow should be pretty good. Nice numbers of cutthroat trout patrol these waters, scooping up most anything that resembles a bug. But, as with almost all Uintas lakes, the fishing can change from year to year. If Crow Lake doesn't meet your expectations, there are several lakes close by that can be tested. Travel north about a mile to DG–6, DG–9, and DG–10. These lakes are all worth a try, and any one of them may be red-hot.

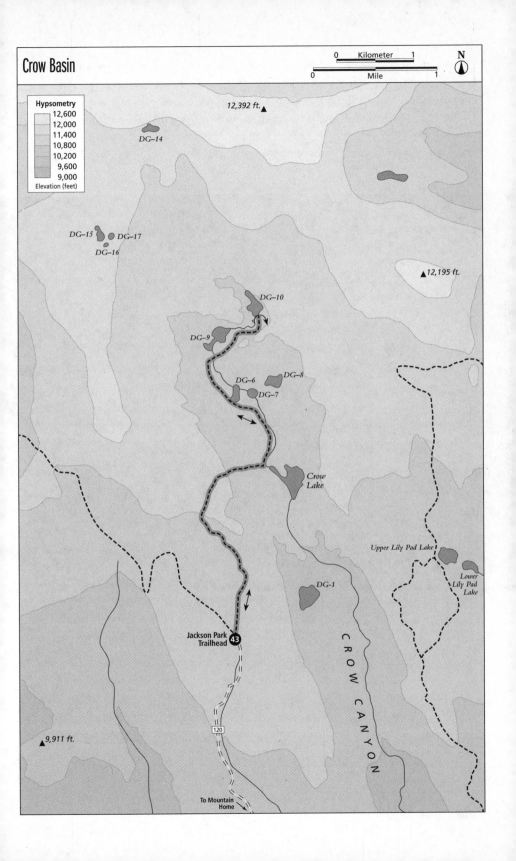

Another mile of riding northwest will put you into a cluster of lakes that rarely see anglers (DG–14, DG–15, DG–16, and DG–17). They are not fit for camping but can provide a lot of fishing fun. Cutthroat trout in various sizes and numbers make things very interesting. These lakes make an excellent day hike for anyone camped at Crow Lake. There is very little horse pasture up this way, and the only drinking water to speak of is from springs emerging from the talus slope at DG–14.

Columbine flowers in Crow Basin

44 Bollie Lake

The avid outdoorsman should have great expectations of Bollie Lake. Fast fishing has been reported for pan-size brookies, and the open picturesque shorelines make for easy fly casting. Excellent campsites and horse pasture exist by the lush meadows that are interspersed with pines.

Start: Dry Gulch trailhead
Distance: 12.0 miles out and back
Destination elevation: 10,660 feet
Approximate hiking time: 8 hours
Difficulty: Moderate
Usage: Light
Nearest town: Duchesne, Utah
Drainage: Dry Gulch

Maps: USGS Mt. Emmons and USGS Bollie Lake; USDA Forest Service High Uintas Wilderness; Trails Illustrated High Uintas Wilderness
Trail contacts: Ashley National Forest, Forest Supervisor, 355 North Vernal Ave., Vernal, UT 84078, (435) 781-1181; Duchesne Ranger District, 85 West Main, Duchesne, UT 84021, (435) 738-2482

Finding the trailhead: From Heber City, take US 40 east 69 miles to Duchesne. Turn north onto SR 87 and travel 14 miles to Mountain Home. Follow Moon Lake Road north 4 miles to where Yellowstone River Road intersects on the east side. Follow Yellowstone River Road another 4 miles past Hell's Canyon Road. From the Center Park–Swift Creek junction, follow Yellowstone River Road northeast about 3 miles to a four-wheel-drive road (#119) that winds southeast then east about 5 miles to Jackson Park Road (#120). About 3 miles northwest up Jackson Park Road, it turns into a rough jeep road. It is really quite inaccessible, even with four-wheel drive. This is Jackson Park trailhead. The Dry Gulch trailhead is 2 miles east of the Jackson Park Road turnoff to Dry Gulch Road (#122) and another 4 miles to Dry Gulch trailhead.
There are no facilities at either of these trailheads.

The Hike

Several different starting points can be used to reach Bollie Lake. All access points are about the same distance, but the old logging road that ventures past Jefferson Park is the most feasible route. Access to the logging road can only be obtained by foot or on horseback. Dry Gulch Road has been barricaded about 4.0 miles from the turnoff of Road 119. From the trailhead, hike along an old jeep road 1.5 miles north to the trail. The beginning portion of this trail is a little hard to find and difficult to follow for the first 0.25 mile. Follow a hit-or-miss trail 2.0 miles east to the old logging road. Then follow the logging road 2.5 miles north, passing Jefferson Park. Stay with the trail another 1.5 miles west along a canyon rim until you reach Bollie Lake.

Four-wheel drive is advised for access to the Dry Gulch trailhead. If easy car access is what you need, then the best starting point is from the Uintas River Drainage. Starting at U-Bar Ranch, follow the Uintas River Trail 3.0 miles north to Sheep

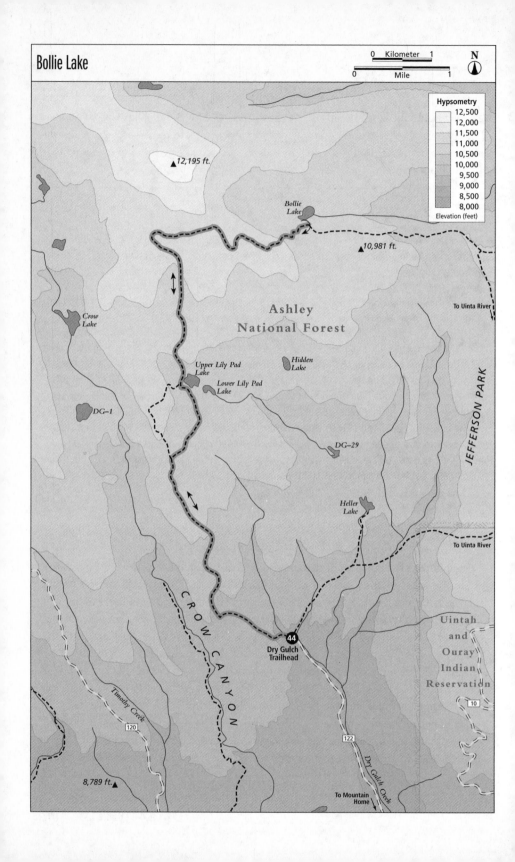

Bollie Lake

Hypsometry
- 12,500
- 12,000
- 11,500
- 11,000
- 10,500
- 10,000
- 9,500
- 9,000
- 8,500
- 8,000

Elevation (feet)

0 Kilometer 1

0 Mile 1

N

▲12,195 ft.

Bollie
Lake

▲10,981 ft.

To Uinta River

Crow
Lake

Ashley
National Forest

Upper Lily Pad
Lake

Hidden
Lake

Lower Lily Pad
Lake

DG–1

DG–29

JEFFERSON PARK

Heller
Lake

To Uinta River

CROW CANYON

44
Dry Gulch
Trailhead

Uintah
and
Ouray
Indian
Reservation

10

Timothy Creek

120

122

Dry Gulch Creek

8,789 ft.▲

To Mountain
Home

Bridge. Then take the Chain Lakes Trail 1.0 mile west to the top of some steep switchbacks. Here an old sheep trail heads south then west 3.5 miles to the lake.

This trek also features a loop trail. If you are like us, taking the same old route back to the car can be boring. For a change of scenery, we suggest taking the trail back over Flat Top Mountain, then past Lily Pad Lakes.

Lily Pad Lakes are in a beautiful meadow surrounded by timber. There are excellent campsites here, and horse munchies abound in the area. Upper Lily Pad Lake provides the better fishing.

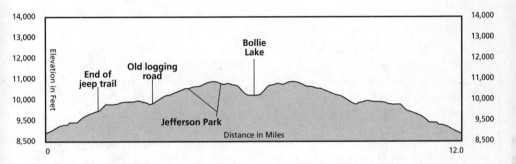

45 Chain Lakes

Chain Lakes are three connecting reservoirs and one natural lake. Campsites and horse pasture are somewhat limited at all four lakes, but they receive heavy camping and fishing anyway. During the late summer months, the reservoirs experience serious fluctuation, and angling pressure decreases rapidly. However, from July to mid-August pan-size brookies are abundant at all reservoirs and should produce fast fishing. Chain #4 is a natural lake located on a plateau. Anglers don't utilize this lake as much as the others, but this is often the best fishing hole during late summer.

Start: Uintas trailhead
Distance: 16.0 miles out and back
Destination elevation: 10,580 feet
Approximate hiking time: 10 hours
Difficulty: Moderate—some steep sections
Usage: Heavy
Nearest town: Roosevelt, Utah
Drainage: Uintas River

Maps: USGS Bollie Lake and USGS Mt. Emmons; USDA Forest Service High Uintas Wilderness; Trails Illustrated High Uintas Wilderness
Trail contacts: Ashley National Forest, Forest Supervisor, 355 North Vernal Ave., Vernal, UT 84078, (435) 781-1181; Duchesne Ranger District, 85 West Main, Duchesne, UT 84021, (435) 738-2482

Finding the trailhead: From Heber City, take US 40 east 99 miles to Roosevelt. Then take SR 121 north for 11 miles to Neola. Head north 17 miles on Road 118 to Wandin and Uintas Campgrounds. The trailhead is located 0.8 mile past the Uintas Campground.

The Uintas trailhead has room for twenty vehicles; amenities include toilets and a stock ramp. There is no water at the trailhead. Camping is available at Uintas Campground.

The Hike

A good place to set up base camp is Pippen Lake (sometimes called Island Lake). It sits in a meadow 0.5 mile southwest of Lower Chain's outlet. Pippen is distinguished by a small island near the south end of the shore and has excellent meadowland campsites. Plenty of horse pasture dominates the surrounding terrain. Pippen is one of the better fly-fishing lakes in the Uintas River Drainage and sustains moderate angling use throughout the summer. You should have no problem filling your skillet with fresh mountain brook trout.

If you're looking to get off the beaten path, Oke Doke Lake is a good spot. This handsome lake is just 1.0 mile from Chain #4. From the fourth Chain Lake or Roberts Pass, head west along the south side of the ridge that extends from Mount Emmons. Oke Doke Lake is on the eastern base of Mount Emmons in a high cirque. No campsites or horse pasture exists. Light angling pressure often means exciting fishing for cunning cutthroat trout.

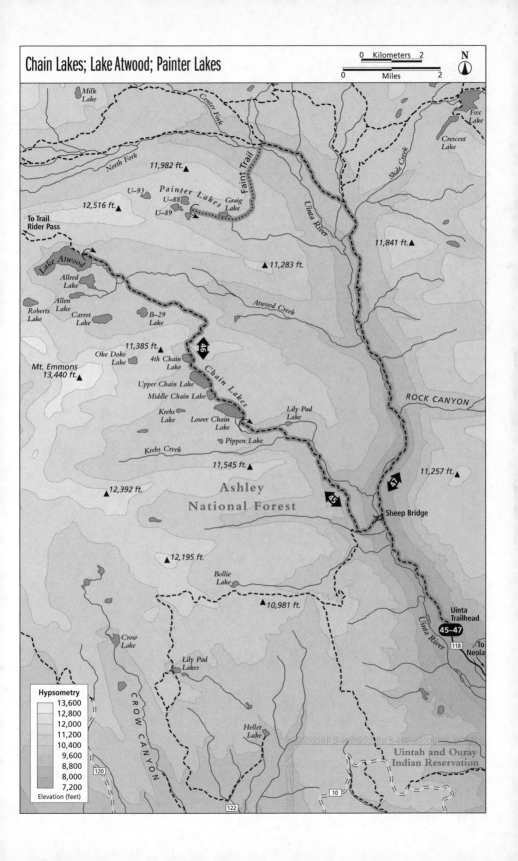

Chain Lakes; Lake Atwood; Painter Lakes

Milk
Lake

Fox
Lake

Center Fork

Crescent
Lake

North Fork

11,982 ft. ▲

Painter Lakes

U–93

Faint Trail

Graig
Lake

Shale Creek

12,516 ft. ▲

U–88

U–89

To Trail
Rider Pass

11,841 ft. ▲

Uinta River

Lake Atwood

11,283 ft. ▲

Allred
Lake

Atwood Creek

Allen
Lake

Roberts
Lake

Carrot
Lake

B–29
Lake

11,385 ft. ▲

Oke Doke
Lake

Chain Lakes

46

4th Chain
Lake

Mt. Emmons
13,440 ft. ▲

Upper Chain Lake

ROCK CANYON

Middle Chain Lake

Krebs
Lake

Lily Pad
Lake

Lower Chain
Lake

Pippen Lake

11,257 ft. ▲

Krebs Creek

11,545 ft. ▲

47

12,392 ft. ▲

Ashley

45

National Forest

Sheep Bridge

12,195 ft. ▲

Bollie
Lake

10,981 ft. ▲

Uinta
Trailhead

45–47

Crow
Lake

Uinta River

118

To
Neola

Lily Pad
Lakes

Hypsometry

Elevation (feet)
13,600
12,800
12,000
11,200
10,400
9,600
8,800
8,000
7,200

120

C R O W   C A N Y O N

Heller
Lake

Uintah and Ouray
Indian Reservation

122

10

Access to Chain Lakes begins at the Uintas trailhead. Take the Uintas River Trail 3.0 miles north to Sheep Bridge. Proceed east across the footbridge and up a thousand feet of switchbacks. Catch your breath, then follow the trail northwest to Krebs Basin and Lower Chain Lake. No overnight horse grazing is allowed from 0.25 mile on either side of the trail from Lower Chain Lake to Upper Chain Lake.

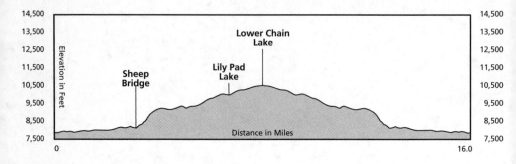

46 Lake Atwood

Lake Atwood houses one of the largest brook trout populations in the High Uintas. With this in mind, you just may want to throw your line in here and forget about all the surrounding lakes. Bad decision! Atwood receives most of the attention in this basin, and angling may be hampered by semi-crowded shorelines. Allred and Mt. Emmons Lakes have the same problem. Although fast fishing usually occurs, so do a lot of people. This is partly because Atwood and Allred offer the best camping opportunities in Atwood Basin. Lake Atwood loses much of its appeal later in the summer, when it draws down about 15 feet.

See map on page 111.
Start: Uintas trailhead
Distance: 27.2 miles out and back
Destination elevation: 11,030 feet
Approximate hiking time: 16 hours
Difficulty: Moderate—some steep sections
Usage: Moderate
Nearest town: Roosevelt, Utah
Drainage: Uintas River

Maps: USGS Bollie Lake and USGS Mt. Emmons; USDA Forest Service High Uintas Wilderness; Trails Illustrated High Uintas Wilderness
Trail contacts: Ashley National Forest, Forest Supervisor, 355 North Vernal Ave., Vernal, UT 84078, (435) 781-1181; Duchesne Ranger District, 85 West Main, Duchesne, UT 84021, (435) 738-2482

Finding the trailhead: From Heber City, take US 40 east 99 miles to Roosevelt. Then take SR 121 north for 11 miles to Neola. Head north 17 miles on Road 118 to Wandin and Uintas Campgrounds. The trailhead is located 0.8 mile past the Uinta Campground.
   The Uinta trailhead has room for twenty vehicles; amenities include toilets and a stock ramp. There is no water at the trailhead. Camping is available at Uinta Campground.

The Hike

From Uinta trailhead, take the Uinta River Trail 3.0 miles north to Sheep Bridge. Cross the bridge and climb 1,000 feet of switchbacks over 5.0 miles to Lower Chain Lake. Continue on the same trail 2.0 miles over a pass and into the Atwood Creek Drainage. Lake Atwood is 3.6 miles northwest along the trail from the top of the pass.

   Other lakes in Atwood Basin include Roberts, George Beard, Carrot, and B–29. Roberts Lake is a typical alpine lake located in a cirque basin 1.0 mile southwest of Atwood. Follow a faint trail 1.5 miles west from Mt. Emmons Lake. No campsites exist in this small windy basin, so angling pressure remains light for feisty cutthroat trout.

   Two miles west on the trail from Atwood lies George Beard Lake (U–21). This lake sits in windswept terrain just below Trail Rider Pass. Most people ignore this water because there is no shelter, but this makes perfect conditions for the avid

Most anglers headed to the Uintas are not looking for trophy fish, but big fish can be caught at many lakes. This big brook trout was caught in the Atwood Basin.

PHOTO BY CORDELL ANDERSEN

angler. That is, if there's fast fishing for wild trout—and there is. George Beard Lake contains a huge supply of wild brookies. Another lake that might be worth checking out, U–19, sits just 0.5 mile south of George Beard. Not many anglers make it this far.

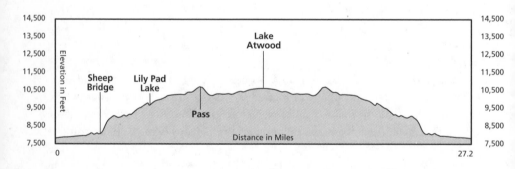

47 Painter Lakes

Painter Lakes take after their name. They are scattered about like little dabs of acrylic on a painter's palette. This beautiful wilderness is characterized by gentle rolling hills and timbered terrain. Due to the remoteness and difficult travel to this basin, Painter Lakes remain blissfully free of people and debris.

See map on page 111.
Start: Uinta trailhead
Distance: 30.5 miles out and back
Destination elevation: 11,030 feet
Approximate hiking time: 18 hours
Difficulty: High—cross-country travel
Usage: Light
Nearest town: Roosevelt, Utah
Drainage: Uinta River

Maps: USGS Fox Lake and USGS Kings Peak; USDA Forest Service High Uintas Wilderness; Trails Illustrated High Uintas Wilderness
Trail contacts: Ashley National Forest, Forest Supervisor, 355 North Vernal Ave., Vernal, UT 84078, (435) 781-1181; Duchesne Ranger District, 85 West Main, Duchesne, UT 84021, (435) 738-2482

Finding the trailhead: From Heber City, take US 40 east 99 miles to Roosevelt. Then take SR 121 north for 11 miles to Neola. Head north 17 miles on Road 118 to Wandin and Uinta Campgrounds. The trailhead is located 0.8 mile past Uinta Campground.

The Uinta trailhead has room for twenty vehicles; amenities include toilets and a stock ramp. There is no water at the trailhead Camping is available at the Uinta Campground.

The Hike

From Uinta trailhead, take the Uinta River Trail 3.0 miles north to Sheep Bridge. Stay on the trail up the Uinta River 9.0 miles to the junction with the trail coming down from Kidney Lakes. Stay left (northwest) 2.0 miles, following the Uinta River to North Fork Park. From North Fork Park, follow a vague trail 2.0 miles south up a steep and rugged 900-foot incline next to a small creek. The first lake you'll run into is Craig.

Craig is the only lake in this basin with a horse pasture; it also contains a good population of cutthroat trout. Although good campsites exist at Craig Lake, better accommodations exist at Painter Lakes U–88 and U–89. Following the inlet of Craig Lake 1.0 mile west, you'll find the first two Painter Lakes. These lakes sit only 100 yards apart. U–88 is the largest lake in the basin, so fishing may be better at this lake than any of the others. Angling pressure is almost nil, and eager brook trout should be fighting one another to get to your lure first. But don't forget U–89. This lake fluctuates like a toilet bowl, but you never know; a big one may be lurking inside. Situated deep in the western part of Painter Lakes Basin is Lake U–93, located 0.75 mile west of U–88. U–93 is above timberline at an elevation of 11,400 feet, and there are no campsites or horse pasture. Angling is unpredictable. These cutthroat either bite or they don't, and if they do, they are small. Unless you're just out for a pleasure stroll, other lakes like U–88 and Craig will better fulfill your fishing desires.

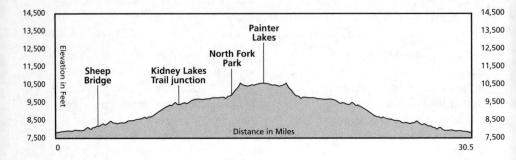

48 Queant Lake

A gentle hike, great camping, and a chance to get away from the campground masses—perhaps these are the reasons Queant Lake is so popular. While you're likely to have neighbors here, it's a whole lot better than spending the night with the RVs and roadside tenters. Besides, not all backpackers are loners. Many actually enjoy a little company, as long as backcountry etiquette is followed.

Start: West Fork Whiterocks trailhead
Distance: 10.0 miles out and back
Destination elevation: 10,652 feet
Approximate hiking time: 7 hours
Difficulty: Easy, but long
Usage: Heavy
Nearest town: Roosevelt, Utah
Drainage: Whiterocks River

Maps: USGS Chepeta Lake; USDA Forest Service High Uintas Wilderness; Trails Illustrated High Uintas Wilderness
Trail contacts: Ashley National Forest, Forest Supervisor, 355 North Vernal Ave., Vernal, UT 84078, (435) 781-1181; Duchesne Ranger District, 85 West Main, Duchesne, UT 84021, (435) 738-2482

Finding the trailhead: From Heber City, take US 40 east 99 miles to Roosevelt. Then take SR 121 north for 11 miles to Neola. Follow SR 121 east about 5 miles to a junction. From the junction, follow a paved road north 3 miles to the town of Whiterocks. Keep on the road, heading north for 4 miles to another junction. At this point, follow Road 117, which winds east then north 18 miles to Pole Creek Junction. Then take Road 110 about 4 miles north to the West Fork junction. From here it's about 1 mile northwest to the West Fork trailhead; the road continues north another 7 miles to the Chepeta trailhead. There are numerous four-wheel-drive roads in the area, so stay on the road most traveled.

West Fork Whiterocks has parking for twenty vehicles, toilets, corrals, and a stock-unloading ramp.

The Hike

From West Fork Whiterocks trailhead, the trail goes northwest 2.0 miles to a junction with the trail to Queant Lake. Turn right (northeast) in 0.5 mile to a small lake, then travel 2.5 miles northwest to the lake.

Queant Lake is big enough to handle several large groups. It's a long walk around its 57 acres, and there are plenty of campsites, horse pasture, and spring water. Look for the latter along the northern shore. You will have little difficulty finding a ready-made camp. All you'll have to do is move in.

If Queant doesn't suit your tastes, head north another 0.75 mile to Ogden Lake. It sees far fewer hikers than Queant and offers just as many amenities. Campsites and horse pasture are abundant, and a large spring flows into the north end.

Angling at Queant, Ogden, and Cleveland Lakes may be only fair. This area does entertain a lot of anglers. Plan on working a little harder here than you would on

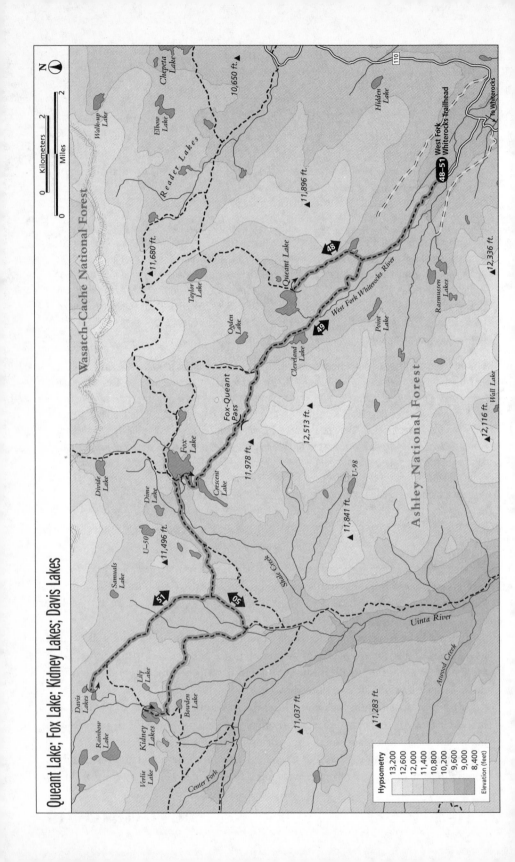

Queant Lake; Fox Lake; Kidney Lakes; Davis Lakes

some of the more remote lakes, and stay with the basics. Small flies (#16) in the late evening and early morning should yield at least enough trout for a pleasant meal. There is also a good-looking stream below Queant that should produce some small trout.

Queant Lake is a great place to introduce someone to backpacking, particularly youngsters. The trip is not taxing, and there is loads of room to run and explore without leaving the proximity of the lake. Everyone has to begin someplace, and Queant Lake provides an ideal setting for beginners. Hey, even we old-timers like a nice, easy outing once in a while.

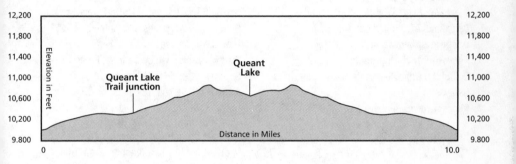

49 Fox Lake

Although Fox is a primitive lake, it just doesn't remind you of a wilderness area. Large groups of campers bring horses loaded with all their "essentials" and begin to party. Don't get us wrong. We like to have fun just as much as the next guy, but we prefer a place that is a little less conspicuous. Fox Lake gets more than its share of high-impact camping.

See map on page 118.
Start: West Fork Whiterocks trailhead
Distance: 17.0 miles out and back
Destination elevation: 10,790 feet
Approximate hiking time: 11 hours
Difficulty: Difficult—due to Fox-Queant Pass
Usage: Heavy
Nearest town: Roosevelt, Utah

Drainage: Uinta River
Maps: USGS Fox Lake; USDA Forest Service High Uintas Wilderness; Trails Illustrated High Uintas Wilderness
Trail contacts: Ashley National Forest, Forest Supervisor, 355 North Vernal Ave., Vernal, UT 84078, (435) 781-1181

Finding the trailhead: From Heber City, take US 40 east 99 miles to Roosevelt. Then take SR 121 north for 11 miles to Neola. Follow SR 121 east about 5 miles to a junction. From the junction, follow a paved road north 3 miles to the town of Whiterocks. Keep on the road, heading north for 4 miles to another junction. At this point, follow Road 117, which winds east then north 18 miles to Pole Creek Junction. Then take Road 110 about 4 miles north to the West Fork junction. From here it's about 1 mile northwest to the West Fork trailhead; the road continues north another 7 miles to the Chepeta trailhead. There are numerous four-wheel-drive roads in the area, so stay on the road most traveled.

West Fork Whiterocks has parking for twenty vehicles, toilets, corrals, and a stock-unloading ramp.

The Hike

The best access to Fox begins at West Fork Whiterocks trailhead. From the trailhead, the trail goes northwest 2.0 miles to a junction with the trail to Queant Lake. Stay left (northwest) for 1.5 miles to Cleveland Lake. It's another 3.5 miles over Fox-Queant Pass to Crescent and Fox Lakes. Another route that is well traveled by horses starts in the Uinta River Drainage. This trail runs next to the Uinta River for 10.0 miles to a three-way junction. At this point, take the northeast trail 3.5 miles up Shale Creek to Fox Lake.

Fox is a fluctuating reservoir that experiences a serious drawdown during the late summer months, and fishing success declines with the water level. Despite this, the lake frequently hosts large groups of Boy Scouts and partygoers alike. Campsites are found around the lake, while horse pastures are located north of Fox and west of Crescent Lake. Overall fishing pressure is considered moderate for brook and cutthroat trout.

Remains of an old cabin at Fox Lake

Just southwest of Fox is Crescent Lake, a long narrow reservoir that fluctuates only moderately. Camping areas are all around the lake, but Scouts often have them occupied during the midsummer months. Angling usage is quite heavy at times. Best results may occur in the late evening while casting off the rocks. Cutthroat trout are the main species, but an occasional brookie may show up.

Other lakes in the Fox Lake area are Dollar, Brook, and Divide. Dollar Lake is sometimes called Dime Lake. This aesthetic lake is in a large meadow 1.0 mile northwest of Fox and features better-than-average campsites along with a generous supply of horse pasture. A good number of pan-size brookies inhabit the lake. As with the other lakes around here, Dollar sometimes receives heavy use from large groups that migrate from Fox Lake. Your best bet to escape the crowds is Brook Lake. It lies 1.0 mile east of Fox near the trail. Camping areas are available, and pressure is remarkably light. There is a 0.25 mile campfire restriction around Fox, Crescent, and Dime Lakes.

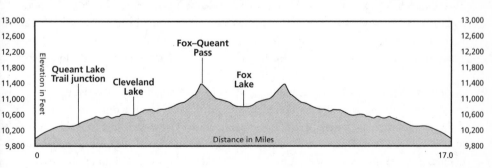

50 Kidney Lakes

Several lakes make up the Kidney Lakes Basin, and most receive substantial camping or fishing use. Kidney Lakes are no exception. Large recreational groups usually occupy both Kidney Lakes. Plenty of campsites can be found between the lakes and around West Kidney. Fishing is often good for brook trout and an occasional 1-pound rainbow. Moose are often seen feeding in the shallows of both Kidney Lakes. Be aware of these large animals, and give them their space. Although usually docile, an upset moose is extremely dangerous.

See map on page 118.

Start: West Fork Whiterocks trailhead
Distance: 26.0 miles out and back
Destination elevation: 10,850 feet
Approximate hiking time: 16 hours
Difficulty: Difficult—due to Fox-Queant Pass
Usage: Heavy
Nearest town: Roosevelt, Utah

Drainage: Uinta River
Maps: USGS Fox Lake; USDA Forest Service High Uintas Wilderness; Trails Illustrated High Uintas Wilderness
Trail contacts: Ashley National Forest, Forest Supervisor, 355 North Vernal Ave., Vernal, UT 84078, (435) 781-1181

Finding the trailhead: From Heber City, take US 40 east 99 miles to Roosevelt. Then take SR 121 north for 11 miles to Neola. Follow SR 121 east about 5 miles to a junction. From the junction, follow a paved road north 3 miles to the town of Whiterocks. Keep on the road, heading north for 4 miles to another junction. At this point, follow Road 117, which winds east then north 18 miles to Pole Creek Junction. Then take Road 110 about 4 miles north to the West Fork junction. From here it's about 1 mile northwest to the West Fork trailhead; the road continues north another 7 miles to the Chepeta trailhead. There are numerous four-wheel-drive roads in the area, so stay on the road most traveled.

West Fork Whiterocks has parking for twenty vehicles, toilets, corrals, and a stock-unloading ramp.

The Hike

Five different access points can be used for the Kidney Lakes area. The shortest route begins at the West Fork Whiterocks trailhead. The others start at Uinta River, Chepeta Lake, Hoop Lake, and Spirit Lake. But they are at least 3 miles longer. Excellent trails exist for each route, and stock-unloading ramps are present at every trailhead except Chepeta Lake.

From West Fork Whiterocks trailhead, the trail goes northwest 2.0 miles to a junction with the trail to Queant Lake. Stay left (northwest) for 1.5 miles to Cleveland Lake. It's another 4.5 miles over Fox-Queant Pass to Crescent and Fox Lakes. After you pass Fox Lake, there's a trail junction with the cutoff trail into the Uinta River Drainage 1.0 mile farther. Stay right (west) 0.5 mile to another trail junction with the trail to Davis Lakes. Stay left (southwest) 0.5 mile to a three-way junction with the trail into Uinta River Drainage. Turn right (northwest) and go 2.0 miles to Kidney Lakes.

For secluded camping, try nearby Bowden or Lily Lake. Bowden has limited campsites but an endless supply of horse pasture. Lily is a quaint little lake surrounded by yellow water lilies. Campsites with horse pastures are just west of the lake. Lily receives only light pressure, even though it's only 0.5 mile from the Kidney Lakes.

Along a well-marked trail, about a mile northwest of Kidney Lakes lies Rainbow Lake. The trail also leads to numerous lakes in the upper northwest portion of the basin. These lakes are in high, windswept country. There are no decent camps up here. Rainbow Lake sees moderate to heavy fishing pressure but is mostly limited to day use. Don't forget about the lakes located above Rainbow Lake. These small bodies of water may bring a nice surprise, and the ones just below are certainly worth checking out. Expect to find a good mixture of brookies, rainbows, and cutthroat.

Nearby Davis Lakes present good angling opportunities too. They are a little over 1.0 mile north of Kidney Lakes and 250 yards north and south of each other. Both lakes get light use, and fly fishing can be fast for pan-size brookies.

There is a 0.25 mile campfire restriction around Kidney Lakes and Verlie Lake.

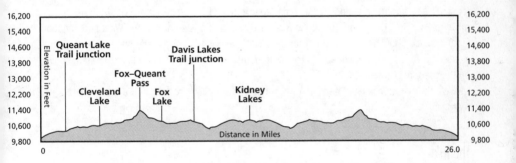

51 Davis Lakes

Nestled in a high cirque, Davis Lakes offer a true alpine experience. The surrounding hills are composed of lush green grasses and scattered pines that may remind you of the Swiss Alps. Equestrians will appreciate all the space, pasture, and water for their animals, as well as the fact that horses cannot really roam any higher.

See map on page 118.
Start: West Fork Whiterocks trailhead
Distance: 27.5 miles out and back
Destination elevation: 11,020 feet
Approximate hiking time: 16 hours
Difficulty: Difficult—due to Fox-Queant Pass
Usage: Light
Nearest town: Roosevelt, Utah

Drainage: Uinta River
Maps: USGS Fox Lake; USDA Forest Service High Uintas Wilderness; Trails Illustrated High Uintas Wilderness
Trail contacts: Ashley National Forest, Forest Supervisor, 355 North Vernal Ave., Vernal, UT 84078, (435) 781-1181

Finding the trailhead: From Heber City, take US 40 east 99 miles to Roosevelt. Then take SR 121 north for 11 miles to Neola. Follow SR 121 east about 5 miles to a junction. From the junction, follow a paved road north 3 miles to the town of Whiterocks. Keep on the road, heading north for 4 miles to another junction. At this point, follow Road 117, which winds east then north 18 miles to Pole Creek Junction. Then take Road 110 about 4 miles north to the West Fork junction. From here it's about 1 mile northwest to the West Fork trailhead; the road continues north another 7 miles to the Chepeta trailhead. There are numerous four-wheel-drive roads in the area, so stay on the road most traveled.

West Fork Whiterocks has parking for twenty vehicles, toilets, corrals, and a stock-unloading ramp.

The Hike

Davis Lakes are a little off the beaten path and don't see a lot of visitors. From West Fork Whiterocks trailhead, the trail goes northwest 2.0 miles to a junction with the trail to Queant Lake. Stay left (northwest) for 1.5 miles to Cleveland Lake. It's another 3.5 miles to Crescent and Fox Lakes. After you pass Fox Lake, there's a trail junction with the cutoff trail into the Uinta River Drainage 1.0 mile farther. Stay right (west) 1.0 mile to another trail junction with the trail to Davis Lakes. Turn right (north) and go 4.3 miles to Davis Lakes.

A loop trail passes just below Davis South. It can be accessed from either Kidney Lakes, or if you're coming from Fox Lake, take the Davis Lakes turnoff about 2.0 miles from Fox Lake. A sign marks the turnoff, and regardless of which way you take to Davis Lakes, the trail is hard to follow in places. Keep your compass and map handy, and keep pointed toward the large cirque in the mountainside.

Best camping facilities are on the south side of Davis South Lake. A spacious existing campsite should accommodate groups of up to eight people. Spring water flows into Davis South along the north shore. There is a 0.25 mile campfire restriction around Davis Lakes.

The north shore is also the deepest and is where most of the fish are. Plump, pan-size brookies can be easily harvested using a small fly or woolly worm. There is plenty of open shoreline where fly casters can have a ball. You won't catch big fish here, but you will probably catch as many as you want, as long you want. Small brook trout also inhabit Davis North Lake but may be tougher to fool. For a change of pace, try fishing the small stream between the lakes or the outlet stream from Davis South.

Don't be surprised to see moose in the area. The large mammals are common between Davis Lakes and Kidney Lakes. Enjoy them at a distance, and you'll probably see them often. There are also deer and elk around, but they are much more wary.

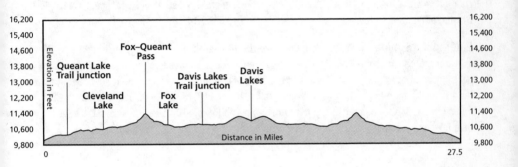

52 Rock Lakes

It is merely 1.4 miles to Lower Rock Lake. However, by the time you shuffle around all the deadfall, it will feel like 2. There is no trail, and lots of rocks add to the challenge of this trek. Even though these lakes lie close to the popular Pole Creek Campground, don't expect many people here.

Start: Pole Creek Lake
Distance: 3.0 miles out and back
Destination elevation: 10,550 feet
Approximate hiking time: 2.5 hours
Difficulty: Moderate—some cross-country travel
Usage: Light
Nearest town: Roosevelt, Utah
Drainage: Whiterocks River

Maps: USGS Rasmussen Lakes; USDA Forest Service High Uintas Wilderness; Trails Illustrated High Uintas Wilderness
Trail contacts: Ashley National Forest, Forest Supervisor, 355 North Vernal Ave., Vernal, UT 84078, (435) 781-1181; Duchesne Ranger District, 85 West Main, Duchesne, UT 84021, (435) 738-2482

Finding the trailhead: From Heber City, take US 40 east 99 miles to Roosevelt. Then take SR 121 north for 11 miles to Neola. Follow SR 121 east about 5 miles to a junction. From the junction, follow a paved road north 3 miles to the town of Whiterocks. Keep on the road, heading north for 4 miles to another junction. At this point, follow Road 117, which winds east then north 18 miles to Pole Creek Junction. Take a left turn, staying on Road 117. Pole Creek Lake is about 1 mile from the junction.

The Hike

Find Rock Lakes by following the inlet of Pole Creek Lake up to a large meadow. Proceed along the south side of the meadow then up a steep incline, while embracing the outlet of Lower Rock Lake. Middle Rock Lake can be easily found by pursuing the inlet of Lower Rock, 200 yards north up a hill. Upper Rock sits across a nasty boulder field, 0.5 mile north of Middle Rock.

Although heavy timber and rock ledges surround Lower and Middle Rock Lakes, some open shoreline is accessible for fishing. The only decent camping areas are found near the center of a crevice on the west side of Lower Rock. One other campsite presents itself along the east side of Middle Rock. Spring water is located on the southwest side of Lower Rock, but no other sources are known throughout this region. Angling should be best at Lower Rock Lake. Brook trout 10 to 14 inches are common. Middle Rock Lake does not receive good water circulation and is not deep enough to retain a respectable population of fish.

Upper Rock Lake sits in a shallow depression on a high, flat bench. Many badgering boulders surround this lake, while rockslides abut the water from the north. Open shorelines present good fly-casting possibilities. But this lake withdraws fairly quickly during the summer months and most often experiences winterkills. After all that's

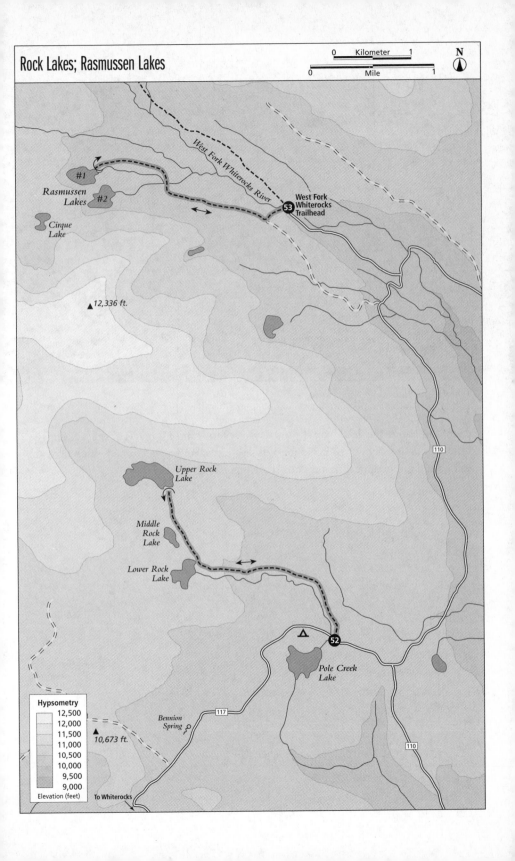

Rock Lakes; Rasmussen Lakes

Rasmussen Lakes

#1

#2

Cirque Lake

West Fork Whiterocks River

West Fork Whiterocks Trailhead

53

▲ 12,336 ft.

Upper Rock Lake

Middle Rock Lake

Lower Rock Lake

110

△

52

Pole Creek Lake

117

Bennion Spring

▲ 10,673 ft.

110

Hypsometry

	12,500
	12,000
	11,500
	11,000
	10,500
	10,000
	9,500
	9,000

Elevation (feet)

To Whiterocks

0   Kilometer   1

0   Mile   1

N

Lower Rock Lake

been said about this lake, you'll probably elect to avoid Upper Rock Lake. On the other hand, the scenery is nice, the solitude is great, and a McDonalds-type drive-in will sound rather appealing on your return trip. Well, maybe.

53 Rasmussen Lakes

There are a lot of well-kept secrets in these mountains, and here is one of them. Rasmussen Lakes offer solitude, fine camping, and good fishing. The only price you'll have to pay for all of this is less than 2 miles of cross-country hiking. Most likely, it's the cross-country part that keeps most visitors away. Whenever access is a little tricky, people seem to shy away. So, if you like to be alone but don't like to hike very far, this could be for you.

See map on page 127.
Start: West Fork Whiterocks trailhead
Distance: 3.6 miles out and back
Destination elevation: 10,473 feet
Approximate hiking time: 3 hours
Difficulty: Moderate—some cross-country travel
Usage: Light
Nearest town: Roosevelt, Utah

Drainage: Whiterocks River
Maps: USGS Rasmussen Lakes; USDA Forest Service High Uintas Wilderness; Trails Illustrated High Uintas Wilderness
Trail contacts: Ashley National Forest, Forest Supervisor, 355 North Vernal Ave., Vernal, UT 84078, (435) 781-1181

Finding the trailhead: From Heber City, take US 40 east 99 miles to Roosevelt. Then take SR 121 north for 11 miles to Neola. Follow SR 121 east about 5 miles to a junction. From the junction, follow a paved road north 3 miles to the town of Whiterocks. Keep on the road, heading north for 4 miles to another junction. At this point, follow Road 117, which winds east then north 18 miles to Pole Creek Junction. Then take Road 110 about 4 miles north to the West Fork junction. From here it's about 1 mile northwest to the West Fork trailhead; the road continues north another 7 miles to the Chepeta trailhead. There are numerous four-wheel-drive roads in the area, so stay on the road most traveled.

West Fork Whiterocks has parking for twenty vehicles, toilets, corrals, and a stock-unloading ramp.

The Hike

To get to Rasmussen Lakes, follow West Fork Creek (starts near the trailhead), and just stay on the south side. The north bank has several inlets that will only serve to get you wet or sidetracked. After a steep, rocky climb through thick pines, you will first come to Rasmussen Lake 2. You could camp here, but camping is better at Rasmussen Lake 1. Press on another 0.25 mile to the northwest.

At Rasmussen 1 there are many nice campsites to choose from, especially on the eastern side of the lake. There is no need to build a new campsite, so please don't. Horse access is possible, but there isn't much to feed them. As for drinking water, plan on bringing plenty or having some means of water purification. No reliable source of spring water exists.

Anglers will want to try both lakes. Each is stocked regularly with brook trout, and fishing pressure is light. This may be a good spot for a day hike mixed with a little fishing. It's certainly close enough to the trailhead for day use. For further adventure, check out Cirque Lake. It is only 0.5 mile southwest of Rasmussen Lakes and has been stocked with grayling. It may or may not be good fishing, but its picturesque glacial setting will certainly be more than worth the effort.

Brook trout, although not native to the Uinta Mountains, are found across the range and often are the first fish many anglers catch.

54 Reader Lake

You might take a hint from this lake's name and bring a good book to read. This is a good place to be alone and relax. Reader Lake is no longer managed as a fishery, but does get some trout moving in from Reader Creek. Here is a respite for the non-fishing backpacker.

Start: Chepeta Lake trailhead
Distance: 8.5 miles out and back
Destination elevation: 10,960 feet
Approximate hiking time: 6 hours
Difficulty: Easy
Usage: Light
Nearest town: Roosevelt, Utah

Drainage: Whiterocks River
Maps: USGS Chepeta Lake; USDA Forest Service High Uintas Wilderness; Trails Illustrated High Uintas Wilderness
Trail contacts: Ashley National Forest, Forest Supervisor, 355 North Vernal Ave., Vernal, UT 84078, (435) 781-1181

Finding the trailhead: From Heber City, take US 40 east 99 miles to Roosevelt. Then take SR 121 north for 11 miles to Neola. Follow SR 121 east about 5 miles to a junction. From the junction, follow a paved road north 3 miles to the town of Whiterocks. Keep on the road, heading north for 4 miles to another junction. At this point, follow Road 117, which winds east then north 18 miles to Pole Creek Junction. Then take Road 110 about 11 miles north to the Chepeta Lake trailhead.

The Hike

Located at the head of Reader Lakes Basin, Reader Lake offers deluxe camping accommodations for the discriminating solitude seeker. Bubbling water, fresh from a mountain spring, is served up cold with every meal. The lake borders timberline and provides a wonderful alpine ambience, complete with light afternoon thundershowers and warm, inviting sunsets. OK, OK, so it's not really as inviting as the travel brochure makes it sound. Reader Lake is subject to the same unpredictable weather, mosquitoes, and hazards as the other 1,000 Uinta lakes. It is better than some and worse than others. However, it is seldom used and is a fine place to shack out for a while and ignore the rest of the world. It's not always the aesthetic place we have described, but it might be.

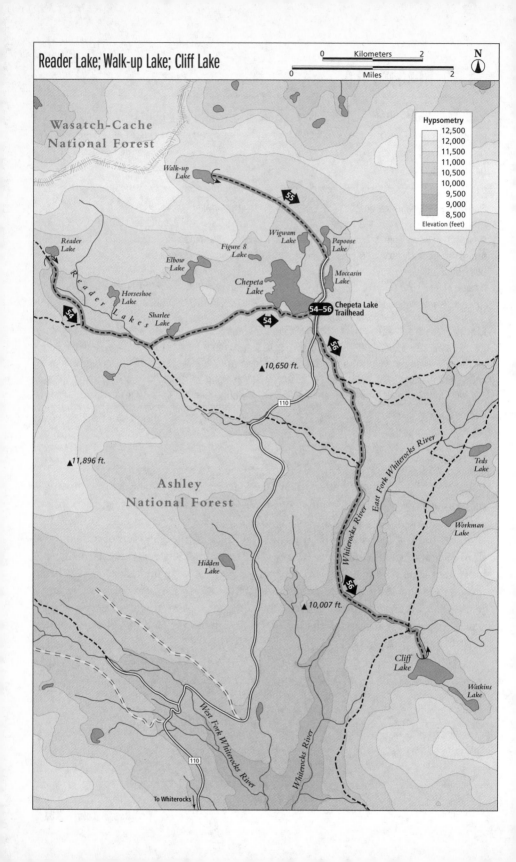

Reader Lake; Walk-up Lake; Cliff Lake

Kilometers

Miles

N

Hypsometry
12,500
12,000
11,500
11,000
10,500
10,000
9,500
9,000
8,500
Elevation (feet)

Wasatch–Cache
National Forest

Walk-up
Lake

55

Reader
Lake

Wigwam
Lake

Papoose
Lake

Figure 8
Lake

Elbow
Lake

Moccasin
Lake

Reader Lakes

Horseshoe
Lake

Chepeta
Lake

54–56

Chepeta Lake
Trailhead

54

Sharlee
Lake

54

56

▲10,650 ft.

110

▲11,896 ft.

Ashley
National Forest

East Fork Whiterocks River

Teds
Lake

Whiterocks River

Workman
Lake

Hidden
Lake

56

▲10,007 ft.

Cliff
Lake

Watkins
Lake

West Fork Whiterocks River

Whiterocks River

110

To Whiterocks

To reach Reader Lake, follow the Highline Trail west from the Chepeta Lake trailhead about 2.5 miles until you reach Reader Creek. Staying on the west side of the creek, follow it northwest another 1.5 miles to Reader Lake. The lake is shallow and only 10 acres in size. It may first appear as a large pond, but there are no other large ponds in the area to confuse it with.

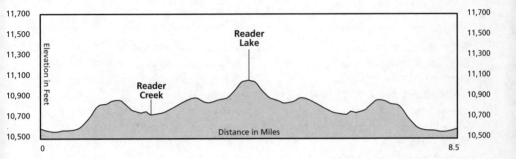

55 Walk-up Lake

Walk-up Lake is not as easy as its name implies. You don't want to be in a hurry going through this country. It's both beautiful and treacherous. But cirque lovers will adore this bowl carved out eons ago when glaciers ruled the High Uintas, and solitude seekers should like this place, since it sees very few visitors.

See map on page 132.
Start: Chepeta Lake trailhead
Distance: 7.5 miles out and back
Destination elevation: 11,114 feet
Approximate hiking time: 5 hours
Difficulty: Moderate–cross-country travel
Usage: Very light
Nearest town: Roosevelt, Utah

Drainage: Whiterocks River
Maps: USGS Chepeta Lake; USDA Forest Service High Uintas Wilderness; Trails Illustrated High Uintas Wilderness
Trail contacts: Ashley National Forest, Forest Supervisor, 355 North Vernal Ave., Vernal, UT 84078, (435) 781-1181

Finding the trailhead: From Heber City, take US 40 east 99 miles to Roosevelt. Then take SR 121 north for 11 miles to Neola. Follow SR 121 east about 5 miles to a junction. From the junction, follow a paved road north 3 miles to the town of Whiterocks. Keep on the road, heading north for 4 miles to another junction. At this point, follow Road 117, which winds east then north 18 miles to Pole Creek Junction. Then take Road 110 about 11 miles north to the Chepeta Lake trailhead.

The Hike

The easiest (but not easy) route is to first go 1.3 miles to Papoose Lake, almost directly north of Chepeta Lake trailhead. From there, hike northwest another 2.5 miles up steep, rocky slopes and meadows. It is a little tricky picking your way through the boulders, so plan on a little extra time.

Cirque lovers will adore this bowl, carved out eons ago when glaciers ruled the High Uintas. Steep slopes drop sharply into the clear water, which reaches a depth of 55 feet. That's pretty deep for a lake of only 18 acres.

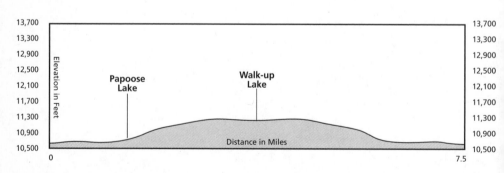

Solitude seekers also should like this place. The lake sees very few visitors throughout the course of a year. You might expect it to receive considerably more pressure due to its proximity to popular Chepeta Lake, but its inaccessibility keeps it a quiet place. Despite its rugged access and appearance, there are some fair campsites located in grassy clearings just above the lake, though we wouldn't recommend these spots during a thunderstorm.

Brook trout are stocked occasionally. In a lake this deep, fish are usually more selective and have more defined feeding times. Early morning and late evening are when you are likely to have success at Walk-up Lake. Just don't expect too much if you take a day hike into here to try some midday angling.

56 Cliff Lake

Simply put—this is quite a quiet, rugged place.

See map on page 132.
Start: Chepeta Lake trailhead
Distance: 11.2 miles out and back
Destination elevation: 10,348 feet
Approximate hiking time: 7 hours
Difficulty: Moderate
Usage: Light
Nearest town: Roosevelt, Utah

Drainage: Whiterocks River
Maps: USGS Chepeta Lake and USGS Paradise Park; USDA Forest Service High Uintas Wilderness; Trails Illustrated High Uintas Wilderness
Trail contacts: Ashley National Forest, Forest Supervisor, 355 North Vernal Ave., Vernal, UT 84078, (435) 781-1181

Finding the trailhead: From Heber City, take US 40 east 99 miles to Roosevelt. Then take SR 121 north for 11 miles to Neola. Follow SR 121 east about 5 miles to a junction. From the junction, follow a paved road north 3 miles to the town of Whiterocks. Keep on the road, heading north for 4 miles to another junction. At this point, follow Road 117, which winds east then north 18 miles to Pole Creek Junction. Then take Road 110 about 11 miles north to the Chepeta Lake trailhead.

The Hike

Cliff Lake can actually be reached by four-wheel-drive road. However, it is not advisable. Just beyond Johnson Creek, the road passes over several severe rough-rock ledges. Then it circles around Dead Horse Park, only to complete its deformity at the lake. To say the least, this road will torture the toughest truck. From Paradise Park Campground, the road to Cliff Lake is graded for about 6.0 miles. The last 3.0 miles is considered a jeep road. Good luck!

An alternate route can be accessed by way of Chepeta Lake. It is only 5.6 miles from here and offers more of a wilderness experience. From Chepeta Lake trailhead, go southeast 0.7 mile to a trail junction. Stay right (south) for 1.0 mile to the Whiterocks River and another trail junction. Cross the river and continue south along the river 2.2 miles to another river crossing. Cross the river and climb 1.7 miles to the lake.

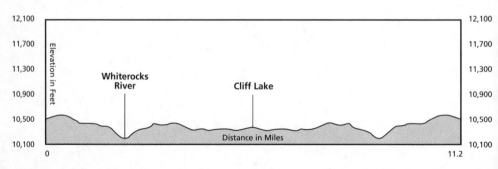

Additional lakes will be unveiled along this trail. Sand, Teds, Workman, and Wooley Lakes are all known to maintain good fly fishing and many good campsites. After you've visited these lakes, you'll wonder why you should even go to Cliff Lake. Well, we don't know. There are no cozy camp spots, and spring water is nonexistent at the lake. However, Cliff Lake does get far less angling attention than any of the other lakes mentioned above.

57 Paul Lake

Fat brook trout inhabit Paul Lake, along with plenty of freshwater shrimp. The fish feed on shrimp and grow big and finicky. You may want to try a piece of shrimp, or a small shrimp fly or scud might work better. Angling usage is light for now, but more and more people are getting good reports about Paul Lake.

Start: Paradise Park trailhead
Distance: 4.0 miles out and back
Destination elevation: 10,630 feet
Approximate hiking time: 4 hours
Difficulty: Moderate—cross-country
Usage: Light
Nearest town: Vernal, Utah
Drainage: Ashley Creek

Maps: USGS Paradise Park; USDA Forest Service High Uintas Wilderness; Trails Illustrated High Uintas Wilderness
Trail contacts: Ashley National Forest, Forest Supervisor, 355 North Vernal Ave., Vernal, UT 84078, (435) 781-1181

Finding the trailhead: From Vernal, drive west 15 miles to LaPoint. Turn north toward the Uinta Mountains on SR 104, then drive another 30 miles to Paradise Park.

The Hike

The best access route follows the inlet of Paradise Park Reservoir to a small meadow. Then head north 1.5 miles up a rugged, timbered incline to Little Elk Lake. From Little Elk, follow a poorly marked trail 0.25 mile north to Paul Lake. Paul is up on a level bench characterized by rugged, timbered slopes and lots of rocks. Keep your map and compass handy when trying to locate this lake. Campsites exist on the west shore, but horses won't find much to eat around here. This is an excellent short hike that offers great potential for fine fishing and solitude. That's a rare combination these days.

Nearby Little Elk Lake contains one good campsite at the south end.

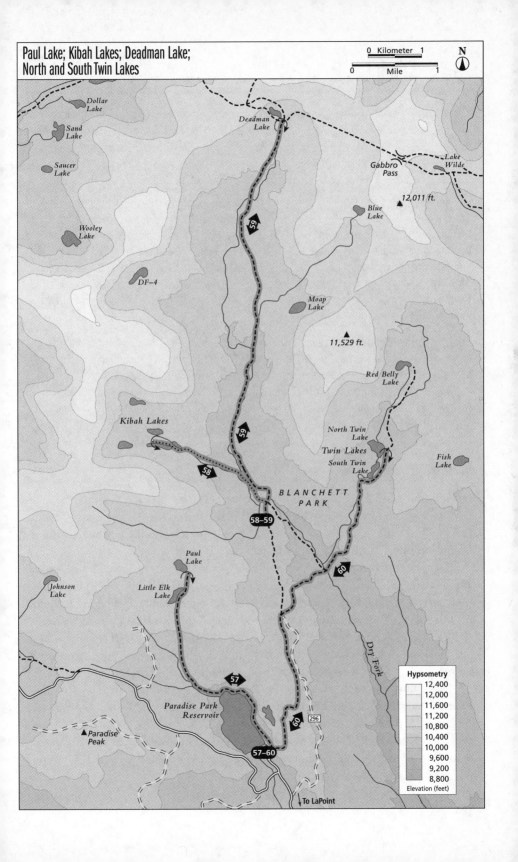

Paul Lake; Kibah Lakes; Deadman Lake; North and South Twin Lakes

0 Kilometer 1

0 Mile 1

N

Dollar Lake

Sand Lake

Saucer Lake

Wooley Lake

DF-4

Kibah Lakes

Johnson Lake

Little Elk Lake

Paul Lake

Paradise Peak

Paradise Park Reservoir

Deadman Lake

59

59

58

58-59

57

60

57-60

Gabbro Pass

Lake Wilde

12,011 ft.

Blue Lake

Moap Lake

11,529 ft.

Red Belly Lake

North Twin Lake

Twin Lakes

South Twin Lake

Fish Lake

BLANCHETT PARK

60

296

Dry Fork

To LaPoint

Hypsometry

12,400
12,000
11,600
11,200
10,800
10,400
10,000
9,600
9,200
8,800
Elevation (feet)

58 Kibah Lakes

Since there are only poor campsites and horse access is nearly impossible, most people visiting Kibah Lakes are on day hikes from Blanchett Park. To reach Blanchett Park, follow a jeep road from Paradise Park Reservoir 4 miles north. Great camping areas and plenty of horse munchies are available at the park.

See map on page 139.
Start: Blanchett Park
Distance: 3.0 miles out and back
Destination elevation: 10,550 feet
Approximate hiking time: 4 hours
Difficulty: Moderate–cross-country
Usage: Moderate
Nearest town: Vernal, Utah

Drainage: Ashley Creek
Maps: USGS Paradise Park; USDA Forest Service High Uintas Wilderness; Trails Illustrated High Uintas Wilderness
Trail contacts: Ashley National Forest, Forest Supervisor, 355 North Vernal Ave., Vernal, UT 84078, (435) 781-1181

Finding the trailhead: From Vernal, drive west 15 miles to LaPoint. Turn north toward the Uinta Mountains, then drive another 30 miles to Paradise Park. You can start hiking from here, but if you have sturdy four-wheel drive, keep heading north another 4 miles to Blanchett Park.

If you're coming from the Salt Lake City area, begin your journey to Paradise Park at Roosevelt. Take SR 121 north 10 miles to Neola. Keep following SR 121 another 14 miles east to the small community of LaPoint.

The Hike

No real trail exists to Kibah Lakes. From Blanchett Park, go cross-country 1.0 mile northwest over some nasty boulder fields to East Kibah (DF–11). This lake is identified by a rockslide along the north shore and a wet meadow to the northwest. Fishing is spotty at times, but occasionally a large trout can be netted.

Right next door to the southwest of East Kibah sits Finger Kibah. This lake takes after its name, as its shape portrays a finger. Angling should be a little faster here. Brook trout survive well in this lake, and a superb population is steadily maintained. A panful of "finger lickin'" trout are in order here, so bring along your frying pan and stove.

One-half mile west of Finger Kibah, you'll find West Kibah Lake. It rests at the base of a talus slope in the southwest corner of Kibah Basin. Fishing usage is light to moderate for brook trout, and it is possible to camp overnight here utilizing a primitive campsite.

Three hundred yards northwest of East Kibah is Island Kibah (DF–16). Surrounded by rocky, timbered ridges, a small island protrudes from its shallow water. Angler use is moderate for brookies.

North Kibah (DF–15) is located about 1.0 mile northwest of East Kibah. Because of low water levels during late summer, it tends to experience fish winterkill. However, this may be a good lake to catch some solitude.

59 Deadman Lake

Although Deadman Lake lies in unsheltered, windy terrain, it gets frequent visits from Scouts. A few fair campsites are found along the south shore, but horse pasture is a scarce commodity. Three other lakes reside near the head of Dry Fork Creek. From Deadman, these lakes are 1.5 to 5 miles away.

See map on page 139.
Start: Blanchett Park
Distance: 10.0 miles out and back
Destination elevation: 10,790 feet
Approximate hiking time: 7 hours
Difficulty: Moderate
Usage: Heavy
Nearest town: La Point, Utah

Drainage: Ashley Creek
Maps: USGS Whiterocks Lake; USDA Forest Service High Uintas Wilderness; Trails Illustrated High Uintas Wilderness
Trail contacts: Ashley National Forest, Forest Supervisor, 355 North Vernal Ave., Vernal, UT 84078, (435) 781-1181

Finding the trailhead: From Vernal, drive west 15 miles to LaPoint. From LaPoint, travel a paved road 7 miles north to a junction. Take the left-hand road 23 miles northwest to Paradise Park. You can start hiking from here, but if you have sturdy four-wheel drive, keep heading north another 4 miles to Blanchett Park.

If you're coming from the Salt Lake City area, begin your journey to Paradise Park at Roosevelt, Utah. Take SR 121 north 10 miles to Neola. Keep following SR 121 another 14 miles east to the small community of LaPoint.

The Hike

Deadman Lake can be reached from several access points, but the trail from Blanchett Park is the most feasible. From Paradise Park, go 4.0 miles up the four-wheel-drive road to Blanchett Park at the end of the road. Deadman Lake is 5.0 miles up a good trail following Dry Fork Creek. The trail splits in two directions upon reaching the lake. The east trail ventures over Gabbro Pass and into Lakeshore Basin; the west trail disperses into Whiterocks, Beaver Creek, and Carter Creek Drainages.

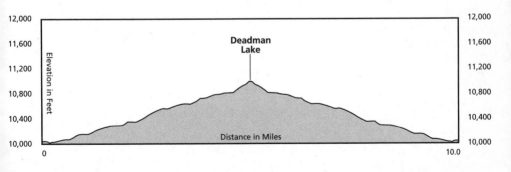

Reach Blue Lake by traveling 1.5 miles southeast from Deadman Lake over a bald mountain. This scenic lake sits at the top of a windswept basin on the northeast side of Dry Fork. No campsites exist. Blue Lake contains an excellent supply of hungry brook trout. Watch out for sheep dip here. In the midsummer months, rotational sheep grazing depreciates the aesthetic value of this beautiful basin.

From Blue, another scenic lake is easily reached—Moap Lake. It is just a little over 1.0 mile south of Blue Lake at the base of a steep talus slope within a small cirque. No fish exist here, but it's a beautiful spot for solitude seekers and hermits.

If remote fishing is what you're after, then DF–4 is your kind of lake. Find it by following Reynolds Creek 1.0 mile to its spring source. Then head 1.0 mile over rough boulders into a cirque basin. Due to the rugged terrain, there are no camping areas. Angler utilization is very light, and fishing is often hot for feisty cutthroat trout. Allow yourself plenty of time to get back to base camp before dark!

60 North and South Twin Lakes

Twin Lakes lie in marshy terrain characterized by open meadows interspersed with timber. Although these lakes receive heavy usage, many camping areas are available, especially around South Twin Lake. However, spring water can only be found at North Twin. Horse pasture is present at either lake, but South Twin has more. During summer, angling usage remains steady, and fishing is usually good.

See map on page 139.
Start: Paradise Park trailhead
Distance: 10.0 miles out and back
Destination elevation: 10,300 feet
Approximate hiking time: 7 hours
Difficulty: Moderate
Usage: Heavy
Nearest town: Vernal, Utah

Drainage: Ashley Creek
Maps: USGS Paradise Park; USDA Forest Service High Uintas Wilderness; Trails Illustrated High Uintas Wilderness
Trail contacts: Ashley National Forest, Forest Supervisor, 355 North Vernal Ave., Vernal, UT 84078, (435) 781-1181

Finding the trailhead: From Vernal, drive west 15 miles to LaPoint. Turn north toward the Uinta Mountains, and drive another 30 miles to Paradise Park. You can start hiking from here.

The Hike

Two different starting points can be used for reaching Twin Lakes. Blanchett Park is closer, but adventurers without a four-wheel-drive vehicle prefer the Paradise Park trailhead. On the other hand, Blanchett Park offers great campsites for day hikers making the trek to the Twin or Kibah Lakes. From Paradise Park, follow the Dry Fork Trail 3.5 miles north to Dry Fork Creek. The Twin Lakes Trail then heads 1.5 miles northeast to the lake. After the first mile past Paradise Park, the trail crosses several logging roads. During this 2.0-mile stretch, the trail and rock cairns are difficult to locate.

If heavy pressure crimps your camping style, try Red Belly Lake. It receives a little less usage but gets some day use from hikers staying at Twin Lakes. Red Belly

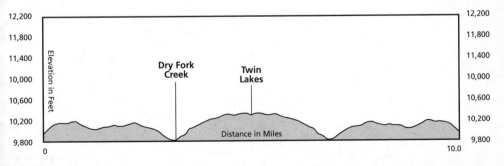

is located 1.0 mile north of Twin Lakes on the Dry Fork Trail. Campsites and horse pasture are on the southeast side of the lake. Angling pressure is considered moderate.

Another nice excursion from North Twin is Fish Lake. Begin near the east inlet of North Twin Lake. From the inlet, follow a hit-or-miss forest service trail 2.5 miles east to Fish. This pretty lake is at the foot of steep talus slopes on the west side of Marsh Peak. Meadows scattered with timber surround the outer portions of Fish Lake, along with good campsites and spring water. Heavy usage is usually encountered throughout July and August. However, natural reproduction enables trout to survive the heavy pressure.

Litterbugs often plague all the lakes mentioned. Practice low-impact techniques, and leave this area better than you found it.

61 Lakeshore Lake

If sightseeing is on your agenda, then Lakeshore is a great place to visit. This picture-perfect lake rests in a meadow encased by partly timbered slopes and rolling tundra. It reminded us of the scenery in the classic movie *The Sound of Music*. You should have seen Brad running down the hill much like Julie Andrews.

Start: Leidy Peak trailhead, at the east end of the Highline Trail
Distance: 9.0 miles out and back
Destination elevation: 10,792 feet
Approximate hiking time: 6 hours
Difficulty: Moderate
Usage: Moderate
Nearest town: Vernal, Utah

Drainage: Ashley Creek
Maps: USGS Leidy Peak; USDA Forest Service High Uintas Wilderness; Trails Illustrated High Uintas Wilderness
Trail contacts: Ashley National Forest, Forest Supervisor, 355 North Vernal Ave., Vernal, UT 84078, (435) 781-1181

Finding the trailhead: From Vernal, take the Red Cloud Loop Road toward East Park Reservoir; continue on toward Hacking Lake. You can camp at Hacking Lake or drive up the road another mile to the Leidy Peak trailhead at the eastern end of the Highline Trail. The total distance from Vernal is about 32 miles.

The Hike

The shortest route begins at Leidy Peak trailhead, on the east end of the Highline Trail above Hacking Lake; the other starts at Ashley Twin Lakes. Both trails are well marked, but the trail from Hacking Lake is difficult to follow as it goes around Leidy Peak. The Hacking Lake route is at least a mile shorter and can be reached by car. Ashley Twin Lakes can only be reached by jeep, after figuring out your way through a maze of brutally rocky roads. Take our word on this one—use the Highline trailhead by Hacking Lake.

From Leidy Peak trailhead, go 0.5 mile south to a trail junction. Stay right and go 1.5 miles around the south side of Leidy Peak to another trail junction. Stay left (west) and travel 2.0 miles to a fork. Stay left (west), go 0.1 mile to a second junction, and turn left (southeast). Lakeshore Lake is 0.9 mile from the second fork.

Lakeshore Lake is named for the basin. It is just off a good forest service trail in the upper end of Lakeshore Basin. Good campsites are present, along with an abundant supply of horse pasture and spring water. However, sheep grazing can foul the surrounding watershed. It would be a good idea to take precautions where drinking water is concerned.

Known as a decent fishing lake, Lakeshore holds a good population of fish. You should be able to catch enough for a tasty shore lunch.

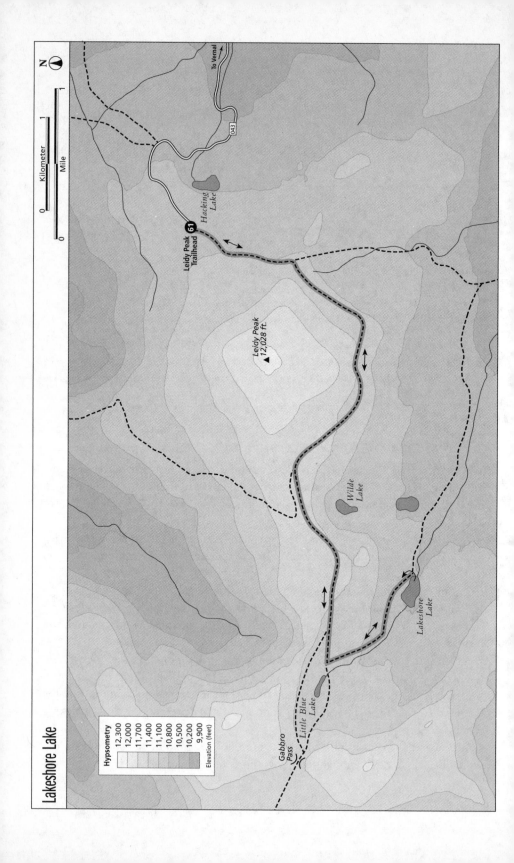

Lakeshore Lake

Hypsometry
12,300
12,000
11,700
11,400
11,100
10,800
10,500
10,200
9,900
Elevation (feet)

N

Kilometer
0   1
Mile
0   1

Leidy Peak Trailhead
61

Hacking Lake

To Vernal

043

Leidy Peak
▲ 12,028 ft.

Wilde Lake

Lakeshore Lake

Little Blue Lake

Gabbro Pass

Another lake in Lakeshore Basin is Little Blue, a cirque lake that sits on the trail 1.0 mile northwest of Lakeshore Lake at the base of Gabbro Pass. Do you like wind? You can have as much as you want here. During unsettled weather, the wind blows constantly and continues to blow even when you least expect it. No campsites or trout exist here, but several springs pop up around the lake.

There seems to be plenty of confusion as to which lake is really Wilde Lake. The USGS maps name the lake we call Little Blue as Wilde Lake, as do the signs you'll encounter. But the DWR booklet describes it as we have in this book. We've gone with the DWR on other inconsistencies, so we will stick with them on this one too. They have been right more than wrong.

Take your time as you explore this wonderful wilderness—and definitely take your camera.

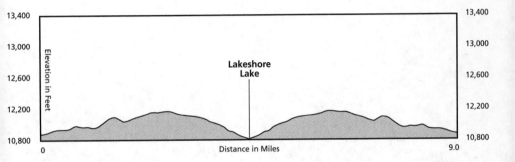

North Slope

The North Slope is heavily wooded and wetter than the South Slope. The hikes are generally shorter and not as steep. There is not as much space, but there is plenty to go around. Crowds are generally lighter on the North Slope, since people who live along the populous Wasatch Front tend to choose the South Slope hikes. Road access can be problematic on some drainages, and four-wheel drive is recommended for some trailheads.

Bald Lake

62 North Erickson Lake

There aren't many lakes in the High Uintas capable of yielding trout as big as North Erickson Lake does while requiring such a short, easy hike.

Start: End of Upper Setting Road
Distance: 5.6 miles out and back
Destination elevation: 10,020 feet
Approximate hiking time: 4 hours
Difficulty: Easy—one steep section
Usage: Moderate
Nearest town: Kamas, Utah
Drainage: Weber River

Maps: USGS Erickson Basin; USDA Forest Service High Uintas Wilderness; Trails Illustrated High Uintas Wilderness
Trail contacts: Wasatch National Forest, Forest Supervisor, 8226 Federal Building, 125 South State St., Salt Lake City, UT 84111; Kamas Ranger District, 50 East Center St., Kamas, UT 84036, (435) 783-4338

Finding the trailhead: From Kamas, take the Mirror Lake Highway (Highway 150) about 10 miles to Upper Setting Road. Turn left onto the dirt road, and twist your way up the mountain until the road ends. A truck or four-wheel drive is recommended.

The Hike

North Erickson Lake sits at the head of Smith and Morehouse Creek in Erickson Basin. It can be reached from the Smith and Morehouse trailhead, but it is easier to start hiking from the end of Upper Setting Road in the Provo River Drainage. From there it is less than 3.0 miles to North Erickson on a good trail. You have to go over the mountain, but it's not very steep (as mountain passes go). Stay with the trail, or you might walk right past the lake. It is in a bit of a hole surrounded by pines.

The best campsites are on the west side of the lake, just off the trail. Spring water is plentiful around the lake. If you camp on the west side as suggested, an ice-cold spring that feeds into the southwest corner of the lake will serve your water needs nicely.

South Erickson is just a hop, skip, and a jump to the south (0.25 mile). This pretty alpine lake abuts a talus slope and provides some excellent photo opportunities, but camping and fishing are better at North Erickson Lake. Large slickrock formations are prevalent between the two lakes. It is worth the hike over to South Erickson just to experience the unique terrain.

North Erickson Lake

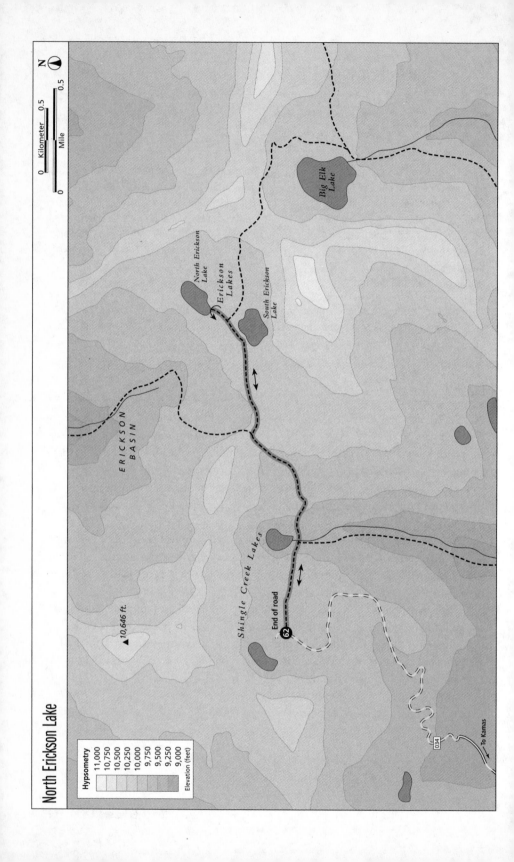

Hypsometry

11,000
10,750
10,500
10,250
10,000
9,750
9,500
9,250
9,000

Elevation (feet)

ERICKSON BASIN

▲ 10,646 ft.

Shingle Creek Lakes

North Erickson Lake

Erickson Lakes

South Erickson Lake

Big Elk Lake

End of road

62

034

To Kamas

N

0   Kilometer   0.5

0   Mile   0.5

Back at North Erickson, the fish await. Actually, you'll probably do most of the waiting. The fish seem to feed mostly at dusk and dawn, especially the big ones. Brook trout exceeding 18 inches in length and 2 pounds in weight can be caught if you're patient—and lucky—enough. Try casting a small fly (#16) with a bubble as far as you can. Be sure to use fresh, supple line. Being able to cast long distances may mean the difference between getting skunked or catching a few alpine lunkers.

63 Abes Lake

Abes Lake sits all alone, and you will likely be too, if you take this short, steep hike from Holiday Park.

Start: Holiday Park trailhead
Distance: 7.0 miles out and back
Destination elevation: 9,820 feet
Approximate hiking time: 5 hours
Difficulty: Moderate
Usage: Light
Nearest town: Oakley, Utah
Drainage: Weber River

Maps: USGS Erickson Basin; USDA Forest Service High Uintas Wilderness; Trails Illustrated High Uintas Wilderness
Trail contacts: Wasatch National Forest, Forest Supervisor, 8226 Federal Building, 125 South State St., Salt Lake City, UT 84111; Kamas Ranger District, 50 East Center St., Kamas, UT 84036, (435) 783-4338

Finding the trailhead: From Oakley, head east on Weber River Road. Follow it about 11 miles until the pavement ends. The road forks there, and the main road swings to the right (south) toward Smith-Morehouse Reservoir. Don't go that way. Stay on the dirt road that goes east, which will end at Holiday Park. There are several trailheads around Holiday Park, so look around for signs indicating the right trail.

The Hike

This lake can be a little tricky to locate. You have to watch for a side trail that branches away to the left from the main canyon about 2.5 miles up the trail. If you miss the cutoff, you will keep going up the Middle Fork of the Weber River until the trail peters out. The last mile to Abes Lake is the steep section, and you should be heading southeast.

Camping at Abes Lake is limited. The terrain is rocky and uneven. Only small camps exist, with perhaps the best one being on the east side of the lake. But it's quiet here and seldom used, so it can provide a wilderness experience with lots of firewood at your disposal. There is a small inlet on the south end. This is a good spot to refill water containers, but purifying is still recommended. The inlet is also a good place to find fish.

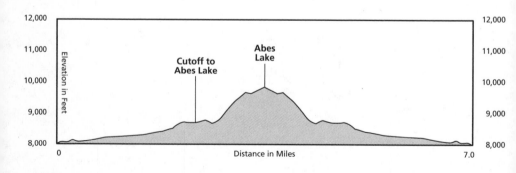

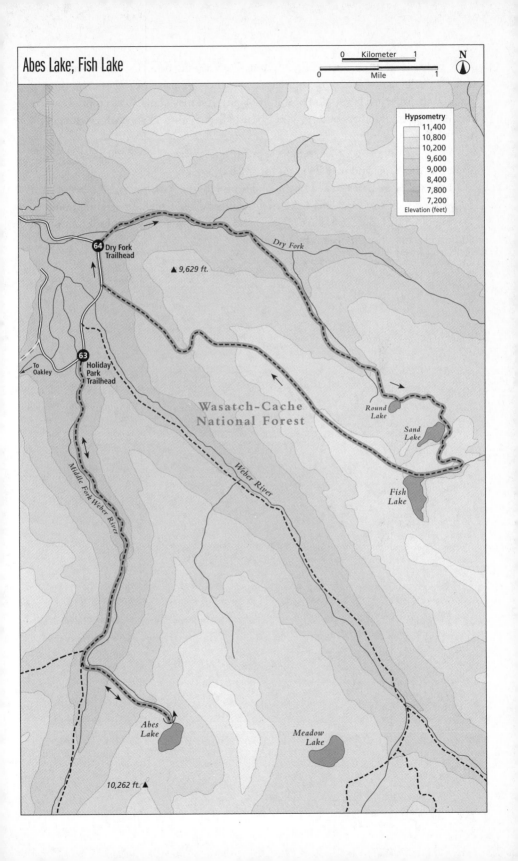

Abes Lake; Fish Lake

Hypsometry
11,400
10,800
10,200
9,600
9,000
8,400
7,800
7,200
Elevation (feet)

64 Dry Fork
Trailhead

Dry Fork

▲ 9,629 ft.

63 Holiday
Park
Trailhead

To
Oakley

Wasatch-Cache
National Forest

Round
Lake

Sand
Lake

Middle Fork Weber River

Weber River

Fish
Lake

Abes
Lake

Meadow
Lake

10,262 ft. ▲

Cutthroat trout dominate these waters. They reach about 15 inches but can be quite a challenge to catch. As with larger fish, they are particular about the time of day and the offering. If you don't hit it just right, you may come away empty-handed. There are good numbers of trout here, so just keep trying and you will eventually fill the frying pan.

There are not many other angling opportunities nearby. Tiny Neil Lake is 0.5 mile south of Abes Lake and may be good for small brookies.

These lakes are best reached by the trail from Holiday Park but can also be reached by heading west from Lovenia Lake over a rugged saddle, then descending 600 feet. Having done this route, we don't recommend it. It is not as easy as it looks on paper, and it's certainly not an option by horseback.

64 Fish Lake

Despite the elevation gain, many enthusiastic people find the Dry Fork Loop Trail a rewarding day hike. Backpackers with heavy loads usually avoid this steep, rugged trail. But experienced horseback riders discover this trek isn't so difficult after all.

See map on page 153.
Start: Holiday Park (Dry Fork trailhead)
Distance: 9.0-mile loop
Destination elevation: 10,180 feet
Approximate hiking time: 6 hours
Difficulty: Moderate—some steep sections
Usage: Heavy
Nearest town: Oakley, Utah
Drainage: Weber River

Maps: USGS Whitney Reservoir; USDA Forest Service High Uintas Wilderness; Trails Illustrated High Uintas Wilderness
Trail contacts: Wasatch National Forest, Forest Supervisor, 8226 Federal Building, 125 South State St., Salt Lake City, UT 84111; Kamas Ranger District, 50 East Center St., Kamas, UT 84036, (435) 783-4338

Finding the trailhead: From Oakley, head east on the Weber River Road and follow it until the pavement ends. The road forks there, and the main road swings to the right (south) toward Smith-Morehouse Reservoir. Don't go that way. Stay on the dirt road that goes east, which ends at Holiday Park. There are several trailheads around Holiday Park, so look around for signs indicating the right trail.

The Hike

The main starting point is located on the east side of Holiday Park at the Dry Fork trailhead. The other connecting trail begins 0.5 mile south of the Dry Fork trailhead, but it is hard to locate unless you've made this trip before. From the Dry Fork trailhead, follow a well-marked trail 2.0 miles east to a shallow river crossing. At this point, the trail twists another 1.5 miles southeast up a 1,300-foot incline to Round Lake. A large outlet releases a good supply of water that provides a wannabe waterfall that crosses the trail just before arrival. This small lake has good campsites all around it, but it's heavily used and degraded by refuse.

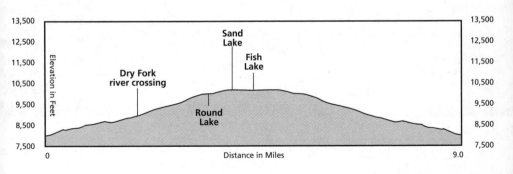

Following the loop trail 0.5 mile east to Sand Lake, you'll obtain the privilege of being hosted by righteous scenery comprising beautiful, timbered mountains and distant peaks. Sand Lake has only a couple of good campsites and no spring water, but fishing is fast and furious for small grayling.

Arctic grayling inhabit Fish Lake too. This lake sits another 0.5 mile south on the loop trail from Sand Lake. Fish Lake is surrounded by alpine mountains and pretty talus slopes that abut the water from the west. Running water is plentiful at three different outlets, but camping areas are limited due to rocky terrain. Angling is only fair but could be better from an inflatable raft.

Leaving Fish Lake, the loop trail proceeds west and up across a steep incline to the top of a scenic ridge. From here a hit-or-miss trail gradually declines down the ridgetop for about 3.0 miles. A well-defined trail then drops off the south side of the ridge and down a steep incline, intersecting a logging road that winds down to the Dry Fork trailhead. Total distance around the loop is 9.0 miles.

Fish Lake

65 Notch Lake

Going down anyone? Boy, you sure don't find many hikes like this one in the High Uintas. You actually get to hike downhill on the hike in. A fast hiker should be able to cover the entire distance in an hour. But coming back out may be a bit slower, as you'll have to make up 500 feet of elevation.

Start: Bald Mountain trailhead
Distance: 4.6 miles out and back
Destination elevation: 10,300 feet
Approximate hiking time: 3 hours
Difficulty: Easy
Usage: Heavy
Nearest town: Kamas, Utah
Drainage: Weber River

Maps: USGS Mirror Lake; USDA Forest Service High Uintas Wilderness; Trails Illustrated High Uintas Wilderness
Trail contacts: Wasatch National Forest, Forest Supervisor, 8226 Federal Building, 125 South State St., Salt Lake City, UT 84111; Kamas Ranger District, 50 East Center St., Kamas, UT 84036, (435) 783-4338

Finding the trailhead: From Kamas, take the Mirror Lake Highway (Highway 150) 30 miles to Bald Mountain overlook. About 0.5 mile north of the overlook is the turnoff to Bald Mountain.

Bald Mountain has space for twenty-five cars and offers picnic tables and toilets. No drinking water is available at the trailhead.

The Hike

Notch Lake lies at the east base of Notch Mountain and is visible from the trail. From Bald Mountain trailhead, the trail goes west and then northwest 2.3 miles to the lake. It is actually a reservoir that fluctuates quite a bit as the summer progresses. Notch usually drops more than 20 feet and loses about half its surface size. Campsites are abundant and spacious, so don't worry about a place to stay, although you might have some company. Spring water flows just west of the lake.

Notch is stocked with brook trout, but heavy pressure is to blame for only fair fishing. Bait anglers can expect to have some luck here, as well as fly fishers. Many high-country lakes offer poor fishing for bait anglers, but Notch is one of the exceptions.

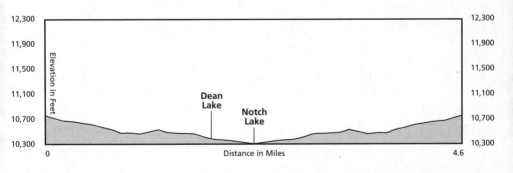

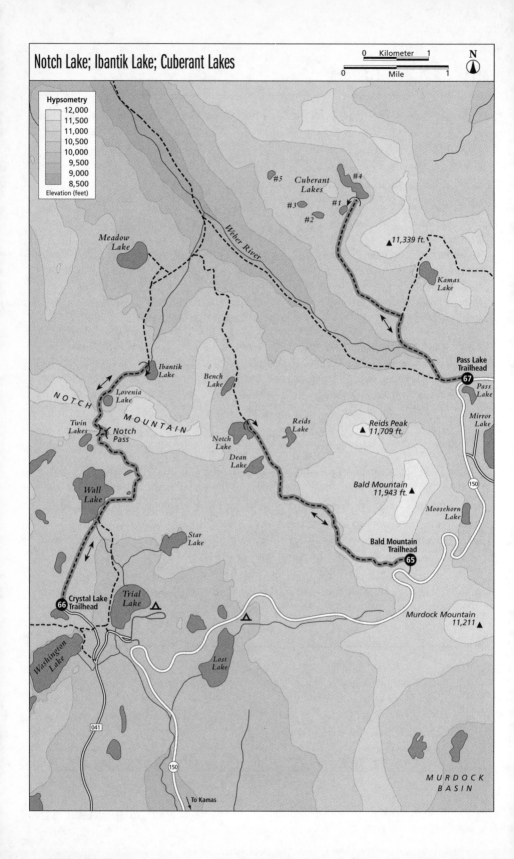

Notch Lake; Ibantik Lake; Cuberant Lakes

Hypsometry

12,000
11,500
11,000
10,500
10,000
9,500
9,000
8,500

Elevation (feet)

Kilometer

Mile

N

#5

Cuberant Lakes

#4

#3

#1

#2

▲11,339 ft.

Kamas Lake

Meadow Lake

Weber River

Pass Lake Trailhead

67

Pass Lake

Ibantik Lake

Bench Lake

NOTCH

Lovenia Lake

MOUNTAIN

Twin Lakes

Notch Pass

Notch Lake

Reids Lake

Reids Peak
▲ 11,709 ft.

Mirror Lake

150

Dean Lake

Bald Mountain
11,943 ft. ▲

Wall Lake

Moosehorn Lake

Star Lake

Bald Mountain Trailhead

65

Crystal Lake Trailhead

66

Trial Lake

Murdock Mountain
11,211 ▲

Washington Lake

Lost Lake

041

150

To Kamas

MURDOCK BASIN

There are a couple of other lakes nearby. Give them a try if Notch doesn't fill your needs. Bench Lake is just 0.5 mile north, and Dean Lake is 0.5 mile south of Notch Lake. Bench Lake often experiences winterkills but receives far less camping pressure. This scenic alpine lake is a great place for a small party to camp if you don't care if you catch fish.

If you don't want to hike back up to the trailhead, then park another vehicle at the Crystal Lake trailhead near Trial Lake. From Notch Lake, follow the trail north a couple of miles around the mountain, then south over Notch Pass (gorgeous), and then down to the Crystal Lake trailhead. The entire loop, from Bald Mountain trailhead to Crystal Lake trailhead, makes an easy and scenic day hike. After all, it's downhill almost all the way.

66 Ibantik Lake

The trail goes right over Notch Pass. Even if you don't visit Ibantik Lake, you should hike to the top of Notch Pass and gaze into the deep turquoise depths of Lovenia Lake directly below. Absolutely gorgeous! Words cannot describe its beauty. Pictures cannot depict its depth, nor the feeling you get at the top of a cliff looking down. The view is a must for hikers searching for awesome alpine scenery.

See map on page 158.
Start: Crystal Lake trailhead
Distance: 6.6 miles out and back
Destination elevation: 10,100 feet
Approximate hiking time: 5 hours
Difficulty: Moderate—steep over Notch Pass
Usage: Heavy
Nearest town: Kamas, Utah
Drainage: Weber River

Maps: USGS Mirror Lake; USDA Forest Service High Uintas Wilderness; Trails Illustrated High Uintas Wilderness
Trail contacts: Wasatch National Forest, Forest Supervisor, 8226 Federal Building, 125 South State St., Salt Lake City, UT 84111; Kamas Ranger District, 50 East Center St., Kamas, UT 84036, (435) 783-4338

Finding the trailhead: From Kamas, take the Mirror Lake Highway (Highway 150) 27 miles to Trial Lake. Exit west onto a paved road, and travel about a mile to a fork in the road. Then turn north for another mile to the trailhead.

This is a popular trailhead with room for fifty-seven vehicles and has nice toilet facilities. Water and other amenities can be found at Trial Lake Campground.

The Hike

The trail from Crystal Lake trailhead goes north 1.1 mile to Wall Lake. There is a trail junction here with the trail coming from Trial Lake. Continue to the left (north) 1.6 miles past Lovenia Lake on the west side of the trail to the notch in Notch Mountain. Ibantik Lake is 0.6 mile northeast of the Notch.

Campsites exist at Lovenia Lake, but there are better ones and fewer people at Ibantik. There is more room for the crowds to disperse once you reach Ibantik Lake.

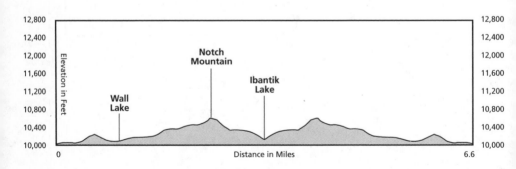

Lovenia Lake from Notch Pass near Ibantik Lake

It is well suited for a half-day hike or a quick overnighter. Some backpackers can't get to the trailhead until evening. Ibantik might be ideal for someone getting a late start—it is easily reached within 2 hours of Crystal Lake trailhead.

Day anglers frequently try their luck in this area. Lovenia, Ibantik, and Meadow Lakes to the north all receive frequent plants of brook and cutthroat trout. The fishing may be good or poor, depending on the time of year, the time of day, or your own fishing skill. Keep in mind that these lakes get heavy pressure, so don't be surprised if many of the fish are wary—or have already been caught.

67   Cuberant Lakes

Most of the Cuberant Lakes are nestled in the pines, except for Cuberant #4, which sits against a talus slope in a picture-book setting. Lake #4 is by far the largest and deepest of the Cuberant Lakes. This is a relatively short and easy hike for these mountains.

See map on page 158.
Start: Pass Lake trailhead
Distance: 5.0 miles out and back
Destination elevation: 10,420 feet
Approximate hiking time: 4 hours
Difficulty: Moderate
Usage: Moderate
Nearest town: Kamas, Utah
Drainage: Weber River

Maps: USGS Mirror Lake; USDA Forest Service High Uintas Wilderness; Trails Illustrated High Uintas Wilderness
Trail contacts: Wasatch National Forest, Forest Supervisor, 8226 Federal Building, 125 South State St., Salt Lake City, UT 84111; Kamas Ranger District, 50 East Center St., Kamas, UT 84036, (435) 783-4338

Finding the trailhead: From Kamas, take the Mirror Lake Highway (Highway 150) 32 miles to Pass Lake. The trailhead is on the opposite side of the road from the lake.

The Hike

Cuberant Lake #2 is the best place to camp among the five Cuberant Lakes. However, you may want to camp at Cuberant #3. It is the only lake around with possible spring water. These lakes are all a little different from one another, and whether you are on a day hike or an overnighter, it is rewarding to experience each one and enjoy what each has to offer.

Park at the Pass Lake trailhead, just across the road from Pass Lake. Or park at Pass Lake and catch the trail behind the guardrail where the road makes a 90-degree turn. Watch the trail signs closely; before long, about 1.2 miles, you'll be branching off the main trail (north) toward Kamas Lake. After another 0.5 mile, take another fork

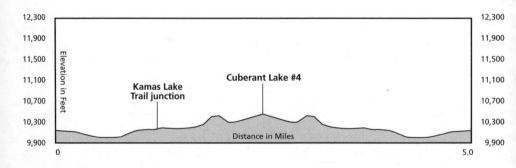

northwest leading to Cuberant Lakes. If all goes according to plan, you will arrive at Cuberant Lake #1 first.

Fishing is generally good at these lakes for mostly pan-size cutthroat and brook trout, although a few large fish can occasionally be fooled. All the lakes, except Cuberant #5, are stocked regularly. A fly-and-bubble combination is effective around here. The fish like tiny flies, but there isn't much space for traditional fly casting. The conifers surrounding these lakes are notorious for gobbling up ill-presented flies. But the pines offer camouflage that can be used to your advantage when stalking wary trout in these small lakes.

If you like calm, shade, quiet, and lots of pine trees, then you will enjoy the Cuberant Basin. It's a great place to catch a nap and a few trout. Bring along the mosquito repellent, because there won't be much wind to help keep the bugs at bay.

68 Ruth Lake

When you get to Ruth Lake, don't forget to look behind you. Hayden Peak looms larger than life just across the canyon to the west. The view from Ruth Lake is a must for shutterbugs looking for some real photo trophies. You'll want to hang this one on your wall.

Start: Ruth Lake trailhead
Distance: 1.6 miles out and back
Destination elevation: 10,340 feet
Approximate hiking time: 1 hour
Difficulty: Easy
Usage: Heavy
Nearest town: Evanston, Wyoming
Drainage: Bear River

Maps: USGS Mirror Lake; USDA Forest Service High Uintas Wilderness; Trails Illustrated High Uintas Wilderness
Trail contacts: Wasatch National Forest, Forest Supervisor, 8226 Federal Building, 125 South State St., Salt Lake City, UT 84111; Bear River Ranger Station, 32 miles south of Evanston, Wyoming, on the Mirror Lake Highway, (435) 642-6662

Finding the trailhead: From Evanston, take the Mirror Lake Highway (Highway 150) about 42 miles to the Ruth Lake trailhead, which is a roadside pull-off with a sign pointing to Ruth Lake. There are nice restrooms and paved parking.

The Hike

This is a short, easy hike that even kids enjoy. Recently the trail has been posted with nature signs, and there are a variety of natural sights along the way. Everything from miniature meadows and waterfalls to playful chipmunks are scattered along this hike that goes only 0.8 mile west of the trailhead and back. Of course you can go farther if you like. There are several other small lakes in the area. You can spend just a couple of hours or a couple of days exploring this basin. The trail dissolves at Ruth Lake though, so have your map and compass handy if you're continuing on.

Camping and fishing pressure is heavy at Ruth Lake, but the crowds fan out past this point. The fish in these parts see mostly day-use anglers. If you are one of them, the most productive fishing times are early morning and late evening. The hike in/out is short enough that you should have no problem managing your hike around prime fishing hours. If it's fish you're after, don't stop at Ruth Lake very long. You will probably have better success at nearby lakes such as Hayden, Cutthroat, Jewel, and Teal.

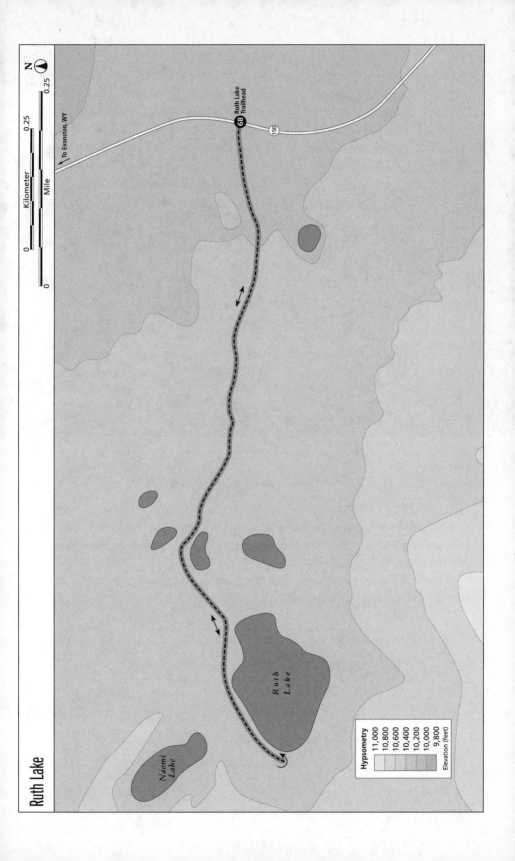

Ruth Lake

Naomi Lake

Ruth Lake

Ruth Lake Trailhead

68

150

To Evanston, WY

N

Kilometer
0   0.25   0.25

Mile
0   0.25

Hypsometry
11,000
10,800
10,600
10,400
10,200
10,000
9,800

Elevation (feet)

Scenes like this one at Ruth Lake are why people return for a lifetime of discovery in the Uinta Mountains.
PHOTO BY MATT McKELL/Utah Division of Wildlife Resources

As with any popular area, litter can be a problem. But this area seems to be well preserved. Let's keep it that way. Pack out what you pack in, and avoid building any new fire rings.

A marked, but faint, trail leads south from Ruth Lake and ties into the trail leading from Scout Lake to Lofty Lake.

69 Whiskey Island Lake

All right, who names these lakes anyway? With Bourbon Lake and Whiskey Springs close by, someone must have been on an all-nighter when it came time to issuing names. Solitude seekers will enjoy Whiskey Island. Few visit this rugged basin, but those who do will say it's easily worth the trip—for the aesthetics. If you're looking for a short, interesting hike where you can really get away from everyone, then this is a good bet. It's quiet. You can meditate. Maybe you'll catch a glimpse of an eagle riding the updraft by the steep talus ridge. Most certainly you could tan (or burn) yourself, just lying back next to the turquoise waters.

Start: End of the dirt road
Distance: 2.6 miles out and back
Destination elevation: 10,340 feet
Approximate hiking time: 2 hours
Difficulty: Moderate—cross-country hiking
Usage: Light
Nearest town: Evanston, Wyoming
Drainage: Bear River

Maps: USGS Whitney Reservoir; USDA Forest Service High Uintas Wilderness; Trails Illustrated High Uintas Wilderness
Trail contacts: Wasatch National Forest, Forest Supervisor, 8226 Federal Building, 125 South State St., Salt Lake City, UT 84111; Bear River Ranger Station, 32 miles south of Evanston, Wyoming, on the Mirror Lake Highway, (435) 642-6662

Finding the trailhead: From Evanston, take the Mirror Lake Highway (Highway 150) about 40 miles to an old, and the first, unmarked dirt road on the west side of Highway 150 south of Sulphur Campground. The road is very rough. Most people prefer to walk the road rather than drive it.

The Hike

Whiskey Island can be real tough to reach. If you choose the most direct route, you'll run right into several tricky boulder fields and deadfall timber. Instead, stay close to the mountain, and you should be able to skirt around all the trouble. There is no trail, so keep your map and compass handy. But you really can't miss this glacial cirque if you just follow the bottom of the ridge.

As for fishing, who knows what to expect. The Utah state record for grayling was caught here at one point. The lake does have a history of winterkill. There are no other fishing opportunities in the immediate area, unless you go all the way back to where you started hiking and drop into Bourbon Lake.

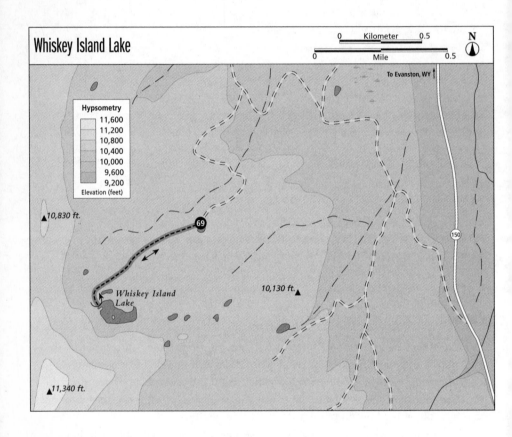

Whiskey Island Lake can be difficult to reach, but the views are worth it.
PHOTO BY MATT MCKELL/UTAH DIVISION OF WILDLIFE RESOURCES

Those into mountaineering should enjoy this trek. Immediately to the northwest of Whiskey Island is a "chute" that will allow a steep climb to the ridgetop. From the top, you can see down the other side into the Dry Fork arm of the Weber River Drainage. That's Fish Lake in the distance. Looking back toward Whiskey Island is another incredible view. Notice the boulder fields that you hopefully avoided on your way in.

70 Hell Hole Lake

Hell Hole is a gamble for anglers. Some years it's hot, and some years it's not. It all depends on the planting schedules, winter survival, and catch-and-release rates. It is a relatively small lake (8.5 acres) and could be fished out if people keep more than they eat for dinner.

Start: Main Fork trailhead
Distance: 10.0 miles out and back
Destination elevation: 10,340 feet
Approximate hiking time: 7 hours
Difficulty: Moderate
Usage: Moderate
Nearest town: Evanston, Wyoming
Drainage: Bear River

Maps: USGS Christmas Meadows; USDA Forest Service High Uintas Wilderness; Trails Illustrated High Uintas Wilderness
Trail contacts: Wasatch National Forest, Forest Supervisor, 8226 Federal Building, 125 South State St., Salt Lake City, UT 84111; Bear River Ranger Station, 32 miles south of Evanston, Wyoming, on the Mirror Lake Highway, (435) 642-6662

Finding the trailhead: From Evanston, take the Mirror Lake Highway (Highway 150) about 34 miles. The unmarked trail starts just off Highway 150. Look right across the road from the Gold Hill turnoff.

The Hike

From Highway 150, hike the old jeep trail for about 1.0 mile. Hikers will come across a gravel road limited to authorized vehicles only. Follow the road about 1.5 miles to a stream channel. Look for a trail sign before crossing the bridge and then follow the trail for 2.5 miles to the lake.

Most of the lake is shallow, which makes for good morning and evening fishing for healthy cutthroat trout. During midday the only feasible spot to fish is the deeper northeast corner of the lake. A small rubber raft may be worthwhile here. Maybe there are deeper holes out in the middle that the fish retreat to during the day. No other fishing opportunities exist nearby if Hell Hole doesn't produce.

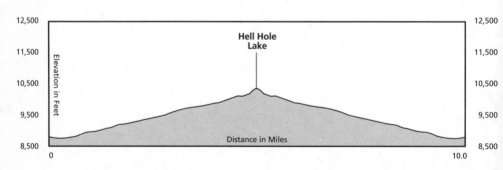

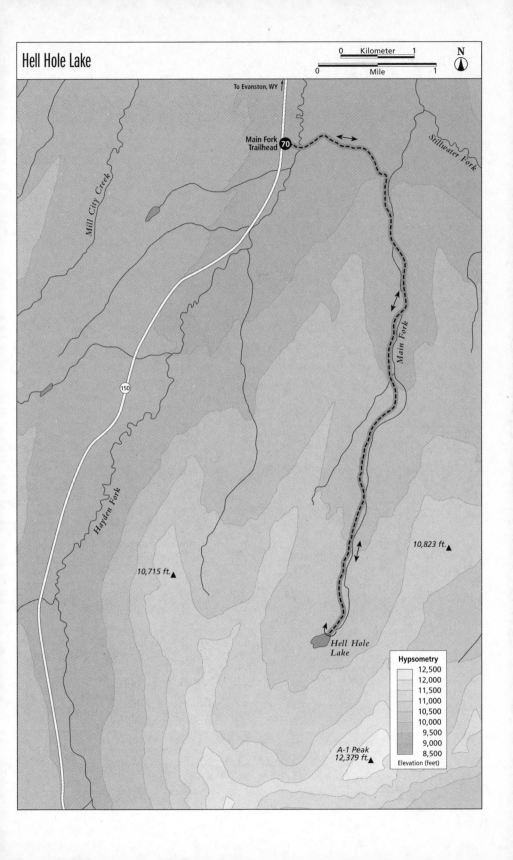

Hell Hole Lake

Kilometer
0 1
Mile
0 1

N

To Evanston, WY

Mill City Creek

Stillwater Fork

Main Fork
Trailhead 70

Main Fork

150

Hayden Fork

10,823 ft. ▲

10,715 ft. ▲

Hell Hole
Lake

Hypsometry

	Elevation (feet)
	12,500
	12,000
	11,500
	11,000
	10,500
	10,000
	9,500
	9,000
	8,500

A-1 Peak
12,379 ft. ▲

Hell Hole does have a lot to offer, especially if you are looking for a short week-end trip. Excellent campsites are available for backpackers and equestrians. The latter would probably prefer the east side of the lake for horse pasture, while backpackers should like the west side and its pine-sheltered camps. A good spring flows into the northeast corner of the lake.

71 Ryder and McPheters Lakes

As elaborate as it may seem, the Stillwater Trail is a little deceiving as far as the difficulty of this hike is concerned. It's not the elevation gain that will discourage the soul, but lots of rocks and many mud holes may dampen spirits. The trail does pick up some altitude. However, it is an effortless climb until the Kermsuh-Ryder junction. Then the trail proceeds up, up, and up.

Start: Christmas Meadows trailhead
Distance: 17.0 miles out and back
Destination elevation: 10,620 feet
Approximate hiking time: 11 hours
Difficulty: Moderate—one steep section
Usage: Moderate
Nearest town: Evanston, Wyoming
Drainage: Bear River
Maps: USGS Christmas Meadows and USGS Hayden Peak; USDA Forest Service High Uintas

Wilderness; Trails Illustrated High Uintas Wilderness
Trail contacts: Wasatch National Forest, Forest Supervisor, 8226 Federal Building, 125 South State St., Salt Lake City, UT 84111; Bear River Ranger Station, 32 miles south of Evanston, Wyoming, on the Mirror Lake Highway, (435) 642-6662

Finding the trailhead: From Evanston, take the Mirror Lake Highway (Highway 150) south about 33 miles to the Christmas Meadows turnoff. Follow a good dirt road south about 4 miles to the trailhead.

Christmas Meadows has fifteen parking places and a stock ramp. The nearby campgrounds have toilets and water. This popular trail leads into some of the most spectacular scenery in the High Uintas.

The Hike

Ryder and McPheters Lakes occupy Middle Basin; Mount Agassiz, Spread Eagle, and Hayden are the dominant surrounding peaks. Ryder sits at the foot of three connecting ridges characterized by wind and steep, rocky ledges. Beautiful meadows intersperse the pines, while trickles of water cascade off the cliffs, adding to the aesthetics.

Access begins at the south end of Christmas Meadows Campground. An excellent trail parallels the Stillwater River all the way to Middle Basin. For the last 1.5 miles, the trail departs from the river and is hard to follow, but rock cairns clearly mark the way.

Other lakes in the vicinity are BR–17 and 18. These lakes are located on the south side of Ryder, where you'll find good campsites and an abundant supply of spring water. BR–17 and 18 also contain good populations of brook trout and only receive half the angling pressure of Ryder.

McPheters is another popular fishing hole. This lake is located 0.5 mile north of Ryder on some bedrock shelves next to a talus slope. Campsites are not present in

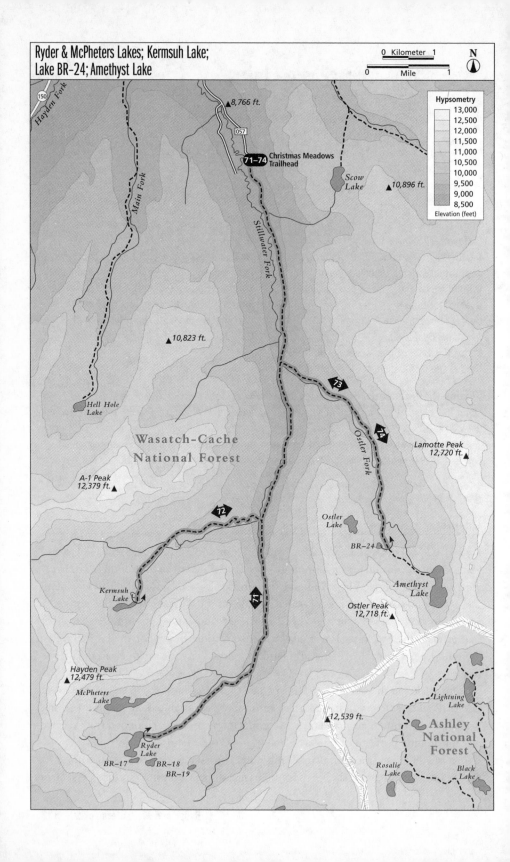

Ryder & McPheters Lakes; Kermsuh Lake; Lake BR–24; Amethyst Lake

N

0 Kilometer 1

0 Mile 1

Hypsometry
13,000
12,500
12,000
11,500
11,000
10,500
10,000
9,500
9,000
8,500
Elevation (feet)

Hayden Fork

150

8,766 ft.

057

71–74 Christmas Meadows Trailhead

Main Fork

Scow Lake

▲ *10,896 ft.*

Stillwater Fork

▲ *10,823 ft.*

73

Ostler Fork

74

Lamotte Peak 12,720 ft. ▲

Hell Hole Lake

Wasatch-Cache National Forest

A-1 Peak 12,379 ft. ▲

72

Ostler Lake

BR–24

Kermsuh Lake

Amethyst Lake

71

Ostler Peak 12,718 ft. ▲

Hayden Peak 12,479 ft. ▲

McPheters Lake

Lightning Lake

▲ *12,539 ft.*

Ashley National Forest

Ryder Lake

BR–17   *BR–18*

BR–19

Rosalie Lake

Black Lake

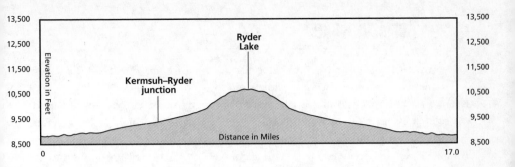

the immediate vicinity but can be found nearby. Due to open terrain, firewood is extremely sparse but can be gathered near the camping areas to the south. Plenty of spring water endows McPheters, along with pan-size cutthroat trout.

If solitude is what you're looking for, Meadow Lake (BR–19) is a good place to visit. Meadow sits 0.5 mile east of BR–18 in rocky, timbered country. This lake plays host to good camping areas and excellent spring water. Deepwater channels circulate through the middle of this shallow lake, which may produce fairly good fishing.

72 Kermsuh Lake

Do you want to get lost? No, we're not talking about losing your direction, but we are contemplating losing the vast majority of crowds that trample the Stillwater Trail. Kermsuh is a gorgeous, isolated lake situated in rocky, timbered country just inside the wilderness area. Upon arrival you'll be greeted by several high peaks, including Hayden, Kletting, and A–1. These major peaks have connecting ridges that almost completely enclose the West Basin. This feature, and the fact that Kermsuh is the only lake in the basin, makes the area a remote and peaceful place.

See map on page 174.
Start: Christmas Meadows trailhead
Distance: 13.6 miles out and back
Destination elevation: 10,300 feet
Approximate hiking time: 9 hours
Difficulty: Moderate—one steep section
Usage: Light
Nearest town: Evanston, Wyoming
Drainage: Bear River

Maps: USGS Christmas Meadows and USGS Hayden Peak; USDA Forest Service High Uintas Wilderness; Trails Illustrated High Uintas Wilderness
Trail contacts: Wasatch National Forest, Forest Supervisor, 8226 Federal Building, 125 South State St., Salt Lake City, UT 84111; Bear River Ranger Station, 32 miles south of Evanston, Wyoming, on the Mirror Lake Highway, (435) 642-6662

Finding the trailhead: From Evanston, take the Mirror Lake Highway (Highway 150) south about 33 miles to the Christmas Meadows turnoff. Follow a good dirt road south about 4 miles to the trailhead.

Christmas Meadows has fifteen parking places and a stock ramp. The nearby campgrounds have toilets and water. This popular trail leads into some of the most spectacular scenery in the High Uintas.

The Hike

From Christmas Meadows, follow the Stillwater Fork Trail 4.5 miles to a posted sign at the Kermsuh-Ryder junction. The Kermsuh Lake Trail heads southwest to and across a narrow footbridge that scaffolds over the Stillwater Fork River. After the river crossing, you'll encounter several steep switchbacks, and startling scenes of a deep river gorge can be spotted at the end of every other cutback. The trail then gradually climbs to a marshy meadow where rock cairns, tree blazes, and short segments of trail mark the rest of the way.

Kermsuh is mostly visited by day hikers. This trek may be questionable for a day hike, but we think it is right on the borderline of what is and what isn't. Allow yourself at least 8 hours for a single-day excursion, including half an hour for a shoreline lunch and a couple of 15-minute breaks. A healthy hiker can make the round-trip in 9 hours, but allow extra time for fishing, photography, or relaxing.

Angling pressure is usually very light for cutthroat in the 12-inch class. Fishing is unpredictable but has been known to be good in the early summer months. Due to the rocky terrain that surrounds this lake, no decent campsites exist. Running water is no problem here, and horse pasture can be found at a small meadow to the south.

This one is for the solitude seeker or the explorer. Go seek!

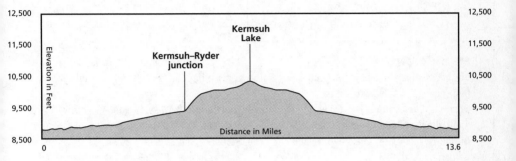

73 Lake BR-24

In honor of all the great nameless lakes in the High Uintas, we just had to spotlight one of the best. Some of the lakes without names are the least visited and have become some of the real jewels of the area. If solitude and a chance for some unspoiled fishing rank high on your list, then try the lakes with no names, especially the ones with no trails. That being said, BR-24 is known as Emerald Lake in some hiking circles.

See map on page 174.
Start: Christmas Meadows trailhead
Distance: 10.6 miles out and back
Destination elevation: 10,460 feet
Approximate hiking time: 7 hours
Difficulty: Moderate—one steep section
Usage: Moderate
Nearest town: Evanston, Wyoming
Drainage: Bear River

Maps: USGS Christmas Meadows; USDA Forest Service High Uintas Wilderness; Trails Illustrated High Uintas Wilderness
Trail contacts: Wasatch National Forest, Forest Supervisor, 8226 Federal Building, 125 South State St., Salt Lake City, UT 84111; Bear River Ranger Station, 32 miles south of Evanston, Wyoming, on the Mirror Lake Highway, (435) 642-6662

Finding the trailhead: From Evanston, take the Mirror Lake Highway (Highway 150) south about 33 miles to the Christmas Meadows turnoff. Follow a good dirt road south about 4 miles to the trailhead.

Christmas Meadows has fifteen parking places and a stock ramp. The nearby campgrounds have toilets and water. This popular trail leads into some of the most spectacular scenery in the High Uintas.

The Hike

From Christmas Meadows trailhead, the trail goes 3.0 miles south along the Stillwater Fork of the Bear River to the turnoff to Lake BR-24 and Amethyst Lake. The trail then follows the Ostler Fork 2.3 miles to Lake BR-24.

Well, we mentioned what to look for in a nameless lake, and BR-24 doesn't seem to fit the stereotype. It receives its share of visitors, its few fish are wary, and the main trail passes right by it. But it is still a gem! Its excellent campsites are the best in Amethyst Basin, with spring water at the lake and horse pasture nearby. BR-24 is a great place to camp if you are going to visit Amethyst Lake. Campsites at Amethyst Lake are above timberline and offer little shelter, firewood, spring water, or horse pasture. Staying at BR-24, you'll have all the commodities you need. It's only a brisk 20-minute walk from BR-24 to Amethyst Lake for some grand sightseeing and fast fishing for lots of pan-size brook trout.

Fishing at BR-24 is unpredictable. A few large cutthroat trout patrol these sparkling waters, and they didn't get big by being stupid. You will have to be extremely lucky or tricky to hook one of these spooky lunkers. But you might fool a smaller

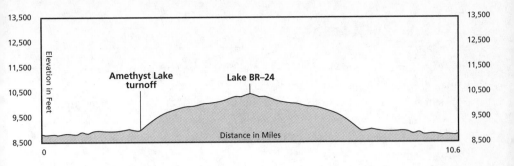

trout or two. If you would like some trout larger than what Amethyst offers, try Ostler Lake. It is less than 0.5 mile northwest of BR–24 and frequently yields cutthroat in the 1-pound class.

Like Amethyst Lake, BR–24 is emerald green—thus its adopted name—in color due to turbidity. It is fairly shallow and therefore casts its own unique shade of turquoise. It is a great place to sit back and just enjoy the placid scenery while a pan of trout sizzle on the fire. Catch the fish at Amethyst, then retire to BR–24 for the evening.

Hayden Peak provides a stunning background to Emerald Lake, indicated on many maps as BR–24.

PHOTO BY MATT McKELL/UTAH DIVISION OF WILDLIFE RESOURCES

74 Amethyst Lake

Set in the top of a glacial cirque, this is one of the prettiest alpine lakes in the High Uintas. A few small pines dot its shores, and the massive cliffs and talus slopes add grandeur to the emerald-green waters. This large lake (42.5 acres) attracts moderate crowds because of its scenery and frequently fast fishing. The hike in is only 6.0 miles each way, but it seems longer. Two thousand feet of elevation is a lot to gain in such a short distance.

See map on page 174.
Start: Christmas Meadows trailhead
Distance: 12.0 miles out and back
Destination elevation: 10,750 feet
Approximate hiking time: 8 hours
Difficulty: Moderate—one steep section
Usage: Moderate
Nearest town: Evanston, Wyoming
Drainage: Bear River

Maps: USGS Christmas Meadows; USDA Forest Service High Uintas Wilderness; Trails Illustrated High Uintas Wilderness
Trail contacts: Wasatch National Forest, Forest Supervisor, 8226 Federal Building, 125 South State St., Salt Lake City, UT 84111; Bear River Ranger Station, 32 miles south of Evanston, Wyoming, on the Mirror Lake Highway, (435) 642-6662

Finding the trailhead: From Evanston, take the Mirror Lake Highway (Highway 150) south about 33 miles to the Christmas Meadows turnoff. Follow a good dirt road south about 4 miles to the trailhead.

Christmas Meadows has fifteen parking places and a stock ramp. The nearby campgrounds have toilets and water. This popular trail leads into some of the most spectacular scenery in the High Uintas.

The Hike

The trail starts at beautiful Christmas Meadows and is maintained well for the entire hike. It parallels the Stillwater Fork of the Bear River half of the way, which presents many tempting fishing holes. After 3.0 miles, the trail forks to the left (southeast). Follow the trail up Ostler Fork 2.3 miles to Lake BR–24 and another 0.7 mile to Amethyst Lake. There's a lot to see along the route, so take your time and enjoy the hike.

Brook trout are active all around Amethyst Lake, but the best spots seem to be on the east side or the deeper southwest corner. Small flies draw attention on about every other cast, and even more regularly during the evening. During midday, try small spinners in the deeper sections. You'll have no trouble filling the frying pan here, but this is not the best place to set up your kitchen.

Excellent campsites are available at BR–24 about a mile below Amethyst Lake. This tiny lake is also emerald in color due to turbidity. Several springs emerge here, and horse pasture is close by in the lower meadows. There is a small population of cutthroat, but don't plan on them for dinner. They are extremely wary. Firewood is limited, unless you care to walk west into the woods a few hundred yards.

Ostler Lake, 0.5 mile to the northwest of BR–24, should have fewer people if you are looking to be alone. It has a few rough campgrounds and several springs. Cutthroat and brookies grow larger at Ostler, so don't be surprised if you hook into one weighing well over a pound. However, fishing is kind of slow, especially when compared to Amethyst Lake.

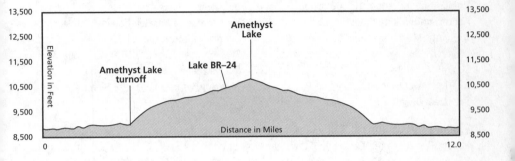

75 Scow Lake

Day hikers looking for solitude will like this area. On weekdays, expect to have the whole place to yourself—unless a herd of elk happens to be passing through.

Start: East Fork Bear River trailhead
Distance: 6.6 miles out and back
Destination elevation: 10,100 feet
Approximate hiking time: 5 hours
Difficulty: Moderate—some steep, cross-country travel
Usage: Moderate
Nearest town: Evanston, Wyoming
Drainage: Bear River

Maps: USGS Christmas Meadows; USDA Forest Service High Uintas Wilderness; Trails Illustrated High Uintas Wilderness

Trail contacts: Wasatch National Forest, Forest Supervisor, 8226 Federal Building, 125 South State St., Salt Lake City, UT 84111; Bear River Ranger Station, 32 miles south of Evanston, Wyoming, on the Mirror Lake Highway, (435) 642-6662

Finding the trailhead: From Evanston, take the Mirror Lake Highway (Highway 150) south about 30 miles to the East Fork of the Bear River turnoff. This road is often referred to as the North Slope Road. Follow this road east 1.5 miles to a junction. Take Road 059 south about 4 miles to East Fork Bear River trailhead. You may need a four-wheel-drive vehicle for the last mile when wet.

This trailhead is within the Hinckley Scout Ranch, previously known as the East Fork Bear River Boy Scout Camp. The parking spots are often filled with visitors to the ranch.

The Hike

Scow Lake can be reached from either the Boundary Creek Trail, at the East Fork Bear River Drainage, or the Wolverine Trail, located by the Bear River Stillwater Road. Both trails connect near the Boundary Creek trailhead, but the East Fork access is about 1.5 miles shorter. Follow the Boundary Creek Trail 2.5 miles south to a small meadow. Then depart from the trail, continuing south 0.75 mile through heavy timber to the lake.

This meadow lake sits on a ridge between the Stillwater and Boundary Creek Drainages. Heavy timber surrounds the lake, along with a few spring-fed meadows.

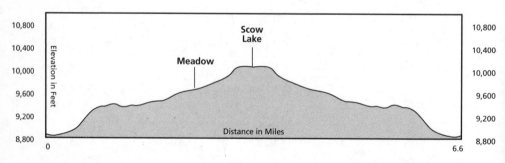

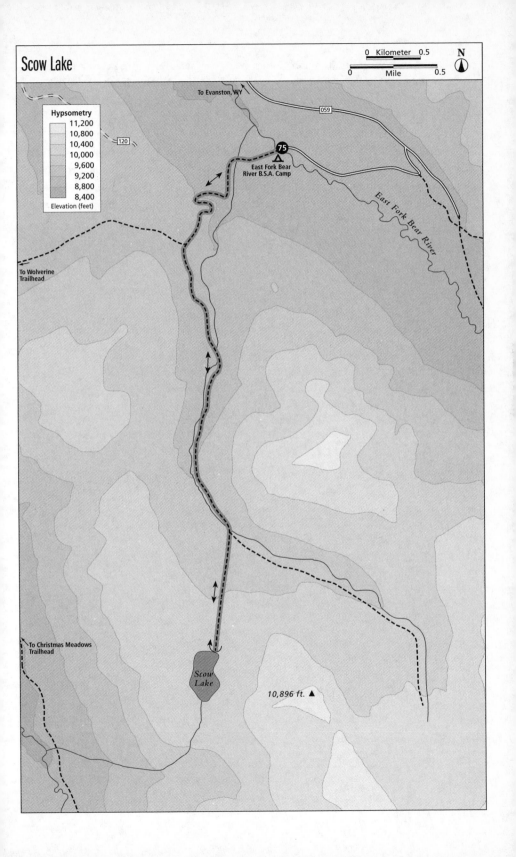

Scow Lake

To Evanston, WY

059

120

75
East Fork Bear
River B.S.A. Camp

East Fork Bear River

Hypsometry

11,200
10,800
10,400
10,000
9,600
9,200
8,800
8,400
Elevation (feet)

To Wolverine
Trailhead

To Christmas Meadows
Trailhead

Scow
Lake

10,896 ft. ▲

Campsites and horse goodies are numerous in the area, but spring water is usually only available in the early summer months. Due to the shallow depth of this lake, it often winterkills. However, brook trout are stocked on a rotational basis. This lake also sustains lots of bugs and mosquitoes, so remember the repellent.

If Scow doesn't fit your fancy, we suggest trying Baker Lake at the end of the Boundary Creek Trail. The last 0.75 mile is hard to follow, which makes Baker Lake difficult to find. Baker is characterized by a large meadow with a gradual timbered slope located on the south end. Good camping areas and plenty of horse pasture exist, and spring water can be found 0.25 mile north of the outlet. Fishing is considered unpredictable. Hearsay warns that brook trout are most often wary.

76 Priord and Norice Lakes

The East Fork Bear River Drainage receives moderate to heavy usage from Boy Scouts and camera-clickers alike. A Boy Scouts of America camp is located 0.5 mile north of the main trailhead. So don't be alarmed if you see a bunch of khaki-green men and kids congregated at any one spot.

Start: East Fork Bear River trailhead
Distance: 16.5 miles out and back
Destination elevation: 10,470 feet
Approximate hiking time: 11 hours
Difficulty: Moderate
Usage: Moderate
Nearest town: Evanston, Wyoming
Drainage: Bear River

Maps: USGS Red Knob; USDA Forest Service High Uintas Wilderness; Trails Illustrated High Uintas Wilderness
Trail contacts: Wasatch National Forest, Forest Supervisor, 8226 Federal Building, 125 South State St., Salt Lake City, UT 84111; Bear River Ranger Station, 32 miles south of Evanston, Wyoming, on the Mirror Lake Highway, (435) 642-6662

Finding the trailhead: From Evanston, take the Mirror Lake Highway (Highway 150) south about 30 miles to the East Fork of the Bear River turnoff. This road is often referred to as the North Slope Road. Follow this road east 1.5 miles to a junction. Take Road 059 south about 4 miles to East Fork Bear River trailhead. You may need a four-wheel-drive vehicle for the last mile when wet.

The Hike

Start your journey on the East Fork Bear River Trail, 0.5 mile southeast of the B.S.A. turnoff. Follow the East Fork Trail 4.0 miles southeast to the Right Hand–Left Hand Fork Trail junction. Then go south on the Right Hand Fork Trail. The trail deteriorates when traveling through bogs and deadfall. When this occurs, following the stream will take you to Norice Lake. From Norice, the trail becomes difficult to locate. Just head south for 0.5 mile, then west 0.25 mile, and you'll find Priord Lake.

Priord sits at the head of the Right Hand Fork Drainage. A rugged cirque basin encircles this timberline lake, and the lake itself is a pretty emerald green. Camping areas exist east of the lake, and spring water is present. However, horse pasture and firewood are limited. Windy conditions may hinder fly casting, but the fish should be cooperative, since Priord Lake only receives light fishing use for cutthroat trout.

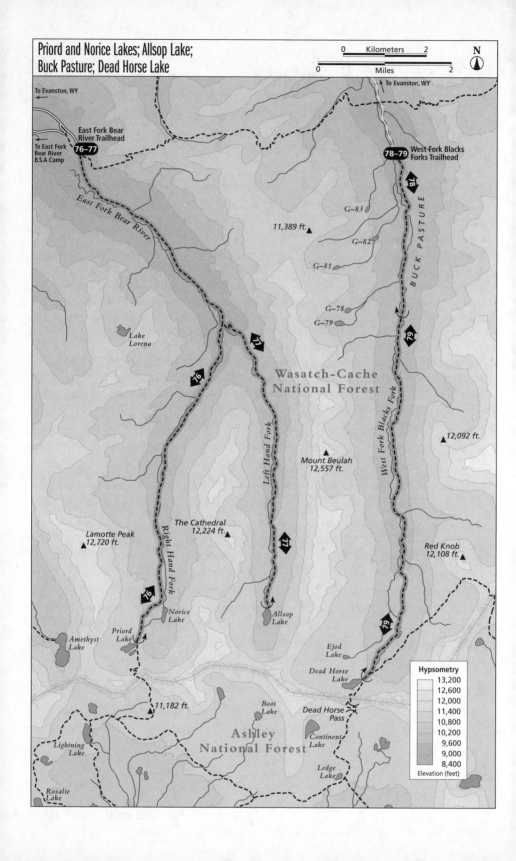

Priord and Norice Lakes; Allsop Lake; Buck Pasture; Dead Horse Lake

To Evanston, WY

To Evanston, WY

East Fork Bear
River Trailhead

76–77

To East Fork
Bear River
B.S.A Camp

78–79   West Fork Blacks
Forks Trailhead

78

East Fork Bear River

G–83

11,389 ft.

G–82

G–81

BUCK PASTURE

G–78

G–79

Lake
Lorena

77

Wasatch-Cache
National Forest

79

76

12,092 ft.

Left Hand Fork

West Fork Blacks Fork

Mount Beulah
12,557 ft.

The Cathedral
12,224 ft.

77

Lamotte Peak
12,720 ft.

Right Hand Fork

Red Knob
12,108 ft.

76

Norice
Lake

Allsop
Lake

79

Priord
Lake

Amethyst
Lake

Ejod
Lake

Dead Horse
Lake

11,182 ft.

Boot
Lake

Dead Horse
Pass

Hypsometry

13,200

Lightning
Lake

Ashley
National Forest

Continent
Lake

12,600
12,000
11,400
10,800
10,200
9,600
9,000
8,400

Rosalie
Lake

Ledge
Lake

Elevation (feet)

Lamotte Peak

Norice is shallow, but despite the depth, this lake contains an excellent population of cutthroat trout. Norice is a meadow lake that is quite boggy in spots. This means one thing: It is a perfect breeding ground for bugs and mosquitoes. Don't forget your repellent!

77 Allsop Lake

What a pretty hike. The East Fork Bear River Trail caresses a wide, flowing river while steering leisurely by ruins of old log cabins, lush green meadows, and sky-reaching pines. Possible camping areas exist all along the river and all the way to the Allsop-Priord junction. After the junction, the Left Hand Fork Trail ascends high along the side of a steep ravine. Here you'll find a stunning overlook of consecutive waterfalls gushing down a sheer rock canyon.

See map on page 186.
Start: East Fork Bear River trailhead
Distance: 17.0 miles out and back
Destination elevation: 10,580 feet
Approximate hiking time: 11 hours
Difficulty: Moderate—one steep section
Usage: Moderate
Nearest town: Evanston, Wyoming
Drainage: Bear River

Maps: USGS Red Knob; USDA Forest Service High Uintas Wilderness; Trails Illustrated High Uintas Wilderness
Trail contacts: Wasatch National Forest, Forest Supervisor, 8226 Federal Building, 125 South State St., Salt Lake City, UT 84111; Bear River Ranger Station, 32 miles south of Evanston, Wyoming, on the Mirror Lake Highway, (435) 642-6662

Finding the trailhead: From Evanston, take the Mirror Lake Highway (Highway 150) south about 30 miles to the East Fork of the Bear River turnoff. This road is often referred to as the North Slope Road. Follow this road east 1.5 miles to a junction. Take Road 059 south about 4 miles to East Fork Bear River trailhead.

The Hike

Start your journey on the East Fork Bear River Trail, 0.5 mile south of the B.S.A. turnoff. Follow the East Fork Trail 4.0 miles southeast to the Right Hand–Left Hand Fork Trail junction. Turn left (east) up Left Hand Fork. Allsop Lake is 4.5 miles up Left Hand Fork. The Allsop Lake Trail slowly gains altitude as exotic mountain peaks appear through the tops of gangling conifers. Once you've worked your way out of these tall strands of trees, a tantalizing view of The Cathedral and Allsop Basin is sighted just beyond a long stretch of meadows.

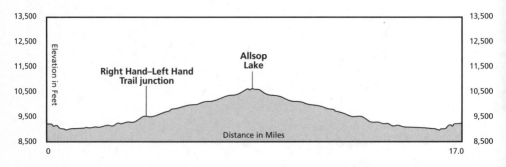

Allsop Lake is a good place to set up a tent, do some fishing, and take in the sights.
PHOTO BY CORDELL ANDERSEN

Allsop is a beautiful bluish-green lake nestled within a spectacular talus and timbered, sloped basin. Excellent campsites with superb spring water sources are plentiful at the lake, while horse pasture can be found nearby or downstream. Fishing for cutthroat trout is often consistent around these parts, and open shorelines make fly-casting quite easy. However, sudden stiff winds may ravage a long-distance cast. It's probably a wise decision to pack some spinners or bait for those unexpected gusts. Other angling prospects can be found in the Left Hand or East Fork of the Bear River. Tasty trout populate these deluxe fishing holes as well.

78 Buck Pasture

Some people would rather fish or camp by a stream than at a lake. There are many benefits to stream camping, especially if you can seclude your camp away from the trail. Any hikers you bump into will just be passing through, the fishing pressure is light, and there is plenty of firewood available. It sounds kind of like a well-kept secret to me, doesn't it? If you would like to try the stream-camping experience, there's no better place than Buck Pasture.

See map on page 186.
Start: West Fork Blacks Fork trailhead
Distance: 7.0 miles out and back
Destination elevation: 9,800 feet
Approximate hiking time: 4.5 hours
Difficulty: Easy
Usage: Moderate
Nearest town: Evanston, Wyoming
Drainage: West Fork Blacks Fork

Maps: USGS Red Knob; USDA Forest Service High Uintas Wilderness; Trails Illustrated High Uintas Wilderness
Trail contacts: Wasatch National Forest, Forest Supervisor, 8226 Federal Building, 125 South State St., Salt Lake City, UT 84111; Bear River Ranger Station, 32 miles south of Evanston, Wyoming, on the Mirror Lake Highway, (435) 642-6662

Finding the trailhead: From Evanston, take the Mirror Lake Highway (Highway 150) south about 30 miles to the East Fork of the Bear River turnoff. This road is often referred to as the North Slope Road. Follow this road east 15 miles to a four-way junction. At this point, follow a good dirt road (Road 063) south until you come to a stream crossing. From here you'll need a high-clearance four-wheel-drive vehicle to safely cross the river—and to negotiate the rocks and mud holes that lie ahead.

The trailhead has room for fifteen vehicles but no campsites, toilets, or drinking water.

The Hike

Buck Pasture is a 2-mile-long beautiful meadow spanning a good portion of the hike to Dead Horse Lake. The West Fork of the Blacks Fork River runs right through the middle of it. This river houses many small trout, and maybe even a few old smart ones. They are bound to be a little wary, since they live in a small stream in an open meadow. Cutthroat and brookies thrive in this ice-cold water, so don't feel guilty about keeping enough for lunch.

Several marginal campsites are noticeable from the trail, but it would be better to leave the trail and explore a bit. Move back into the trees to find a camp away from the wet meadow; otherwise you may have more mosquitoes than you bargained for. Sheep are a smelly problem at times and may be another reason to camp away from the meadows. Horses will have no trouble finding pasture in this lush meadow, but they can easily wander—better hobble them.

Many anglers overlook the great fishing that can be had in small streams like the Little West Fork Blacks Fork River.

Photo by Matt McKell/Utah Division of Wildlife Resources

Stream water is plentiful of course. It looks crystal clear, but you would be wise to purify it. There is lots of livestock upstream, and the dreaded giardia bug is probably lurking about. Springs may be in the area, depending on where you stake your claim. Maybe you'll be lucky enough to find a spring, but don't count on it.

To the west of Buck Pasture lie several small no-name lakes that receive very few visitors. Mostly they are stocked with brook trout. They may provide fast fishing, or they might be duds. Get your compass, check your map, and find G–78. This is probably your easiest access into the area. Follow the same ridgeline north or south to some of the lakes.

Upon returning to camp, we think you'll particularly enjoy having the river sing you to sleep at night. That's just one of the perks of camping by a river. The others you will discover for yourself.

79 Dead Horse Lake

Follow one of the prettiest trails to one of the prettiest lakes in the High Uintas. The West Fork Blacks Fork Trail parallels a river by the same name almost all the way to Dead Horse Lake. It's pure torture to take an avid stream angler on this hike. He or she will constantly be tempted to cast into the many pools that beckon for anglers to try their luck. If you have the time, do it. It may be the best fishing you'll find on this hike.

See map on page 186.

Start: West Fork Blacks Fork trailhead

Distance: 16.0 miles out and back

Destination elevation: 10,878 feet

Approximate hiking time: 11 hours

Difficulty: Moderate

Usage: Moderate

Nearest town: Evanston, Wyoming

Drainage: West Fork Blacks Fork

Maps: USGS Red Knob and USGS Explorer Peak; USDA Forest Service High Uintas Wilderness; Trails Illustrated High Uintas Wilderness

Trail contacts: Wasatch National Forest, Forest Supervisor, 8226 Federal Building, 125 South State St., Salt Lake City, UT 84111; Bear River Ranger Station, 32 miles south of Evanston, Wyoming, on the Mirror Lake Highway, (435) 642-6662

Finding the trailhead: From Evanston, take the Mirror Lake Highway (Highway 150) south about 30 miles to the East Fork of the Bear River turnoff. This road is often referred to as the North Slope Road. Follow this road east 15 miles to a four-way junction. At this point, follow a good dirt road (Road 063) south until you come to a stream crossing. From here you'll need a high-clearance four-wheel-drive vehicle to safely cross the river—and to negotiate the rocks and mud holes that lie ahead.

The trailhead has room for fifteen vehicles but no campsites, toilets, or drinking water.

The Hike

Dead Horse Lake sits at the base of the mountain, right at the edge of timberline. Its turquoise waters present a picture-book setting, if sheep don't happen to be grazing in the area at the time. From the trailhead, the trail follows West Fork south for 7.8 miles to a trail junction with the trail to Red Knob. Stay right and go 0.2 mile to the lake. Immediately south of the lake is Dead Horse Pass. The trail is not easily visible from across the lake, but it is there. Some years it may be late July before you will be able to cross this pass. We haven't figured out if Dead Horse Pass is named for Dead Horse Lake or vice versa. The pass looks like it could be lethal for horses; on the other hand, the lake looks much like a horse head when viewed from the pass. But then, who cares about such trivia when you are surrounded by such magnificent alpine terrain?

Campsites are plentiful on the north side of Dead Horse Lake. Firewood and spring water are not so plentiful. Plan on purifying all your drinking water and searching deep into the timber for fuel wood.

Fishing is not very good at Dead Horse Lake (too many anglers). If you're looking for some faster finny action, trek over to Ejod Lake, just 0.25 mile northwest of Dead Horse Lake. Expect to catch enough pan-size cutthroat for dinner. If Ejod doesn't pan out, don't forget the great-looking stream you passed on your hike to Dead Horse Lake.

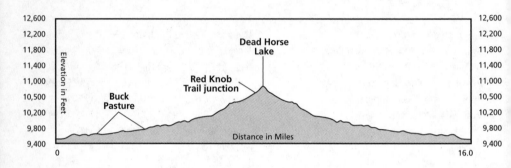

80 East Fork Blacks Fork

Some high mountain passes are inaccessible much of the summer. Red Knob is no exception. After a long, hard winter, the northeast side of Red Knob Pass is plagued with snowdrifts until the middle of August. You may try your luck during late July, but it could be a rugged trip. Snowdrifts are difficult to cross when hoisting a heavy pack; so is the East Fork River when the glaciers melt and fill its banks to capacity. Even when these mountains experience a light winter, Red Knob should not be attempted from the East Fork Trail until mid-July.

Start: East Fork Blacks Fork trailhead
Distance: 20.0 miles out and back
Destination elevation: 12,200 feet
Approximate hiking time: 14 hours
Difficulty: Moderate—several river crossings
Usage: Light
Nearest town: Evanston, Wyoming
Drainage: East Fork Blacks Fork

Maps: USGS Mt. Lovenia; USDA Forest Service High Uintas Wilderness; Trails Illustrated High Uintas Wilderness
Trail contacts: Wasatch National Forest, Forest Supervisor, 8226 Federal Building, 125 South State St., Salt Lake City, UT 84111; Bear River Ranger Station, 32 miles south of Evanston, Wyoming, on the Mirror Lake Highway, (435) 642-6662

Finding the trailhead: From Evanston, take the Mirror Lake Highway (Highway 150) south about 30 miles to the East Fork of the Bear River turnoff. This road is often referred to as the North Slope Road. Follow this road east about 20 miles to a junction just past Lyman Lakes. Then take the south road (Road 065) just a little over 5 miles to East Fork Blacks Fork trailhead.

This trailhead has ten parking places at the upper trailhead and twenty at the lower trailhead. Good campsites and toilets are located at the upper trailhead.

The Hike

East Fork has no lakes. The main purpose of this drainage is as a route for hikers making the 50-mile trek from the Highline trailhead or the 26-mile loop trail that ventures around Mount Lovenia, the upper Lake Fork Drainage, and then back through Little East Fork. The trail begins at the footbridge northeast of the East Fork Campground. From the bridge, follow a well-used trail 1.0 mile south to another footbridge that crosses over the Little East Fork River. Just beyond the bridge, the trail forks to the right and to the left. Both trails take off to the south, then connect again in the upper portion of the Lake Fork Drainage. From the fork, it is 10 miles to Red Knob Pass.

Scenery in the East Fork Blacks Fork is spectacular. Mount Lovenia and other high peaks surround the narrow, ridged canyons, which sometimes stay snowcapped year-round. Beautiful lodgepole pines cover the valley floor, while prolonged rivers

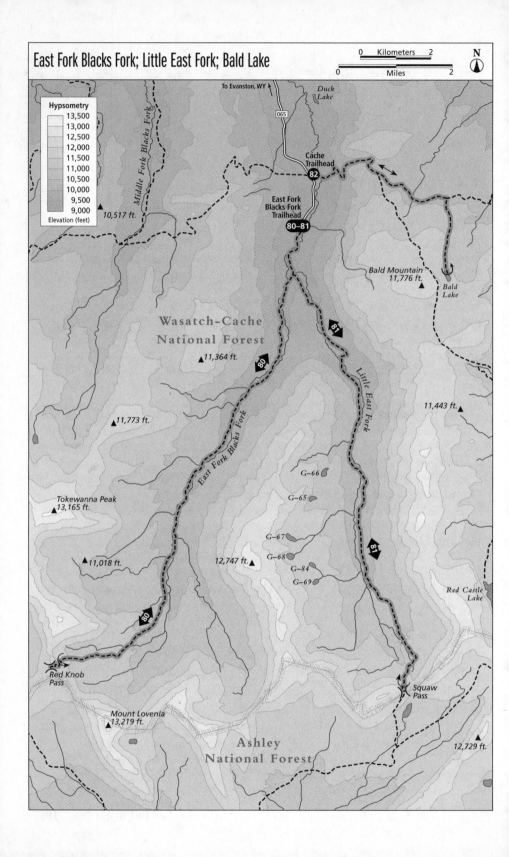

East Fork Blacks Fork; Little East Fork; Bald Lake

Kilometers 0 — 2
Miles 0 — 2

N

To Evanston, WY

Duck Lake

065

Cache Trailhead
82

East Fork Blacks Fork Trailhead
80–81

Hypsometry

	Elevation (feet)
	13,500
	13,000
	12,500
	12,000
	11,500
	11,000
	10,500
	10,000
	9,500
	9,000

Middle Fork Blacks Fork

▲ 10,517 ft.

Bald Mountain 11,776 ft. ▲

Bald Lake

Wasatch-Cache National Forest

▲ 11,364 ft.

80

81

Little East Fork

11,443 ft. ▲

▲ 11,773 ft.

East Fork Blacks Fork

G–66

G–65

Tokewanna Peak
▲ 13,165 ft.

G–67

G–68

81

▲ 11,018 ft.

12,747 ft. ▲

G–84

G–69

Red Castle Lake

80

Red Knob Pass

Squaw Pass

Mount Lovenia
▲ 13,219 ft.

Ashley National Forest

▲ 12,729 ft.

ease through the misty meadows. Scenic campsites can be found along the trail, and firewood is plentiful for the overnight camper.

Occasionally, moose can be spotted grazing in the open meadows. It is a good idea to keep your distance from these animals. Moose are sometimes intrepid and may attack.

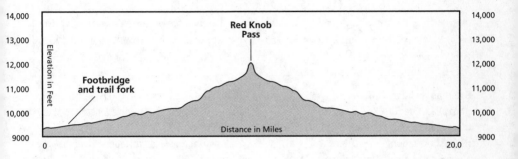

81　Little East Fork

Open, windswept tundra dotted with alpine lakes characterize this remote hike. The Little East Fork Blacks Forks Drainage has several tiny, high lakes that almost nobody visits. Camping opportunities are few, firewood is scarce, spring water is hard to find, horse pasture is scant, and there are no trails to the lakes. All of these factors add up to no visitors. But if you're looking for solitude and a chance to discover some unknown fishing waters, here it is. You've got to have a sense of adventure, but you'll know you've been to some of the least-traveled country these mountains have to offer.

See map on page 196.
Start: East Fork Blacks Fork trailhead
Distance: 12.0 to 20.0 miles out and back
Highest elevation: 11,527 feet
Approximate hiking time: 8 to 14 hours
Difficulty: Moderate
Usage: Light
Nearest town: Evanston, Wyoming
Drainage: East Fork Blacks Fork

Maps: USGS Mt. Lovenia; USDA Forest Service High Uintas Wilderness; Trails Illustrated High Uintas Wilderness
Trail contacts: Wasatch National Forest, Forest Supervisor, 8226 Federal Building, 125 South State St., Salt Lake City, UT 84111; Bear River Ranger Station, 32 miles south of Evanston, Wyoming, on the Mirror Lake Highway, (435) 642-6662

Finding the trailhead: From Evanston, take the Mirror Lake Highway (Highway 150) south about 30 miles to the East Fork of the Bear River turnoff. This road is often referred to as the North Slope Road. Follow this road east about 20 miles to a junction just past Lyman Lakes. Then take the south road (Road 065) just a little over 5 miles to East Fork Blacks Fork trailhead.

This trailhead has ten parking places at the upper trailhead and twenty at the lower trailhead. Good campsites and toilets are located at the upper trailhead.

The Hike

The trail forks about 0.7 mile from the East Fork Blacks Fork trailhead, where the East Fork and the Little East Fork come together. Follow the trail to the left (southeast). From this point it's 4.0 miles to where you might turn to G–66 and G–65. Go another 1.5 miles to the creek coming from G–67 and G–68. Go another 1.5 miles to the creek from G–84 and G–69. It is about 2.3 miles to Squaw Pass from there.

G–66 is the most logical choice to establish a base camp. There are several campsites, and spring water can be found. It is also the first lake you will encounter. You will need a topographical map and a compass to find G–66, or any of these lakes.

The lakes still carry numbers as names to most hikers, but they have also taken on names over the years according to forest service officials. They are G-65 (Jarrod Lake); G-66 (Lake Nikki); G-67 (Lake Kelli); G-68 (Lake Kimberly) and G-69 (Chad Lake).

Little East Fork Blacks Fork from Squaw Pass

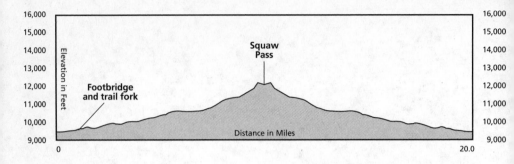

Fishing opportunities may be great, or they may be lousy. Stocking schedules are irregular, and winterkill could take its toll, but the fishing may still be excellent at times. You'll just have to take your chances. There are several of these small lakes within a few miles of one another. Try several. A good horse can make its way around up here, but there isn't much pasture available. You may want to camp by the lower meadows if you have a horse.

The Little East Fork Trail serves as the main sheep thoroughfare for the upper portions of the Lake Fork Drainage. If you take either route after mid-July, be prepared to encounter flocks of sheep. Take precautions where drinking water is concerned.

82 Bald Lake

Bald Lake is probably the only lake in the Smiths Fork Drainage containing campsites that still only receive light fishing and camping use. This natural cirque lake harbors a large population of brook trout. Stocking has been discontinued, since natural reproduction has consistently met its quota. You should have no problem filling your skillet here.

Bald Lake sits near a glacial talus slope with a snowy ice pack that is the main source of water for this alpine lake. Small, stunted pines dot the north and east shorelines where a few sheltered campsites are found. Just south of the lake, a spectacular panorama of the upper Smiths Fork Drainage awaits your viewing.

See map on page 196.
Start: Cache trailhead
Distance: 10.0 miles out and back
Destination elevation: 11,030 feet
Approximate hiking time: 7 hours
Difficulty: Moderate—some steep, cross-country travel
Usage: Light
Nearest town: Mountain View, Wyoming
Drainage: Smiths Fork

Maps: USGS Bridger Lake and USGS Mt. Powell; USDA Forest Service High Uintas Wilderness; Trails Illustrated High Uintas Wilderness
Trail contacts: Wasatch National Forest, Forest Supervisor, 8226 Federal Building, 125 South State St., Salt Lake City, UT 84111; Mountain View Ranger District, 321 Highway 414, PO Box 129, Mountain View, WY 82939, (307) 782-6555

Finding the trailhead: From Evanston, take the Mirror Lake Highway (Highway 150) south about 30 miles to the East Fork of the Bear River turnoff. This road is often referred to as the North Slope Road. Follow this road east about 20 miles to a junction just past Lyman Lakes. Then take the south road (Road 065) for 4 miles. This is a small, undeveloped trailhead. Some hikers use the East Fork Blacks Fork trailhead another mile down the road.

The Hike

This hike begins from either East Fork Blacks Fork or Mansfield Meadows Road. The latter is easier. From Mansfield Meadows Road, follow the West Fork Smiths

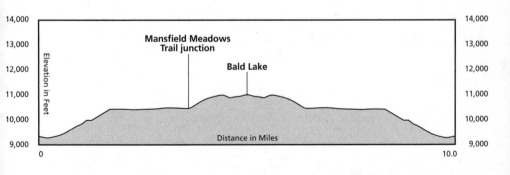

Fork Trail 3.5 miles south to the Mansfield Meadows Trail junction. At this point, follow the stream southwest another 1.5 miles to Bald Lake.

No other lakes exist in the vicinity; Bald Lake is alone. Chances are you will be too if you choose this hike. Here's a great place to spend the weekend and beat the crowds. Relax, breathe deep, and enjoy it.

83 Red Castle Lakes

Red Castle Lake is one of the largest and deepest lakes in the High Uintas. Red Castle is set in a beautiful steep-walled basin. The reddish-colored mountain is shaped like a medieval castle.

Start: China Meadows trailhead
Distance: 22.0 miles out and back
Destination elevation: 11,295 feet
Approximate hiking time: 14 hours
Difficulty: Moderate—one steep section
Usage: Moderate
Nearest town: Mountain View, Wyoming
Drainage: Smiths Fork

Maps: USGS Bridger Lake and USGS Mt. Powell; USDA Forest Service High Uintas Wilderness; Trails Illustrated High Uintas Wilderness
Trail contacts: Wasatch National Forest, Forest Supervisor, 8226 Federal Building, 125 South State St., Salt Lake City, UT 84111; Mountain View Ranger District, 321 Highway 414, PO Box 129, Mountain View, WY 82939, (307) 782-6555

Finding the trailhead: From Mountain View, take Highway 410 south about 6 miles to a junction. Then take Road 017, a well-maintained gravel road, south about 12 miles to a fork. Head west on Road 072, which winds about 4 miles to China Meadows.

The China Meadows trailhead has fifty parking places and offers campsites, toilets, corrals, and a stock ramp.

The Hike

From China Meadows trailhead, the trail follows the East Fork Smiths Fork River south 3.5 miles to the Henrys Fork Trail junction. Continue southwest 0.7 mile to another junction. Stay left, following the river. In about 1.5 miles the trail crosses a tributary of the creek and encounters another junction 0.5 mile farther on. Stay left and go 0.8 mile to another trail junction. Go right for 0.6 mile; at the next trail junction stay left and go 0.2 mile to Lower Red Castle Lake. Red Castle Lake is another 3.2 miles from the lowest end of Lower Red Castle Lake.

Campsites are nonexistent near the lake but can be found, along with running water, at the timbered area to the north. Angling and camping usage is excessively heavy on weekends, and fishing is considered only fair for pan-size cutthroat. Because of the size, depth, and popularity of this lake, an inflatable raft may increase the number and size of fish in your creel. If inflatables are used, use extreme caution. Red Castle is subject to sudden high winds and rapid weather changes. Life jackets are essential!

Lower Red Castle is a popular scenic lake resting in a large alpine meadow. Camping and fishing pressure are extremely heavy here too, but good campsites are available. If there has been a heavy snowpack, you should be able to rustle up some spring water, but firewood is scarce due to overuse.

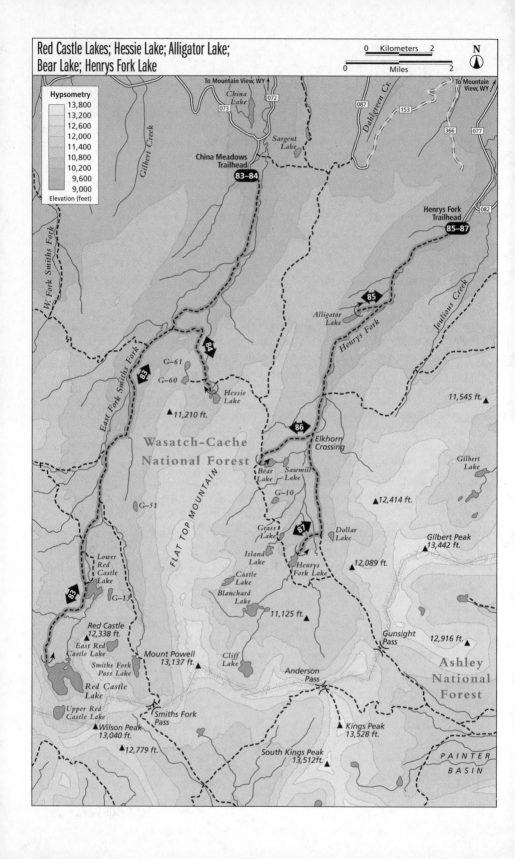

Red Castle Lakes; Hessie Lake; Alligator Lake; Bear Lake; Henrys Fork Lake

0   Kilometers   2
0   Miles   2

N

Hypsometry

13,800
13,200
12,600
12,000
11,400
10,800
10,200
9,600
9,000

Elevation (feet)

To Mountain View, WY

China Lake
072
073
087
153
366
077

Sargent Lake

China Meadows Trailhead
83–84

To Mountain View, WY

Henrys Fork Trailhead
85–87
082

Gilbert Creek

W. Fork Smiths Fork

Dahlgreen Cr.

Joplious Creek

85
Alligator Lake

Henrys Fork

84

G–61

G–60

83

East Fork Smiths Fork

Hessie Lake

▲ 11,210 ft.

11,545 ft. ▲

86
Elkhorn Crossing

Wasatch-Cache National Forest

Gilbert Lake

G–51

FLAT TOP MOUNTAIN

Bear Lake

Sawmill Lake

G–10

▲12,414 ft.

Grass Lake

87

Dollar Lake

Gilbert Peak
13,442 ft. ▲

Lower Red Castle Lake

Island Lake

Henrys Fork Lake

▲12,089 ft.

Castle Lake

83

G–13

Blanchard Lake

▲ 11,125 ft.

Gunsight Pass

12,916 ft. ▲

Red Castle
12,338 ft. ▲

East Red Castle Lake

Smiths Fork Pass Lake

Mount Powell
13,137 ft. ▲

Cliff Lake

Anderson Pass

Ashley National Forest

Red Castle Lake

Upper Red Castle Lake

Smiths Fork Pass

▲Wilson Peak
13,040 ft.

Kings Peak
13,528 ft. ▲

▲12,779 ft.

South Kings Peak
13,512 ft. ▲

P A I N T E R

B A S I N

East Red Castle Lake sits at the base of Red Castle Peak.
Photo by Matt McKell/Utah Division of Wildlife Resources

Upper Red Castle is in a rugged cirque basin, just 0.125 mile south of Red Castle. This lake is known as a poor fishery, but occasionally a large cutthroat trout is netted. No camping areas exist in this windy basin, but spring water is abundant.

East Red Castle is in a steep-walled basin at the east base of Red Castle Peak. Ice-cold spring water can be acquired from several different sources, but campsites, firewood, and horse pasture are not readily available. However, there are several good camping areas in the timbered areas to the northeast, along with a generous supply of horse pasture. You can easily reach East Red Castle from the inlet of Lower Red Castle Lake by picking your way up a steep hill to the east, then around the mountain.

This lake receives moderate fishing pressure for large but wary cutthroat trout. Try a #16 red or black ant at sundown. If the weather is foul, which happens a lot up here, tie on a small silver spinner. It's okay to fish in the rain if you can stay dry, but if the lightning starts, head for shelter.

Smiths Fork Pass Lake is said to have better angling. This lake is noted for its open terrain and irregular shorelines that make fly casting a pleasure. Due to the nature of this country, prospects for campsites and firewood are poor. Good camping areas and shelter are located in the wooded areas to the north, and spring water is present

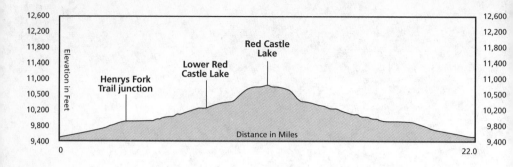

around the lake. This lake is next to the trail in a large cirque basin, 11.0 miles from either China Meadows or the East Fork Blacks Fork Campground.

Compared with most trails in the High Uintas, the East Fork Smiths Fork Trail is like a freeway. It is well groomed, and superb bridges are built over every major river crossing. But don't let these statements fool you. After a hard rain, horses and cows riddle the trail with tracks of slippery, slimy mud holes.

From China Meadows, the trail gradually picks up altitude for the first 7.0 miles. Shortly after you pass Broadbent Meadow, you'll encounter several steep switchbacks. The trail levels off while passing Lower Red Castle Lake but sharply gains elevation the last mile.

Red Castle is one of the most distinct landmarks in the Uinta Mountain range and certainly one of the most photogenic.

Photo by Matt McKell/Utah Division of Wildlife Resources

84 Hessie Lake

Expect heavy weekend pressure at this popular lake. Several well-used camping areas are found along the east and south sides of the lake. However, firewood is limited. Heavily timbered shorelines make fly casting difficult, and for some reason cutthroat trout are quite skeptical. But by late evening, the fish become a little hungry and not so particular.

See map on a page 204.
Start: China Meadows trailhead
Distance: 11.5 miles out and back
Destination elevation: 10,620 feet
Approximate hiking time: 7.5 hours
Difficulty: Moderate
Usage: Heavy
Nearest town: Mountain View, Wyoming
Drainage: Smiths Fork

Maps: USGS Bridger Lake and USGS Mt. Powell; USDA Forest Service High Uintas Wilderness; Trails Illustrated High Uintas Wilderness
Trail contacts: Wasatch National Forest, Forest Supervisor, 8226 Federal Building, 125 South State St., Salt Lake City, UT 84111; Mountain View Ranger District, 321 Highway 414, PO Box 129, Mountain View, WY 82939, (307) 782-6555

Finding the trailhead: From Mountain View, take Highway 410 south about 6 miles to a junction. Then take Road 017, a well-maintained gravel road, south about 12 miles to a fork. Head west on Road 072, which winds about 4 miles to China Meadows.

The China Meadows trailhead has fifty parking places and offers campsites, toilets, corrals, and a stock ramp.

The Hike

This heavily timbered lake lies at the base of a rocky point in the East Fork of Smiths Fork Drainage. Access starts at the south side of China Meadows Campground. Take the East Fork trail 3.5 miles south to the Henrys Fork Trail junction. Then head east toward Henrys Fork 2.0 miles to the Hessie Lake turnoff. Travel another 0.25 mile west and you'll be at Hessie Lake.

A couple of other lakes in the proximity of Hessie are G–60 and G–61. These lakes are easily located by following their outlet stream that crosses the trail just east

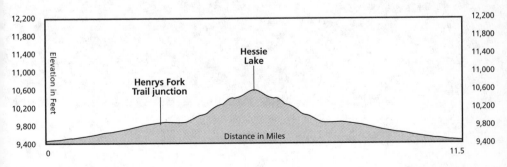

of the Hessie Lake turnoff. G–60 is the first lake you'll run into. This small meadow lake is situated at the base of a timbered ridge. Excellent campsites can be found near the lake, and plenty of horse pasture and spring water are available. Light to moderate fishing pressure is sustained by stocked brook trout.

Find G–61 by following the inlet of G–60 up a steep, timbered ridge 0.125 mile to the south. This shallow lake sits in partially timbered terrain at the base of Flat Top Mountain. Camping areas are present, and lots of horse pasture can be found in the large park to the west and north. Spring water is limited, especially in the late summer months. G–61 is subject to winterkill, but it has been experimentally stocked with brook trout anyway. You might want to give it a try. This lake receives little angling use, which means it could produce a big thrill.

Hessie Lake is accessed via the China Meadows trailhead.
PHOTO BY MATT MCKELL/UTAH DIVISION OF WILDLIFE RESOURCES

85 Alligator Lake

No, this lake is not a swamp where alligators or snakes feed. In fact, it's rather uncommon to encounter any reptile above 9,000 feet in the High Uintas. However, Alligator Lake can be exploited by human creatures. Dominant pressure persists on weekends, but during the weekdays you should experience solitude.

See map on page 204.
Start: Henrys Fork trailhead
Distance: 5.4 miles out and back
Destination elevation: 10,033 feet
Approximate hiking time: 4 hours
Difficulty: Easy
Usage: Heavy
Nearest town: Mountain View, Wyoming
Drainage: Henrys Fork

Maps: USGS Gilbert Peak NE; USDA Forest Service High Uintas Wilderness; Trails Illustrated High Uintas Wilderness
Trail contacts: Wasatch National Forest, Forest Supervisor, 8226 Federal Building, 125 South State St., Salt Lake City, UT 84111; Mountain View Ranger District, 321 Highway 414, PO Box 129, Mountain View, WY 82939, (307) 782-6555

Finding the trailhead: From Mountain View, take Highway 410 south about 6 miles to a junction. Then take SR 017, a well-maintained gravel road, south about 12 miles to a fork. The east road (Road 077) heads south about 5 miles to Henrys Fork.

Henrys Fork trailhead has fifty parking places and is equipped with toilets, campsites, corrals, and a stock ramp.

The Hike

To reach Alligator Lake, follow the Henrys Fork Trail 2.0 miles to a spur trail that parallels the outlet. Good to excellent camping areas exist all around the lake, and angling is considered decent for pan-size brookies. The best fishing should take place along the north side. The south side is relatively shallow for some distance out.

There are four or five campsites with tables, toilets, and fireplaces at the trailhead. Plenty of parking is available for hikers and equestrians, and a good road will ease you into the location. Alligator Lake would make a nice day excursion for kids while the old folks just lie back and enjoy a nap.

86 Bear Lake

Surrounded by mature pines, Bear Lake offers a quiet picture-book setting for the weary traveler. Its deep, placid waters seem to beckon, "Rest here, rest here." And a lot of hikers do. Bear Lake receives its share of backpackers that come to visit the popular Henrys Fork Drainage. You might have some company here, but there are plenty of nice campsites, and the thick pines will serve as privacy barriers.

See map on page 204.
Start: Henrys Fork trailhead
Distance: 13.0 miles out and back
Destination elevation: 10,767 feet
Approximate hiking time: 8 hours
Difficulty: Moderate
Usage: Moderate
Nearest town: Mountain View, Wyoming
Drainage: Henrys Fork

Maps: USGS Mt. Powell; USDA Forest Service High Uintas Wilderness; Trails Illustrated High Uintas Wilderness
Trail contacts: Wasatch National Forest, Forest Supervisor, 8226 Federal Building, 125 South State St., Salt Lake City, UT 84111; Mountain View Ranger District, 321 Highway 414, PO Box 129, Mountain View, WY 82939, (307) 782-6555

Finding the trailhead: From Mountain View, take Highway 410 south about 6 miles to a junction. Then take Road 017, a well-maintained gravel road, south about 12 miles to a fork. The east road (Road 077) heads south about 5 miles to Henrys Fork.

Henrys Fork trailhead has fifty parking places and is equipped with toilets, campsites, corrals, and a stock ramp.

The Hike

To reach Bear Lake, simply follow the Henrys Fork Trail about 5.0 miles to Elkhorn Crossing. There a sign will direct you west. Just stick with the trail, which passes right next to Bear Lake.

Bring some means of water purification, as there are no springs in the immediate area. If you need spring water, head east 0.25 mile to Sawmill Lake. Horses won't find a lot to eat around these parts, so if you have pack animals, keep going up the trail.

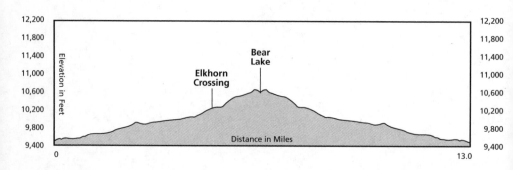

There are numerous existing campsites at Bear Lake. Please don't build any more. As with any heavily used area, use low-impact camping techniques, and lend a hand gathering any leftover litter.

Bear and Sawmill Lakes have good populations of brook trout that provide fast fishing at times. These deep lakes can be fished successfully with either fly or spinner. Just keep your offerings small and work them slowly. You'll catch fish. For a change of pace, try the little creek connecting the two lakes. But practice your stealth. If these wild trout see or hear you, you won't see them.

87 Henrys Fork Lake

Henrys Fork is a beautiful alpine mountain basin. Winding streams flow through misty meadows, and tall pines hiss in the wind while caressing big boulder formations. Campsites are plentiful below timberline, and fishing for brook and cutthroat trout is exciting at most lakes and rivers. Well, there, we said enough. It's a great place to visit. This is a popular destination for Scout groups, so be prepared for company.

See map on page 204.
Start: Henrys Fork trailhead
Distance: 15.0 miles out and back
Destination elevation: 10,830 feet
Approximate hiking time: 10 hours
Difficulty: Moderate
Usage: Heavy
Nearest town: Mountain View, Wyoming
Drainage: Henrys Fork

Maps: USGS Mt. Powell; USDA Forest Service High Uintas Wilderness; Trails Illustrated High Uintas Wilderness
Trail contacts: Wasatch National Forest, Forest Supervisor, 8226 Federal Building, 125 South State St., Salt Lake City, UT 84111; Mountain View Ranger District, 321 Highway 414, PO Box 129, Mountain View, WY 82939, (307) 782-6555

Finding the trailhead: From Mountain View, take Highway 410 south about 6 miles to a junction. Then take Road 017, a well-maintained gravel road, south about 12 miles to a fork. The east road (Road 077) heads south about 5 miles to Henrys Fork.
Henrys Fork trailhead has fifty parking places and is equipped with toilets, campsites, corrals, and a stock ramp.

The Hike

Henrys Fork features an excellent forest service trail that has a gradual climb. However, this trail is not too scenic and seems long until you arrive at Elkhorn Crossing, 5.0 miles from the trailhead. From the crossing, a frail trail heads south across the river and through the basin. Watch for cairns to mark the way. These rock piles are spaced along the trail to Gunsight Pass and beyond. Kings Peak is located on the other side of the pass and is the highest point in Utah (elevation 13,528 feet). After about 2.0 miles, at Dollar Lake turn southwest and go 0.5 mile cross-country to Henrys Fork Lake.

Henrys Fork Lake offers the best accommodations for a base camp. It has several excellent campsites along the east shore and ample running water flowing into and out of the lake. With the exception of Cliff, Castle, and Blanchard, all other lakes in this basin afford good camping areas and shelter.

Fishing can be unpredictable at most lakes and streams in the area. If there is no action at one lake, move to another. There are many to choose from. The best angling might happen at Cliff Lake. For access, follow the inlet of Henrys Fork 1.0 mile south to Blanchard Lake, then follow the inlet of Blanchard another mile south to Cliff. After you pass Blanchard, the terrain is composed of rocky shelves and small waterfalls.

Castle Lake probably receives the least amount of attention in Henrys Fork Basin. Nobody really knows too much about it. We've heard conflicting stories. It may be a good prospect for anglers, or it may just be a stagnant hole.

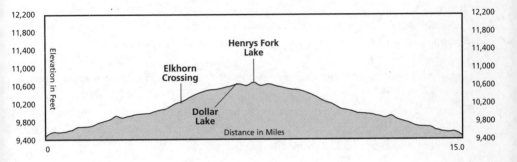

88 Kings Peak via Swift Creek Trailhead

Kings Peak, the highest point in the state of Utah, is the most popular destination of "peak baggers" in the High Uintas and in the entire Beehive State. Novice mountaineers with no special equipment can even reach it. However, it is a long, steep hike to the top of the 13,258-foot summit. Good health and conditioning are a must.

More than 10,000 people attempt to reach the top of Utah each year according to the nonprofit group Friends of Kings Peak (friendsofkingspeak.org).

There are several routes to the top of Kings Peak, all of them long and each providing a different backcountry hiking experience. No matter the route, hikers should plan to head to the top early in the morning and return by early afternoon to avoid the trademark afternoon thunderstorms on the High Uintas. These summer storms frequently include lightning, and the highest point in Utah is the last place you want to be when the electrified bolts are coming from the sky.

Start: Swift Creek trailhead
Distance: 37.4 miles out and back
Destination elevation: 13,528 feet
Approximate hiking time: Variable
Difficulty: Difficult—steep sections
Usage: Light
Nearest town: Duchesne, Utah
Drainage: Yellowstone River

Maps: USGS Garfield Basin, USGS Mount Powell, and USGS Kings Peak; USDA Forest Service High Uintas Wilderness; Trails Illustrated High Uintas Wilderness
Trail contacts: Ashley National Forest, Forest Supervisor, 355 North Vernal Ave., Vernal, UT 84078, (435) 781-1181; Duchesne Ranger District, 85 West Main, Duchesne, UT 84021, (435) 738-2482

Finding the trailhead: From Heber City, take US 40 east 69 miles to Duchesne. Turn north onto SR 87 and travel 14 miles to Mountain Home. Follow Moon Lake Road north 4 miles to where Yellowstone River Road intersects on the east side. Follow Yellowstone River Road another 4 miles past the rough and tumble Hell's Canyon Road. Stay on Yellowstone River Road another 6 miles to the Swift Creek trailhead.

The Swift Creek trailhead can handle parking for twenty-five vehicles and is equipped with campsites, toilets, water, and a stock ramp. Many of the high lakes are 10 to 15 miles away, up steep and rocky terrain. Swift Creek also serves as an optional trailhead for the Yellowstone River Drainage.

The Hike

The trail starts at the Swift Creek trailhead, which serves as the access point to the Swift Creek and Yellowstone Drainages. From the Swift Creek trailhead, it is 0.4 mile until the trail splits at the junction of Trails 057 and 056. Trail 056 climbs up the ridge and into the Swift Creek Drainage and Trail 057 continues up the Yellowstone Drainage. Turn left onto Trail 057; the trail parallels the Yellowstone River for 15.2

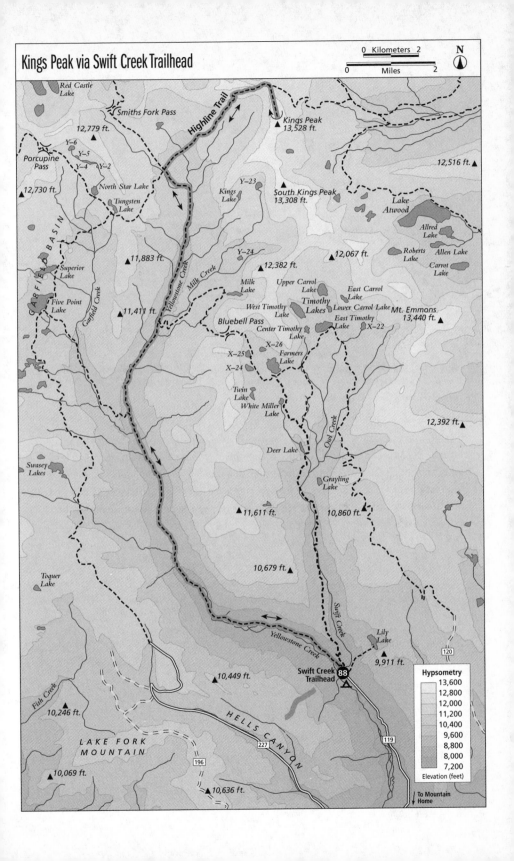

Kings Peak via Swift Creek Trailhead

Red Castle Lake

Smiths Fork Pass

Highline Trail

Kings Peak
13,528 ft.

12,779 ft.

Y–6
Y–5
Y–4   Y–2

Porcupine Pass

12,730 ft.

North Star Lake

Tungsten Lake

12,516 ft.

Kings Lake

Y–23

South Kings Peak
13,308 ft.

Lake Atwood

Allred Lake

GARFIELD BASIN

Superior Lake

11,883 ft.

Y–24

12,382 ft.

12,067 ft.

Roberts Lake

Allen Lake

Carrot Lake

Five Point Lake

11,411 ft.

Garfield Creek

Yellowstone Creek

Milk Creek

Milk Lake

Upper Carrol Lake

East Carrol Lake

Timothy Lakes

Lower Carrol Lake

Mt. Emmons
13,440 ft.

West Timothy Lake

Bluebell Pass

Center Timothy Lake

East Timothy Lake

X–22

X–25

X–26

Farmers Lake

X–24

Twin Lake

White Miller Lake

Owl Creek

12,392 ft.

Deer Lake

Swasey Lakes

Grayling Lake

11,611 ft.

10,860 ft.

10,679 ft.

Toquer Lake

Swift Creek

Lily Lake

9,911 ft.

120

10,449 ft.

Yellowstone Creek

Swift Creek
Trailhead   88

Hypsometry

Fish Creek

10,246 ft.

HELLS CANYON

LAKE FORK MOUNTAIN

227

119

13,600
12,800
12,000
11,200
10,400
9,600
8,800
8,000
7,200

Elevation (feet)

196

10,069 ft.

10,636 ft.

To Mountain Home

Kings Peak from Trail Rider Pass

miles until reaching the junction of Trails 025, 054, and 057. Turn right onto Trail 025 through the alpine and scrub forest to the cirque basin below Kings Peak. Here the trail climbs up Anderson Pass below Kings Peak.

Most people take four days and three nights for this trip. This route gets you away from the crowds of the Henrys Fork, but isn't quite as scenic, with heavy timber lining a lot of the trail until you get closer to Kings Peak.

89 Kings Peak via the Uinta Trailhead

This route to the highest point in Utah is a bit more leisurely than the Swift Creek Trail. There is time to relax, soak up the adventure, and go fishing. The Uinta trailhead could also serve as a great entry for an extended backpacking trip into the High Uintas. Have friends drop you off and meet you at a different trailhead a couple of weeks later.

Start: Uinta trailhead
Distance: 49.0 miles out and back
Destination elevation: 13,528 feet
Approximate hiking time: Variable
Difficulty: Difficult—steep sections
Usage: Light
Nearest town: Roosevelt
Drainage: Uinta River

Maps: USGS Bollie Lake, USGS Mt. Emmons, and USGS Kings Peak; USDA Forest Service High Uintas Wilderness; Trails Illustrated High Uintas Wilderness
Trail contacts: Ashley National Forest, Forest Supervisor, 355 North Vernal Ave., Vernal, UT 84078, (435) 781-1181; Duchesne Ranger District, 85 West Main, Duchesne, UT 84021, (435) 738-2482

Finding the trailhead: From Heber City, take US 40 east 99 miles to Roosevelt. Then take SR 121 north for 11 miles to Neola. Head north 17 miles on Road 118 to Wandin and Uinta Campgrounds. The trailhead is located 0.8 mile past the Uinta Campground.

The Uinta trailhead has room for twenty vehicles; amenities include toilets and a stock ramp. There is no water at the trailhead. Camping is available at Uinta Campground.

The Hike

Hikers should consider this as a multiple-day excursion with plenty to see and fish to catch along the way. Many make this a five-day, four-night outing, and some spend an entire week. Start at the Uinta trailhead and follow the old road 0.8 mile to the Smokey Springs Day Use Area. Then follow the trail along the Uinta River through the forest for 2.2 miles to the sheep bridge crossing the river. The trail splits at this point. Trail 044 heads up the Uinta River Drainage. Cross the bridge and you are on Trail 043. Kings Peak can be reached on either trail, but 043 is the shorter and more scenic route. Once on 043 you will start hitting a series of switchbacks, climbing more than 1,000 feet over 5.0 miles to Lower Chain Lake.

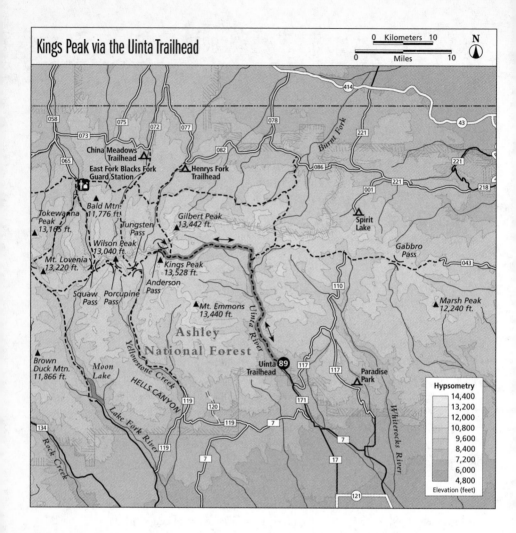

The trail passes the four lakes of Chain Lakes—possible camping areas—and then heads over Roberts Pass to the Lake Atwood Basin. Continue past Lake Atwood—surrounded by Allred Lake, Allen Lake, Carrot Lake, B–29 Lake, and Lake George Beard, all possible camp spots. The main trail then climbs over Trail Rider Pass and drops into the Painter Basin below Kings Peak. Once at the three-way junction of Trails 043, 044, and 025, turn west on 025. In another mile take Trail 068 at the junction to Gunsight Pass and then the Henrys Fork trail to the top.

90 Gilbert Lake

If fly fishing is your thing, then Gilbert Lake might be your idea of heaven. Plenty of open shoreline and lots of eager trout make this a good fly-fishing lake. This lake is a must for fly fishers seeking fast action for brookies and cutthroat trout. Make sure your casting arm is in good shape. It will give out long before the fish do.

Start: West Fork Beaver Creek
Distance: 16.0 miles out and back
Destination elevation: 10,905 feet
Approximate hiking time: 10 hours
Difficulty: Moderate
Usage: Moderate
Nearest town: Mountain View, Wyoming
Drainage: Beaver Creek

Maps: USGS Kings Peak; USDA Forest Service High Uintas Wilderness; Trails Illustrated High Uintas Wilderness
Trail contacts: Wasatch National Forest, Forest Supervisor, 8226 Federal Building, 125 South State St., Salt Lake City, UT 84111; Mountain View Ranger District, 321 Highway 414, PO Box 129, Mountain View, WY 82939, (307) 782-6555

Finding the trailhead: From Mountain View, take Highway 410 south about 6 miles to a junction. Then take Road 017, a well-maintained gravel road, south about 12 miles to a fork. The east road (Road 077) heads south about 5 miles to Henrys Fork. Just before Henrys Fork trailhead, the road splits and Road 058 winds eastward for about 6 miles. When the road splits again, take the right fork onto Road 125. Go about 1 mile, then take another right onto Road 046. You should then be heading south to the trailhead, which is about another 3 miles. The USDA Forest Service map is helpful for finding this one.

The Hike

From the trailhead, the trail heads southwest for 5.5 miles. When the trail turns to the right (west) and begins to climb out of the valley, continue straight (southwest) up the valley, keeping the creek on your left. Gilbert Lake is 2.5 miles up the valley over fairly gentle but brushy terrain.

Equestrians are attracted to this area too. Horse pasture is plentiful around the lush meadows, and flowing water is everywhere. Campsites are well suited to horse travelers who want to set up a large base camp. The best camping is found on the south side of Gilbert Lake or in the trees just north of GR–151. Because of the moist nature of the area, mosquitoes are often a problem. Plan your trip late in the summer, and always bring along sufficient bug dope.

Although Gilbert Lake can offer fine fishing, check out some of the other lakes nearby. They are probably just as good, and maybe even better. South of Gilbert Lake lie GR–151, GR–152, and GR–153. These lakes and their connecting streams are stuffed with fish that seldom see an artificial lure. As with most other High Uinta

Gilbert Lake; Beaver Lake

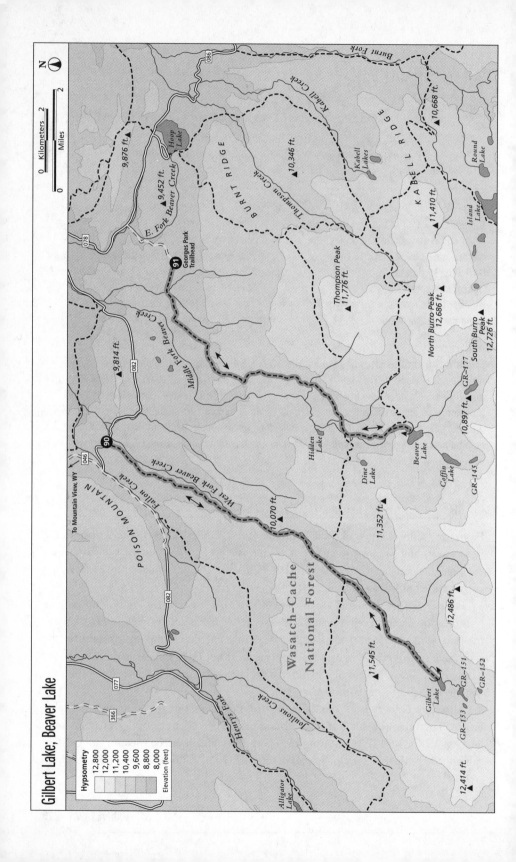

Hypsometry

	12,800
	12,000
	11,200
	10,400
	9,600
	8,800
	8,000

Elevation (feet)

N

0 Kilometers 2
0 Miles 2

To Mountain View, WY

POISON MOUNTAIN

Fallon Creek

West Fork Beaver Creek

Wasatch-Cache National Forest

Jonlions Creek

Henry's Fork

Alligator Lake

12,414 ft.

12,486 ft.

11,545 ft.

11,352 ft.

10,070 ft.

Gilbert Lake

GR-153

GR-151

GR-152

Dine Lake

Hidden Lake

Coffin Lake

GR-145

Beaver Lake

South Burro Peak 12,726 ft.

North Burro Peak 12,686 ft.

GR-177

10,897 ft.

GR

Island Lake

Round Lake

KABELL RIDGE

11,410 ft.

Kabell Lakes

Thompson Peak 11,776 ft.

Thompson Creek

10,346 ft.

BURNT RIDGE

Kabell Creek

Burnt Fork

Hoop Lake

9,876 ft.

9,452 ft.

E. Fork Beaver Creek

Middle Fork Beaver Creek

9,814 ft.

Georges Park Trailhead

91

90

046

082

082

077

366

078

086

lakes, great fishing is never guaranteed. If the lakes are not producing, then check out the streams. They can be hot when the lakes are not.

The trail to Gilbert Lake is sometimes hit-or-miss, so check your map and compass often. There are several wet areas along the route, and a good riding horse or waterproof boots can serve you well to keep your feet dry.

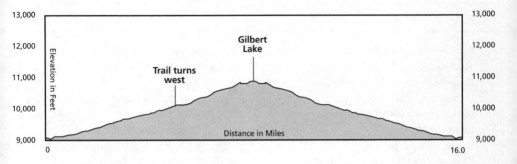

91 Beaver Lake

Beaver Lake is characterized by timbered shorelines, with shallow water prevailing on the east side of the lake. Excellent campsites are in a large park to the west, and several sources of spring water and horse pastures are available in nearby meadows. Brook trout and a few cutthroat inhabit this lake.

See map on page 220.
Start: Georges Park trailhead
Distance: 13.6 miles out and back
Destination elevation: 10,505 feet
Approximate hiking time: 9 hours
Difficulty: Moderate
Usage: Heavy
Nearest town: Mountain View, Wyoming
Drainage: Beaver Creek

Maps: USGS Fox Lake; USDA Forest Service High Uintas Wilderness; Trails Illustrated High Uintas Wilderness
Trail contacts: Wasatch National Forest, Forest Supervisor, 8226 Federal Building, 125 South State St., Salt Lake City, UT 84111; Mountain View Ranger District, 321 Highway 414, PO Box 129, Mountain View, WY 82939, (307) 782-6555

Finding the trailhead: From Mountain View, take WY 414 east then south about 20 miles to Lonetree. Continue south on WY 414 toward Hoop Lake about 9 miles to a junction where Road 058 ventures west to Henrys Fork. Take that road west then south about 3 miles to Georges Park trailhead.

The Hike

Beaver Lake is located in the Middle Fork of Beaver Creek Drainage. From Georges Park trailhead, the trail heads west, then turns to the southwest for 5.5 miles to a fork. Stay to left and go another 1.3 miles to the lake.

Just southwest of Beaver lies Coffin Lake. Coffin gets its name from its oblong shape and small shelves surrounding the water. No trail exists to the lake, but you can find it by following the inlet of Beaver 0.75 mile south then west to the base of some steep talus slopes. Rough and rocky describes the wilderness around this lake. Horse

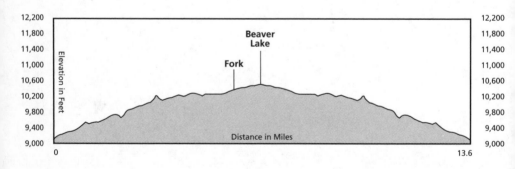

Stunning views of the Middle Fork of the Beaver Creek Drainage are a reward for hiking off-trail to Coffin Lake.
PHOTO BY MATT MCKELL/UTAH DIVISION OF WILDLIFE RESOURCES

travel is quite difficult, and camping areas are a poor prospect. On the bright side, spring water is present, and angling usage is light for unsophisticated cutthroat trout.

Other lakes that you might happen upon in the Beaver Lake Basin are Hidden and Dine. Hidden Lake lies 0.5 mile north of Long Meadow. There is no trail, but access is not difficult. Anglers and backpackers often pass up this lake alike. There is no spring water here, but there are several good camping areas near the inlet.

Discover Dine Lake by following the inlet of Hidden Lake 1.0 mile southwest, or 0.5 mile west of Long Meadow. This lake is surrounded by rocky, timbered terrain and has a talus slope bordering the water on the southwest. Due to the rugged nature of this country, only mediocre campsites are available. There is no horse pasture in the vicinity, but there's plenty of spring water. Although Dine Lake has been stocked throughout the years, it will sometimes experience winterkill during harsh winters.

92 Kabell Lake

Even though Kabell is a popular lake, campsites are scarce and heavy timber surrounds the shoreline. You may ask, "Why then is this lake so popular?" Probably because Kabell is the only lake within a day's hiking distance (round-trip) that can be reached from the ever-popular Hoop Lake.

Start: Hoop Lake trailhead
Distance: 10.4 miles out and back
Destination elevation: 10,348 feet
Approximate hiking time: 7 hours
Difficulty: Easy to moderate
Usage: Moderate
Nearest town: Mountain View, Wyoming
Drainage: Burnt Fork

Maps: USGS Fox Lake; USDA Forest Service High Uintas Wilderness; Trails Illustrated High Uintas Wilderness
Trail contacts: Wasatch National Forest, Forest Supervisor, 8226 Federal Building, 125 South State St., Salt Lake City, UT 84111; Mountain View Ranger District, 321 Highway 414, PO Box 129, Mountain View, WY 82939, (307) 782-6555

Finding the trailhead: From Mountain View, take WY 414 east then south about 20 miles to Lonetree. Continue south on WY 414 about 13 miles to Hoop Lake. The trailhead is on the south side of the lake.

The Hike

To get to Kabell Lake, follow the trail from Hoop Lake 1.0 mile to Kabell Meadows. At the upper portion of the meadows, the trail forks to the south and southwest. From here, take the trail south a couple hundred yards up Kabell Ridge. A side trail then takes off to the southwest, ending at Kabell Lake.

Angler usage is moderate for pan-size cutthroat trout. No decent camping areas are located in the lake vicinity, but a few wannabes with horse pasture exist along the outlet in the meadows to the north. There is spring water on the south side of the lake. You could see a lot of great country, eat lunch at the lake, fish a little, and be back at the campground before dark.

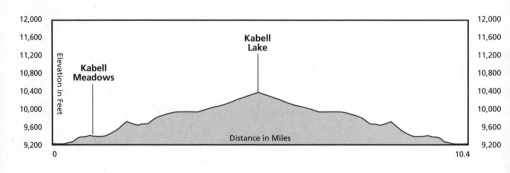

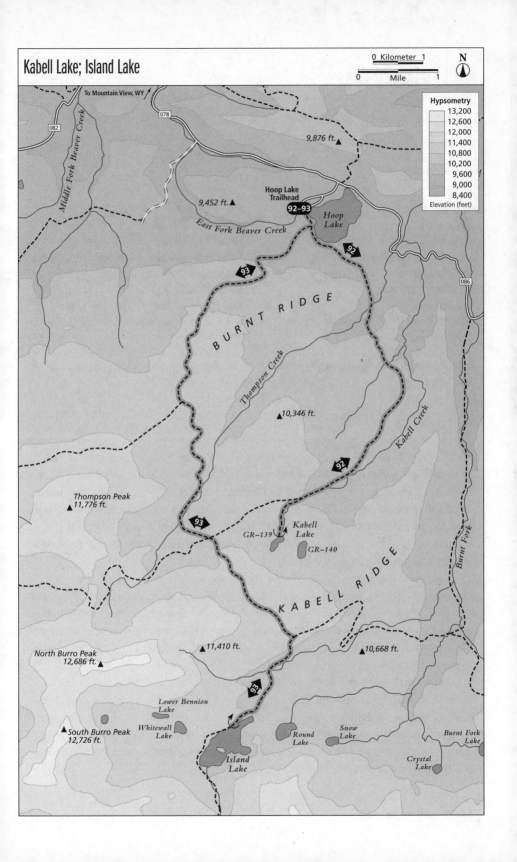

Kabell Lake; Island Lake

0 Kilometer 1

0 Mile 1

N

Hypsometry
13,200
12,600
12,000
11,400
10,800
10,200
9,600
9,000
8,400
Elevation (feet)

To Mountain View, WY

082

078

086

Middle Fork Beaver Creek

9,876 ft. ▲

9,452 ft. ▲

Hoop Lake Trailhead

92–93

92

Hoop Lake

East Fork Beaver Creek

93

B U R N T   R I D G E

Thompson Creek

Kabell Creek

▲10,346 ft.

92

Thompson Peak
▲11,776 ft.

93

GR–139

Kabell Lake

GR–140

K A B E L L   R I D G E

Burnt Fork

North Burro Peak
12,686 ft. ▲

▲11,410 ft.

▲10,668 ft.

93

Lower Bennion Lake

Snow Lake

Burnt Fork Lake

▲ South Burro Peak
12,726 ft.

Whitewall Lake

Round Lake

Crystal Lake

Island Lake

93 Island Lake

Many lakes in the High Uintas claim the name of Island. However, this lake is the king of all the Island Lakes—mainly because it's the biggest. Island Lake is reached from either Hoop or Spirit Lake. The Spirit Lake Trail is about a mile longer, but the elevation gain is 1,000 feet less.

See map on page 225.
Start: Hoop Lake trailhead
Distance: 15.5 miles out and back
Destination elevation: 10,777 feet
Approximate hiking time: 10 hours
Difficulty: Moderate
Usage: Heavy
Nearest town: Mountain View, Wyoming
Drainage: Burnt Fork

Maps: USGS Fox Lake; USDA Forest Service High Uintas Wilderness; Trails Illustrated High Uintas Wilderness
Trail contacts: Wasatch National Forest, Forest Supervisor, 8226 Federal Building, 125 South State St., Salt Lake City, UT 84111; Mountain View Ranger District, 321 Highway 414, PO Box 129, Mountain View, WY 82939, (307) 782-6555

Finding the trailhead: From Lonetree, take Wyoming Highway 414 south about 13 miles to Hoop Lake. The trailhead is on the south side of the lake.

The Hike

From Hoop Lake, the trail climbs southwest up a steep incline then over the more gradual slope of Burnt Ridge 3.5 miles to a trail junction. The trail to the right goes to Beaver Lake. Stay left, descending to Thompson Creek. The trail follows the stream briefly, then crosses it and comes to a trail crossing about 1.8 miles from the last junction. Continue straight across the other trail and climb up and over Kabell Ridge 1.5 miles to another junction with the trail descending into Burnt Creek. Turn right (south) and go 1.0 mile to the lake.

Island is a large alpine lake located in the southwest corner of the Burnt Fork Drainage. It receives fairly heavy usage from Scouts and backpackers alike. Excellent campsites exist around the lake; spring water is located along the south shore. Angling is often good for brook and cutthroat trout using small flies or spinners. Throughout the summer, Island Lake experiences a gradual drawdown as irrigation water is needed downstream.

The farther you get away from Island Lake, the better the solitude. For instance, Round Lake receives only moderate pressure yet features excellent campsites, horse pasture, and spring water.

Snow Lake is impossible for horse travel, which makes fishing pressure for cutthroat trout all the lighter. This lake comes with an excellent source of spring water, but camping areas are nonexistent.

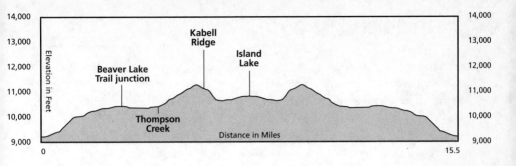

Whitewall and the Bennion Lakes can be worth a visit. They receive light angling use for brook and cutthroat trout. Several springs and campsites with plenty of horse pasture can be found on the west side of Whitewall Lake. Access from Island Lake is west through a large meadow, then up a timbered slope. Get your map and compass out. The best fishing should be at Lower Bennion. Whitewall and Upper Bennion are shallow and often experience winterkill.

94 Tamarack Lake

If you're looking for a nice excursion for the entire family, then Tamarack Lake is a good choice. A well-maintained forest service trail takes off from the southwest side of Spirit Lake Campground. From here, it is only 1.4 miles south then west on the Middle Fork Trail. The trail splits about 1.0 mile from the trailhead, but both trails reunite near the east side of Tamarack Lake. The left-hand trail is a little bit longer but passes Jessen Lake; the right-hand trail heads straight to Tamarack Lake.

Start: Spirit Lake trailhead
Distance: 2.8 miles out and back
Destination elevation: 10,429 feet
Approximate hiking time: 2 hours
Difficulty: Easy
Usage: Heavy
Nearest town: Mountain View, Wyoming
Drainage: Sheep Creek

Maps: USGS Chepeta Lake; USDA Forest Service High Uintas Wilderness; Trails Illustrated High Uintas Wilderness
Trail contacts: Ashley National Forest, Supervisor's Office, 355 North Vernal Ave., Vernal UT 84078, (435) 781-1181; Flaming Gorge Ranger District, 25 West Highway 43, Manila, UT 84046, (435) 784-3445

Finding the trailhead: From Mountain View, take Wyoming Highway 414 east then south about 20 miles to Lonetree. After about 10 miles east on Highway 414 is a three-way junction that provides access to Spirit and Browne Lakes. At this junction, take the south dirt road (Road 221) 13 miles to a junction with a posted sign. Road 001 winds west then south 7 miles to Spirit Lake.

The Spirit Lake trailhead has only five parking places and can accommodate you with excellent campsites, toilets, water, a cafe, horse rentals, and a stock ramp.

The Hike

From Spirit Lake, the trail heads southwest for 0.6 mile to the creek then turns northwest for 0.8 mile to the lake.

Tamarack is the biggest body of water in the Sheep Creek Drainage. Although it receives heavy usage, brook and a few cutthroat trout are maintained by stocking and natural reproduction. The best campsites are on the east side. Perhaps the best campsite is located just a hundred yards south down the trail where it splits off and heads south toward the lake. This site can accommodate a large group. Spring water seeps up along the south shoreline, and horse pasture is present to the east.

Just southeast of Tamarack lies Jessen Lake. Both are about the same type of lake, except Jessen is half the size and has no real campsites. It sits right next to the trail in rocky, timbered country.

If these lakes contain too many people for your taste, try Lost Lake. Get there by following the outlet of Tamarack Lake 0.5 mile northeast. Lost Lake has several campsites to choose from, and angling usage remains relatively light. Fill your canteen before coming here, because there's no spring water in the vicinity. Lost Lake is more

Tamarack Lake; Summit Lake; Daggett Lake; Anson Lakes

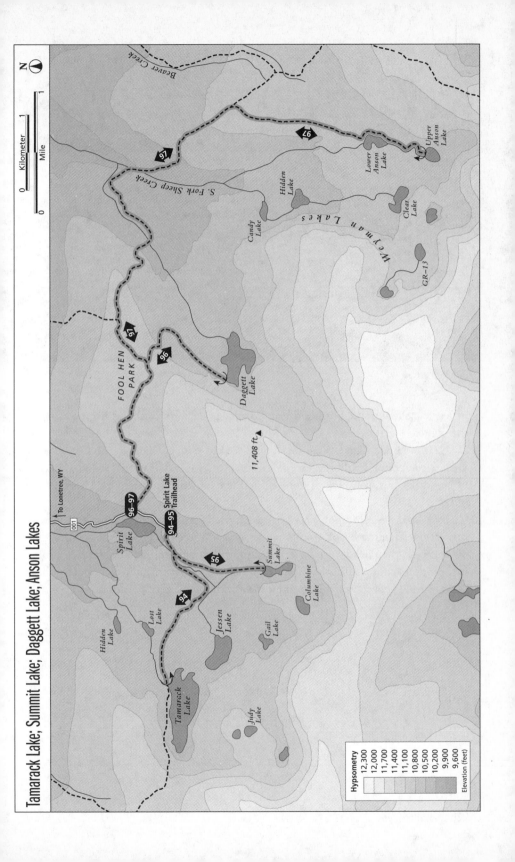

Tamarack Lake

or less a shallow pond, but good water exchange enables cutthroat trout to survive the winter.

Nearby Hidden Lake is another great place to escape. There are no campsites or spring water, but it could produce fast fishing for brookies. It is only 0.25 mile north of Lost Lake, but many hikers don't make the extra effort to see what Hidden Lake offers.

Judy Lake, perched upon a rocky and timbered bench within a scenic alpine basin, can provide fantastic brook trout angling. Follow a steep ridge up the southeast side of Tamarack, then head southwest. Fish a spinner down deep, and get ready for some hard-hitting action. Gail Lake may also produce good opportunities. It receives little attention and is deep enough to support a fair supply of cutthroat trout.

95 Summit Lake

Also named Sasquina Lake, for a beautiful legendary Indian maiden, this lake is seldom visited and has no fish. Going is rough to the lake, but it's worth it.

See map on page 229.
Start: Spirit Lake trailhead
Distance: 2.0 miles out and back
Destination elevation: 10,460 feet
Approximate hiking time: 2 hours
Difficulty: Easy—some cross-country up a steep ravine
Usage: Very light
Nearest town: Mountain View, Wyoming

Drainage: Sheep Creek
Maps: USGS Chepeta Lake; USDA Forest Service High Uintas Wilderness; Trails Illustrated High Uintas Wilderness
Trail contacts: Ashley National Forest, Supervisor's Office, 355 North Vernal Ave., Vernal UT 84078, (435) 781-1181; Flaming Gorge Ranger District, 25 West Highway 43, Manila, UT 84046, (435) 784-3445

Finding the trailhead: From Mountain View, take Wyoming Highway 414 east then south about 20 miles to Lonetree. After about 10 miles east on Highway 414 is a three-way junction that provides access to Spirit and Browne Lakes. At this junction, take the south dirt road (Road 221) 13 miles to a junction with a posted sign. Road 001 winds west then south 7 miles to Spirit Lake.

The Spirit Lake trailhead has only five parking places and can accommodate you with excellent campsites, toilets, water, a cafe, horse rentals, and a stock ramp.

The Hike

To find Summit (Sasquina) Lake, follow the Tamarack Trail 0.25 mile to an open meadow. Take a spur trail south to the base of a rocky ravine. At the top of the ravine lies Summit Lake. There are no fish in this lake, but it is a great place to be alone.

If you want to see some lakes that no one ever really visits, then put on your rock-hopping boots and get ready for some rugged trekking. The lakes we are speaking of are Columbine, Gail, and Judy. These lakes sit in the upper portion of the Middle Fork of Sheep Creek Drainage.

Summit Lake is also known as Sasquina. Years ago a legend was told about its trailhead (Spirit Lake). According to the story, Sasquina was a beautiful Indian maiden. One day while she was picking berries, a strong, handsome Indian chief named Walkara peered through the trees. As he gazed into her eyes of beauty, they became one. However, being from different tribes, they were forbidden to marry. Then one day in the valley of Hickerson Park, the tribes performed a special wedding ceremony. Sasquina and Walkara went on their honeymoon to Spirit Lake. This is where Chief Walkara placed a necklace made from sacred elk bones around her neck.

A few days after their honeymoon, Chief Walkara went in search for food. When he returned, Sasquina was nowhere to be found. He looked for her at all the places they had spent time together, but Sasquina had disappeared. Then he went to the lake they both loved. When he yelled out her name, "Sasquina, Sasquina," out of the lake swam a herd of elk, led by one as white as snow. Sasquina then arose from the lake, wearing the sacred necklace of bones. Legend has it, if you are at Spirit Lake just before dawn, you'll see the spirit of Sasquina rise from the waters.

96 Daggett Lake

We've heard a lot of discouraging stories about Daggett Lake. Some say angling is desperately poor; others tell of the hordes of mosquitoes that can suck you dry. Perhaps these people are misinformed, or maybe they just want to keep a few secrets for themselves. Whatever the reason, we found Daggett to be one of the better rainbow fisheries in the High Uintas. In the short time we spent here, we managed to hook several hefty trout. A small orange fly seemed to get their attention, and bait anglers using green sparkled PowerBait pulled them in just as fast.

See map on page 229.
Start: Spirit Lake
Distance: 5.6 miles out and back
Destination elevation: 10,462 feet
Approximate hiking time: 4 hours
Difficulty: Moderate—some steep sections
Usage: Heavy
Nearest town: Mountain View, Wyoming
Drainage: Sheep Creek

Maps: USGS Whiterocks Lake; USDA Forest Service High Uintas Wilderness; Trails Illustrated High Uintas Wilderness
Trail contacts: Ashley National Forest, Supervisor's Office, 355 North Vernal Ave., Vernal UT 84078, (435) 781-1181; Flaming Gorge Ranger District, 25 West Highway 43, Manila, UT 84046, (435) 784-3445.

Finding the trailhead: From Mountain View, take Wyoming Highway 414 east then south about 20 miles to Lonetree. After about 10 miles east on Highway 414 is a three-way junction that provides access to Spirit and Browne Lakes. At this junction, take the south dirt road (Road 221) 13 miles to a junction with a posted sign. Road 001 winds west then south 7 miles to Spirit Lake.

The trailhead is located next to the road on the east side of Spirit Lake. There are no parking spaces at this trailhead, so use the campground. The lodge at Spirit Lake offers cabins, horse rentals, a cafe with limited hours, toilets, and drinking water.

The Hike

The trail winds around swampy water holes, and a large meadow sits just south of the lake—prime habitat for a large assortment of mosquitoes and other bugs. To avoid these pesky critters, plan your trip after mid–August. By this time, hailstorms and other elements have diminished the insects' numbers.

Access to Daggett begins on the east side of Spirit Lake. Follow a well-groomed trail 1.0 mile east up a steep slope. Then head across Fool Hen Park to a posted sign at the Daggett Lake Trail junction. From here, the trail drops 400 feet down rocky switchbacks and to one of the outlets of Daggett Lake. Proceed along the outlet another 0.75 mile through a couple of boggy meadows and up a boulder ravine.

Daggett Lake plays host to a number of campsites along the northwest shore. Horse pasture is available in a meadow to the north, but spring water is hard to come by. This pretty lake receives moderate to heavy usage. Please help keep it clean.

97 Anson Lakes

People staying at the Spirit Lake Lodge might consider a long day trip to the Weyman Basin and Upper and Lower Anson lakes. The lakes are popular with anglers, but the scenery alone is worth the walk.

See map on page 229.
Start: Spirit Lake
Distance: 13.0 miles out and back
Destination elevation: 10,575 feet
Approximate hiking time: 8 hours
Difficulty: Moderate—some steep sections
Usage: Moderate
Nearest town: Mountain View, Wyoming
Drainage: Sheep Creek

Maps: USGS Whiterocks Lake; USDA Forest Service High Uintas Wilderness; Trails Illustrated High Uintas Wilderness
Trail contacts: Ashley National Forest, Supervisor's Office, 355 North Vernal Ave., Vernal UT 84078, (435) 781-1181; Flaming Gorge Ranger District, 25 West Highway 43, Manila, UT 84046, (435) 784-3445.

Finding the trailhead: From Mountain View, take Wyoming Highway 414 east then south about 20 miles to Lonetree. After about 10 miles east on Highway 414 is a three-way junction that provides access to Spirit and Browne Lakes. At this junction, take the south dirt road (Road 221) 13 miles to a junction with a posted sign. Road 001 winds west then south 7 miles to Spirit Lake.

The trailhead is located next to the road on the east side of Spirit Lake. There are no parking spaces at this trailhead, so use the campground. The lodge at Spirit Lake offers cabins, horse rentals, a cafe, toilets, water, and guide service.

The Hike

From Spirit Lake, follow a well-groomed trail 1.0 mile east up a steep slope and across Fool Hen Park to the turnoff for Daggett Lake. Turn left in 0.5 mile to another junction. Stay right and descend 2.0 miles into South Fork Sheep Creek. After the second creek crossing, the trail climbs then levels off. About 2.0 miles from the creek crossing, turn right, heading south 1.0 mile to Anson Lakes.

The first lake you'll arrive at is Lower Anson. Upper Anson Lake is just a little farther. Follow a scant trail 0.25 mile south as it parallels the east side of the inlet to

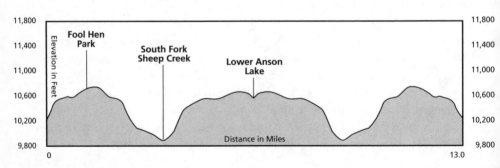

Lower Anson. Both lakes are in rugged and rocky terrain. There is one small camp on the south end of Lower Anson, but the best campsite is located a couple of hundred yards above Lower Anson Lake near the creek.

Fishing should be pretty good if the water is clear. Anson Lakes can get murky during rainy years. Natural reproduction keeps the brook trout population up. In fact, sometimes there are too many trout and they become stunted.

Leave your horses behind at Anson Lakes when traveling into the Weyman Lakes area. Treacherous terrain makes horses impractical. Expect the best fishing at either Clear or Hidden Lake, although Hidden will likely be murky if Anson Lakes are. Clear Lake is always clear and has some fat trout. Candy Lake offers some of the biggest and tastiest trout that will ever tickle your tonsils. Angling is rather slow, but their meat will fulfill your most savory cravings.

98 Lamb Lakes

Just before arrival you might say, "What a bummer." That's because the last mile is extremely rocky and impossible for horse travel. The trail begins on SR 96, just before arriving at Browne Lake. Follow the West Fork Trail 5.5 miles south, then drop over the ridge 1.0 mile west to Bummer Lake.

Start: Browne Lake
Distance: 13.0 miles out and back
Destination elevation: 10,350 feet
Approximate hiking time: 8 hours
Difficulty: Moderate
Usage: Light
Nearest town: Mountain View, Wyoming
Drainage: Carter Creek

Maps: USGS Whiterocks Lake; USDA Forest Service High Uintas Wilderness; Trails Illustrated High Uintas Wilderness
Trail contacts: Ashley National Forest, Supervisor's Office, 355 North Vernal Ave., Vernal UT 84078, (435) 781-1181; Flaming Gorge Ranger District, 25 West Highway 43, Manila, UT 84046, (435) 784-3445

Finding the trailhead: From Mountain View, take Wyoming Highway 414 east then south about 20 miles to Lonetree. After about 10 miles east on Highway 414 is a three-way junction that provides access to Spirit and Browne Lakes. At this junction, take the south dirt road (Road 221) 13 miles to a junction with a posted sign. Browne Lake is 8 miles east on Road 221.

Campsites, toilets, and water are located at Browne Lake, along with three different trailheads. Make sure to start on the right trail.

The Hike

From the trailhead, the trail climbs 2.5 miles to the Sheep Creek Canal, then goes another 2.0 miles to a creek crossing on West Fork. After crossing the creek, the trail climbs the slopes toward the top of the ridge for about 1.0 mile. Before reaching tree line, turn right off the trail and contour 1.0 mile to Lamb Lakes.

Lamb Lakes can provide prime angling. However, fishing is unpredictable. Although these lakes receive little pressure, most have a history of winterkill during long, hard winters. In the summer months, there's an excellent elk population here. Signs of elk are everywhere, but actually seeing these animals can be quite difficult. One sniff, sound, or sight of a human, and the only evidence of their existence will be the sound of hooves pouncing through the trees.

Several lakes occupy Lamb Lakes Basin: Bummer, Mutton, Lamb, Ram, Ewe, GR–20, and GR–21. All of these lakes are in rough and rocky, timbered country, and campsites are few and far between. Except for the Bummer Lake area, spring water can be found at all of the lakes.

To reach Mutton Lake, follow the inlet of Bummer Lake 0.5 mile south. This lake plays host to the best camping areas in Lamb Lakes Basin. Fishing pressure is considered light for stocked brook trout.

Lamb Lakes; Tepee Lakes

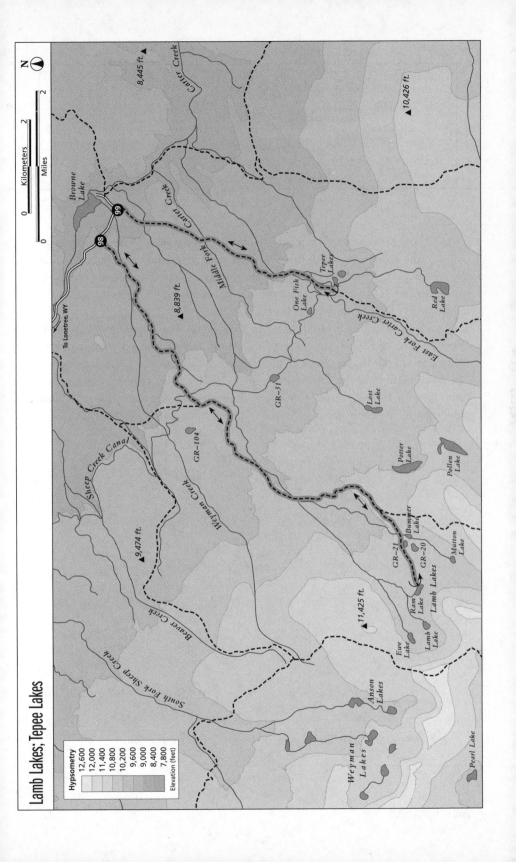

Hypsometry

	Elevation (feet)
	12,600
	12,000
	11,400
	10,800
	10,200
	9,600
	9,000
	8,400
	7,800

N

0   Kilometers   2
0   Miles   2

To Lonetree, WY

Sheep Creek Canal

Browne Lake

99

98

Carter Creek

Carter Creek

8,445 ft. ▲

8,839 ft. ▲

Middle Fork

Carter Creek

10,426 ft. ▲

East Fork Carter Creek

Tepee Lakes

One Fish Lake

Red Lake

GR-31

Lost Lake

9,474 ft. ▲

GR-104

Weymon Creek

Potter Lake

Pollen Lake

GR-21

Bumper Lake

GR-20

Mutton Lake

Ram Lake

Lamb Lakes

Lamb Lake

Ewe Lake

11,425 ft. ▲

Beaver Creek

South Fork Sheep Creek

Weyman Lakes

Anson Lakes

Pearl Lake

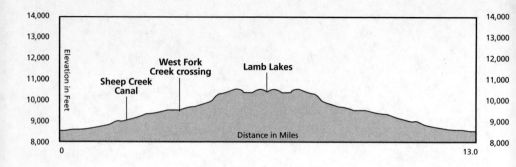

Lamb Lake is next to a steep rocky slope 1.0 mile west of Bummer. There is no trail, and the going gets rough when crossing over rocks and dead timber. This lake may also experience winterkill during harsh winters. For better angling possibilities, try Ram Lake. It is a little deeper and is fed by a fresh supply of spring water. Ram Lake is just 1.0 mile southwest of Bummer Lake.

Ewe Lake is a fishless pond sitting at the base of a talus slope 1.0 mile west of Bummer. The hike is over rough terrain. Ewe can also be reached by dropping over the ridge from the Beaver Creek Trail. There are no campsites or fish, but spring water can be found around the lake. GR–20 and GR–21 receive very light angling pressure. However, fishing is quite slow due to shallow water. Get out and see this remote wilderness. Few people do.

99 Tepee Lakes

While an elevation gain of 1,000 feet in 3.5 miles doesn't sound like much, most of that elevation is picked up during the last mile. For the first couple of miles, the trail topples over several rolling hills. After the second bridge crossing, the trail proceeds up a steady incline. At times this excursion feels like a constant uphill battle. On the other hand, it's rather relaxing on the way out.

See map on page 237.
Start: Browne Lake
Distance: 7.0 miles out and back
Destination elevation: 9,410 feet
Approximate hiking time: 5 hours
Difficulty: Moderate—one steep section
Usage: Heavy
Nearest town: Manila, Utah
Drainage: Carter Creek

Maps: USGS Leidy Peak; USDA Forest Service High Uintas Wilderness; Trails Illustrated High Uintas Wilderness
Trail contacts: Ashley National Forest, Supervisor's Office, 355 North Vernal Ave., Vernal UT 84078, (435) 781-1181; Flaming Gorge Ranger District, 25 West Highway 43, Manila, UT 84046, (435) 784-3445.

Finding the trailhead: From Mountain View, take Wyoming Highway 414 east then south about 20 miles to Lonetree. After about 10 miles east on Highway 414 is a three-way junction that provides access to Spirit and Browne Lakes. At this junction, take the south dirt road (Road 221) 13 miles to a junction with a posted sign. Browne Lake is 8 miles east on Road 221.

Campsites, toilets, and water are located at Browne Lake, along with three different trailheads. Make sure to start on the right trail.

The Hike

From the trailhead, the trail heads south, crossing West Fork then Middle Fork before it reaches East Fork 2.7 miles from the trailhead. The trail then crosses East Fork and continues 0.8 mile to Tepee Lakes.

Tepee Lakes attract a variety of visitors. Boy Scout groups congregate near Browne Lake, and many others use this recreation area. Good campsites and spring water are

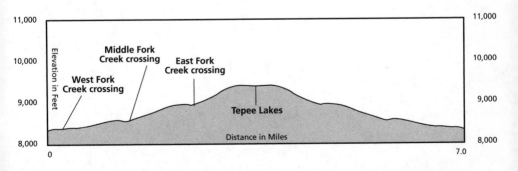

near the west side of the trail of Lower Tepee, and angling is usually good for pan-size brookies. Upper Tepee Lake is somewhat slow for fishing. During hard, cold winters, it often experiences winterkills.

Other good fishing holes in the Middle or East Fork Drainage are Red, Lost, and One Fish Lakes. Red Lake is at the end of a rugged trail, 2.0 miles south of Tepee Lakes. This pretty lake lies beneath Leidy Peak, and angling pressure remains light for stocked brook trout. Lost Lake (also known as Mystery Lake) is a beautiful body of water nestled within a secluded pocket formed by two ridges. Find Lost Lake by following a skimpy trail, which is marked with a posted sign. This would be a good time to break out the map.

One Fish Lake might just be that. You may catch one fish, or you could net a bundle. This lake is surrounded by heavy timber, making back casting impossible. The fly-and-bubble technique can help you avoid these obstacles. Campsites are not available in the immediate vicinity. However, camping areas, spring water, and horse pasture are located 0.125 mile southeast in a large meadow.

100 The Highline Trail

There's a certain breed of backpackers that practically lives on the trail. These are the long-haulers. It takes a lot of stamina and willpower to take on a long hike lasting many days or even weeks. If you are strong enough, crazy enough, and have lots of time, then maybe you can join the elite long-haulers on the Highline Trail.

Start: Highline trailhead (west end) or Leidy Peak trailhead (east end)
Distance: 83.0 miles one way
Highest elevation: 12,600 feet
Approximate hiking time: 55 hours
Difficulty: Extremely difficult
Usage: Moderate
Nearest town: Kamas, Utah (west end), or Manila, Utah (east end)

Maps: USDA Forest Service High Uintas Wilderness; Trails Illustrated High Uintas Wilderness
Trail contacts: Ashley National Forest, Forest Supervisor, 355 North Vernal Ave., Vernal, UT 84078, (435) 781-1181; Duchesne Ranger District, 85 West Main, Duchesne, UT 84021, (435) 738-2482

Finding the trailhead: The Highline is the most popular trail of the High Uintas. From Kamas, take the Mirror Lake Highway (Highway 150) 34 miles to a large sign on the east side of the road that says "Highline Trail." This trailhead has a listed capacity of twenty-four vehicles, but there are often considerably more parked here on busy weekends. This crowded trailhead is equipped with toilets, water, stock ramp, and nearby campsites.

The other end of the trail is at the Leidy Peak trailhead. From Vernal, take the Red Cloud Loop Road toward East Park Reservoir and continue on toward Hacking Lake. You can camp at Hacking Lake, or drive up the road another mile to the Leidy Peak trailhead at the eastern end of the Highline Trail. Total distance from Vernal is about 32 miles.

The Hike

The trail begins at either the Highline trailhead (west end) or at the Leidy Peak trailhead on the eastern end of the High Uinta Mountains. The trail from Leidy Peak starts about 600 feet higher, but that factor will have little effect on the total wear and tear of this lengthy trek. The Highline Trail takes you up and down seven mountain passes. They are (west to east) Rocky Sea, Dead Horse, Red Knob, Porcupine, Tungsten, Anderson, and Gabbro. It is these passes that make this journey something special. From atop the backbone of the High Uintas, you'll witness one spectacular vista after another.

Almost all the Highline experience happens on the south slope of the Uintas. The only exception is where the trail takes a brief detour over Dead Horse Pass into the West Fork Blacks Fork Drainage. After less than 4.0 miles, the trail winds its way back to the south slope over Red Knob Pass.

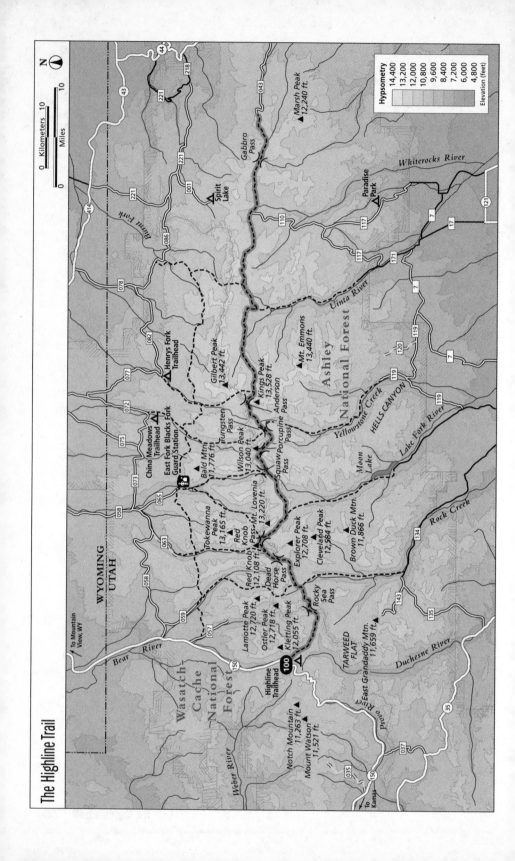

The Highline Trail

N

Hypsometry

14,400
13,200
12,000
10,800
9,600
8,400
7,200
6,000
4,800

Elevation (feet)

0 Kilometers 10
0 Miles 10

WYOMING
UTAH

Wasatch
Cache
National
Forest

Ashley
National
Forest

Bear River
Weber River
Bear River
Blacks Fork
Henry Fork
Smiths Fork
Uinta River
Whiterocks River
Yellowstone Creek
Lake Fork River
Rock Creek
Provo River
Duchesne River
East Grandaddy Mtn.

To Mountain
View, WY

China Meadows
Trailhead

Henrys Fork
Trailhead

Spirit
Lake

East Fork Blacks Fork
Guard Station

Gabbro
Pass

Marsh Peak
12,240 ft.

Paradise
Park

Gilbert Peak
13,442 ft.

Kings Peak
13,528 ft.

Anderson
Pass

Mt. Emmons
13,440 ft.

Tungsten
Pass

Wilson Peak
13,040 ft.

Squaw
Pass

Porcupine
Pass

Bald Mtn.
11,776 ft.

Tokewanna
Peak
13,165 ft.

Red
Knob

Mt. Lovenia
13,220 ft.

Red Knob
Pass

Dead
Horse
Pass

Explorer Peak
12,708 ft.

Cleveland Peak
12,584 ft.

Brown Duck Mtn.
11,866 ft.

HELLS CANYON

Moon
Lake

Lamotte Peak
12,720 ft.

Ostler Peak
12,718 ft.

Kletting Peak
12,055 ft.

Rocky
Sea Pass

Highline
Trailhead

100

Notch Mountain
11,263 ft.

Mount Watson
11,521 ft.

TARWEED
FLAT

East Grandaddy Mtn.
11,659 ft.

To Kamas

218
221
4
43
221
114
221
001
086
078
082
077
072
075
073
065
063
058
058
059
057
150
035
037
85
150
043
110
117
117
117
171
7
17
121
7
119
120
119
119
119
134
143
135

Rocky Sea Pass

Because much of the Highline Trail is above timberline, plan carefully where to spend your nights. Choose camps with pines for shelter from wind and rain. Low stands of pines are also the safest place to be when lightning is flashing. Speaking of bad weather, allow yourself at least a couple of extra days to complete this hike. You might get holed up for a while waiting for the skies to settle down.

It should go without saying that excellent physical conditioning is a prerequisite to this alpine adventure. The steep, rocky miles will tear at your muscles, and the high mountain passes will take your breath away. But then, so will the scenery.

The Art of Hiking

When standing nose to nose with a mountain lion, you're probably not too concerned with the issue of ethical behavior in the wild. No doubt you're just terrified. But let's be honest. How often are you nose to nose with a mountain lion? For most of us, a hike into the "wild" means loading up the SUV with expensive gear and driving to a toileted trailhead. Sure, you can mourn how civilized we've become—how GPS units have replaced natural instinct and Gore-Tex, true grit—but the silly gadgets of civilization aside, we have plenty of reason to take pride in how we've matured. With survival now on the back burner, we've begun to reason—and it's about time—that we have a responsibility to protect, no longer just conquer, our wild places: that they, not we, are at risk. So please, do what you can. The following section will help you understand better what it means to "do what you can" while still making the most of your hiking experience. Anyone can take a hike, but hiking safely and well is an art requiring preparation and proper equipment.

Trail Etiquette

Zero impact. Always leave an area just like you found it—if not better than you found it. Avoid camping in fragile, alpine meadows and along the banks of streams and lakes. Use a camp stove versus building a wood fire, required in some Uinta Mountain locations. Pack up all of your trash and extra food. Bury human waste at least 100 feet from water sources under 6 to 8 inches of topsoil. Don't bathe with soap in a lake or stream—use prepackaged moistened towels to wipe off sweat and dirt, or bathe in the water without soap.

Stay on the trail. It's true, a path anywhere leads nowhere new, but purists will just have to get over it. Paths serve an important purpose; they limit impact on natural areas. Straying from a designated trail may seem innocent but it can cause damage to sensitive areas—damage that may take years to recover, if it can recover at all. Even simple shortcuts can be destructive. Furthermore, creating new trails leads to confusion and may lead to other hikers down the road getting lost. So, please, stay on the trail.

Leave no weeds. Noxious weeds tend to overtake other plants, which in turn affects animals and birds that depend on them for food. To minimize the spread of noxious weeds, hikers should regularly clean their boots, tents, packs, and hiking poles of mud and seeds. Also brush your dog to remove any weed seeds before heading off into a new area.

Keep your dog under control. You can buy a flexi-lead that allows your dog to go exploring along the trail, while allowing you the ability to reel him in should another hiker approach or should he decide to chase a rabbit or deer—and worse for the dog, a porcupine. Always obey leash laws and be sure to bury your dog's waste or pack it in sealed bags.

Respect other trail users. Often you're not the only one on the trail. With the rise in popularity of multiuse trails, you'll have to learn a new kind of respect, beyond the nod and "hello" approach you may be used to. First investigate whether you're on a multiuse trail, and assume the appropriate precautions. When you encounter motorized vehicles (ATVs, motorcycles, and 4WDs), be alert. Though they should always yield to the hiker, often they're going too fast or are too lost in the buzz of their engine to react to your presence. If you hear activity ahead, step off the trail just to be safe. Note that you're not likely to hear a mountain biker coming, so be prepared and know ahead of time whether you share the trail with them. Cyclists should always yield to hikers, but that's little comfort to the hiker. Be aware. When you approach horses or pack animals on the trail, always step quietly off the trail, preferably on the downhill side, and let them pass. If you're wearing a large backpack, it's often a good idea to sit down. To some animals, a hiker wearing a large backpack might appear threatening. Many national forests allow domesticated grazing, usually for sheep and cattle. Make sure your dog doesn't harass these animals, and respect ranchers' rights while you're enjoying yours.

Getting into Shape

Unless you want to be sore—and possibly have to shorten your trip or vacation—be sure to get in shape before a big hike. If you're terribly out of shape, start a walking program early, preferably eight weeks in advance. Start with a 15-minute walk during your lunch hour or after work and gradually increase your walking time to an hour. You should also increase your elevation gain. Walking briskly up hills really strengthens your leg muscles and gets your heart rate up. If you work in a storied office building, take the stairs instead of the elevator. If you prefer going to a gym, walk the treadmill or use a stair machine. You can further increase your strength and endurance by walking with a loaded backpack. Stationary exercises you might consider are squats, leg lifts, sit-ups, and push-ups. Other good ways to get in shape include biking, running, aerobics, and, of course, short hikes. Stretching before and after a hike keeps muscles flexible and helps avoid injuries.

Preparedness

It's been said that failing to plan means planning to fail. So do take the necessary time to plan your trip. Whether going on a short day hike or an extended backpack trip, always prepare for the worst. Simply remembering to pack a copy of the *US Army Survival Manual* is not preparedness. Although it's not a bad idea if you plan on entering truly wild places, it's merely the tourniquet answer to a problem. You need to do your best to prevent the problem from arising in the first place. In order to survive—and to stay reasonably comfortable—you need to concern yourself with the basics: water, food, and shelter. Don't go on a hike without having these bases covered. And don't go on a hike expecting to find these items in the woods.

Water. Even in frigid conditions, you need at least two quarts of water a day to function efficiently. Add heat and taxing terrain and you can bump that figure up to one gallon. That's simply a base to work from—your metabolism and your level of conditioning can raise or lower that amount. Unless you know your level, assume that you need one gallon of water a day. Now, where do you plan on getting the water?

Preferably not from natural water sources. These sources can be loaded with intestinal disturbers, such as bacteria, viruses, and fertilizers. *Giardia lamblia,* the most common of these disturbers, is a protozoan parasite that lives part of its life in water sources. The parasite spreads when mammals defecate in water sources. Once ingested, giardia can induce cramping, diarrhea, vomiting, and fatigue within two days to two weeks after ingestion. Giardiasis is treatable with prescription drugs. If you believe you've contracted giardiasis, see a doctor immediately.

Treating water. The best and easiest solution to avoid polluted water is to carry your water with you. Yet, depending on the nature of your hike and the duration, this may not be an option—one gallon of water weighs 8½ pounds. In that case, you'll need to look into treating water. Regardless of which method you choose, you should always carry some water with you in case of an emergency. Save this reserve until you absolutely need it.

There are three methods of treating water: boiling, chemical treatment, and filtering. If you boil water, it's recommended that you do so for 10 to 15 minutes. This is often impractical because you're forced to exhaust a great deal of your fuel supply. You can opt for chemical treatment, which will kill giardia but will not take care of other chemical pollutants. Another drawback to chemical treatments is the unpleasant taste of the water after it's treated. You can remedy this by adding powdered drink mix to the water. Filters are the preferred method for treating water. Many filters remove giardia, organic and inorganic contaminants, and don't leave an aftertaste. Water filters are far from perfect, as they can easily become clogged or leak if a gasket wears out. It's always a good idea to carry a backup supply of chemical treatment tablets in case your filter decides to quit on you.

Food. If we're talking about survival, you can go days without food, as long as you have water. But we're also talking about comfort. Try to avoid foods that are high in sugar and fat like candy bars and potato chips. These food types are harder to digest and are low in nutritional value. Instead, bring along foods that are easy to pack, nutritious, and high in energy (e.g., bagels, nutrition bars, dehydrated fruit, gorp, and jerky). If you are on an overnight trip, easy-to-fix dinners include rice mixes with dehydrated potatoes, corn, pasta with cheese sauce, and soup mixes. For a tasty breakfast, you can fix hot oatmeal with brown sugar and reconstituted milk powder topped off with banana chips. If you like a hot drink in the morning, bring along herbal tea bags or hot chocolate. If you are a coffee junkie, you can purchase coffee that is packaged like tea bags. You can prepackage all of your meals in heavy-duty sealable plastic bags to keep food from spilling in your pack. These bags can be reused to pack out trash.

Shelter. The type of shelter you choose depends less on the conditions than on your tolerance for discomfort. Shelter comes in many forms—tent, tarp, lean-to, bivy sack, cabin, cave, etc. If you're camping in the desert, a bivy sack may suffice, but if you're above the tree line and a storm is approaching, a better choice is a three- or four-season tent. Tents are the logical and most popular choice for most backpackers, as they're lightweight and packable—and you can rest assured that you always have shelter from the elements. Before you leave on your trip, anticipate what the weather and terrain will be like and plan for the type of shelter that will work best for your comfort level (see Equipment later in this section).

Finding a campsite. If there are established campsites, stick to those. If not, start looking for a campsite early—around 3:30 or 4 p.m. Stop at the first decent site you see. Depending on the area, it could be a long time before you find another suitable location. Pitch your camp in an area that's level Make sure the area is at least 200 feet from fragile areas like lakeshores, meadows, and stream banks. And try to avoid areas thick in underbrush, as they can harbor insects and provide cover for approaching animals.

If you are camping in stormy, rainy weather, look for a rock outcrop or a shelter in the trees to keep the wind from blowing your tent all night. Be sure that you don't camp under trees with dead limbs that might break off on top of you. Also, try to find an area that has an absorbent surface, such as sandy soil or forest duff. This, in addition to camping on a surface with a slight angle, will provide better drainage. By all means, don't dig trenches to provide drainage around your tent—remember you're practicing zero-impact camping.

If you're in bear country, steer clear of creekbeds or animal paths. If you see any signs of a bear's presence (i.e., scat, footprints), relocate. You'll need to find a campsite near a tall tree where you can hang your food and other items that may attract bears, such as deodorant, toothpaste, or soap. Carry a lightweight nylon rope with which to hang your food. As a rule, you should hang your food at least 20 feet from the ground and 5 feet away from the tree trunk. You can put food and other items in a waterproof stuff sack and tie one end of the rope to the stuff sack. To get the other end of the rope over the tree branch, tie a good size rock to it, and gently toss the rock over the tree branch. Pull the stuff sack up until it reaches the top of the branch and tie it off securely. Don't hang your food near your tent! If possible, hang your food at least 100 feet away from your campsite. Alternatives to hanging your food are bear-proof plastic tubes and metal bear boxes.

Lastly, think of comfort. Lie down on the ground where you intend to sleep and see if it's a good fit. For morning warmth (and a nice view to wake up to), have your tent face east.

First Aid

I know you're tough, but get 10 miles into the woods and develop a blister and you'll wish you had carried that first-aid kit. Face it, it's just plain good sense. Many companies produce lightweight, compact first-aid kits. Just make sure yours contains at least the following:

- Band-Aids
- moleskin
- various sterile gauze and dressings
- white surgical tape
- an Ace bandage
- an antihistamine
- aspirin
- Betadine solution
- a first-aid book
- Tums
- tweezers
- scissors
- antibacterial wipes
- triple-antibiotic ointment
- plastic gloves
- sterile cotton tip applicators
- syrup of ipecac (to induce vomiting)
- thermometer
- wire splint

Here are a few tips for dealing with and hopefully preventing certain ailments:

Sunburn. Take along sunscreen or sunblock, protective clothing, and a wide-brimmed hat. If you do get a sunburn, treat the area with aloe vera gel, and protect the area from further sun exposure. At higher elevations, the sun's radiation can be particularly damaging to skin. Remember that your eyes are vulnerable to this radiation as well. Sunglasses can be a good way to prevent headaches and permanent eye damage from the sun, especially in places where light-colored rock or patches of snow reflect light up in your face.

Blisters. Be prepared to take care of these hike-spoilers by carrying moleskin (a lightly padded adhesive), gauze and tape, or adhesive bandages. An effective way to apply moleskin is to cut out a circle of moleskin and remove the center—like a doughnut—and place it over the blistered area. Cutting the center out will reduce the pressure applied to the sensitive skin. Other products can help you combat blisters. Some are applied to suspicious hot spots before a blister forms to help decrease friction to that area, while others are applied to the blister after it has popped to help prevent further irritation.

Insect bites and stings. You can treat most insect bites and stings by applying hydrocortisone 1 percent cream topically and taking a pain medication such as ibuprofen to reduce swelling. If you forgot to pack these items, a cold compress or a paste of mud and ashes can sometimes assuage the itching and discomfort. Remove any stingers by using tweezers or scraping the area with your fingernail or a knife blade. Don't pinch the area, as you'll only spread the venom. Some hikers are highly sensitive to bites and stings and may have a serious allergic reaction that can be life threatening. Symptoms of a serious allergic reaction can include wheezing, an asthmatic attack, and shock. The treatment for this severe type of reaction is epinephrine. If you know that you are sensitive to bites and stings, carry a pre-packaged kit of epinephrine, which can be obtained only by prescription from your doctor.

Ticks. Ticks can carry diseases such as Rocky Mountain spotted fever and Lyme disease. The best defense is, of course, prevention. If you know you're going to be hiking through an area littered with ticks, wear long pants and a long-sleeved shirt. You can apply a permethrin repellent to your clothing and a DEET repellent to exposed skin. At the end of your hike, do a spot check for ticks (and insects in general). If you do find a tick embedded in your skin, coat the insect with petroleum jelly or tree sap to cut off its air supply. The tick should release its hold, but if it doesn't, grab the head of the tick firmly—with a pair of tweezers if you have them—and gently pull it away from the skin with a twisting motion. Sometimes part of the tick lingers. If this happens, try to remove it with a disinfected needle. Clean the affected area with an antibacterial cleanser and then apply triple-antibiotic ointment. Monitor the area for a few days. If irritation persists or a white spot develops, see a doctor for possible infection.

Poison ivy, oak, and sumac. These skin irritants can be found most anywhere in North America and come in the form of a bush or a vine, having leaflets in groups of three, five, seven, or nine. Learn how to spot the plants. The oil they secrete can cause an allergic reaction in the form of blisters, usually about 12 hours after exposure. The itchy rash can last from ten days to several weeks. The best defense against these irritants is to wear clothing that covers the arms, legs, and torso. For summer, zip-off cargo pants come in handy. There are also nonprescription lotions you can apply to exposed skin that guard against the effects of poison ivy/oak/sumac and can be washed off with soap and water. If you think you were in contact with the plants, after hiking (or even on the trail during longer hikes) wash with soap and water. Taking a hot shower with soap after you return home from your hike will also help to remove any lingering oil from your skin. Should you contract a rash from any of these plants, use an antihistamine to reduce the itching. If the rash is localized, create a light bleach/water wash to dry up the area. If the rash has spread, either tough it out or see your doctor about getting a dose of cortisone (available both orally and by injection).

Snakebites. Snakebites are rare in North America. Unless startled or provoked, the majority of snakes will not bite. If you are wise to their habitats and keep a careful eye on the trail, you should be just fine. When stepping over logs, first step on the log, making sure you can see what's on the other side before stepping down. Though your chances of being struck are slim, it's wise to know what to do in the event you are.

If a nonvenomous snake bites you, allow the wound to bleed a small amount and then cleanse the wounded area with a Betadine solution (10 percent povidone iodine). Rinse the wound with clean water (preferably) or fresh urine (it might sound ugly, but it's sterile). Once the area is clean, cover it with triple-antibiotic ointment and a clean bandage. Remember, most residual damage from snakebites, venomous or otherwise, comes from infection, not the snake's venom. Keep the area as clean as possible and get medical attention immediately.

If you are bitten by a venomous snake, remove the toxin with a suctioning device, found in a snakebite kit. If you do not have such a device, squeeze the wound—DO NOT use your mouth for suction, as the venom will enter your bloodstream through the vessels under the tongue and head straight for your heart. Then, clean the wound just as you would a nonvenomous bite. Tie a clean band of cloth snuggly around the afflicted appendage, about an inch or so above the bite (or the rim of the swelling). This is NOT a tourniquet—you want to simply slow the blood flow, not cut it off. Loosen the band if numbness ensues. Remove the band for a minute and reapply a little higher every 10 minutes.

If it is your friend who's been bitten, treat him or her for shock—make the person comfortable, have him or her lie down, elevate the legs, and keep him or her warm. Avoid applying anything cold to the bite wound. Immobilize the affected area and remove any constricting items such as rings, watches, or restrictive clothing—swelling may occur. Once your friend is stable and relatively calm, seek medical attention in the quickest feasible way. The victim should get treatment within 12 hours, ideally, which usually consists of a tetanus shot, antivenin, and antibiotics.

If you are alone and struck by a venomous snake, stay calm. Hysteria will only quicken the venom's spread. Follow the procedure above, and do your best to reach help. When hiking out, don't run—you'll only increase the flow of blood throughout your system. Instead, walk calmly.

Dehydration. Have you ever hiked in hot weather and had a roaring headache and felt fatigued after only a few miles? More than likely you were dehydrated. Symptoms of dehydration include fatigue, headache, and decreased coordination and judgment. When you are hiking, your rate of fluid loss depends on the outside temperature, humidity, altitude, and your activity level. On average, a hiker walking in warm weather will lose four liters of fluid a day. That fluid loss is easily replaced by normal consumption of liquids and food. However, if a hiker is walking briskly in hot, dry weather and hauling a heavy pack, he or she can lose one to three liters of water an hour. It's important to always carry plenty of water and to stop often and drink fluids regularly, even if you aren't thirsty.

Heat exhaustion. Heat exhaustion is the result of a loss of large amounts of electrolytes and often occurs if a hiker is dehydrated and has been under heavy exertion. Common symptoms of heat exhaustion include cramping, exhaustion, fatigue, lightheadedness and nausea. You can treat heat exhaustion by getting out of the sun and drinking an electrolyte solution made up of one teaspoon of salt and one table-spoon of sugar dissolved in a liter of water. Drink this solution slowly over a period of 1 hour. Drinking plenty of fluids (preferably an electrolyte solution/sports drink) can prevent heat exhaustion. Avoid hiking during the hottest parts of the day, and wear breathable clothing, a wide-brimmed hat, and sunglasses.

Hypothermia. Hypothermia is one of the biggest dangers in the backcountry, especially for day hikers in the summertime. That may sound strange, but imagine starting out on a hike in midsummer when it's sunny and 80 degrees out. You're clad in nylon shorts and a cotton T-shirt. About halfway through your hike, the sky begins to cloud up, and in the next hour a light drizzle begins to fall and the wind starts to pick up. Before you know it, you are soaking wet and shivering. More advanced signs include decreased coordination, slurred speech, and blurred vision. When a victim's temperature falls below 92 degrees, the blood pressure and pulse plummet, possibly leading to coma and death.

To avoid hypothermia, always bring a windproof/rainproof shell, a fleece jacket, tights made of a breathable, synthetic fiber, gloves, and hat when you are hiking in the mountains. Learn to adjust your clothing layers based on the temperature. If you are climbing uphill at a moderate pace you will stay warm, but when you stop for a break you'll become cold quickly, unless you add more layers of clothing.

If a hiker is showing advanced signs of hypothermia, dress him or her in dry clothes and make sure he or she is wearing a hat and gloves. Place the person in a sleeping bag in a tent or shelter that will protect him or her from the wind and other elements. Give the person warm fluids to drink and keep him awake.

Frostbite. When the mercury dips below 32 degrees, your extremities begin to chill. If a persistent chill attacks a localized area, say, your hands or your toes, the circu-latory system reacts by cutting off blood flow to the affected area—the idea being to protect and preserve the body's overall temperature. And so it's death by attrition for the affected area. Ice crystals start to form from the water in the cells of the neglected tissue. Deprived of heat, nourishment, and now water, the tissue literally starves. This is frostbite.

Prevention is your best defense against this situation. Most prone to frostbite are your face, hands, and feet, so protect these areas well. Wool is the material of choice because it provides ample air space for insulation and draws moisture away from the skin. Synthetic fabrics, however, have recently made great strides in the cold weather clothing market. Do your research. A pair of light silk liners under your regular gloves is a good trick for keeping warm. They afford some additional warmth, but more importantly they'll allow you to remove your mitts for tedious work without expos-ing the skin.

If your feet or hands start to feel cold or numb due to the elements, warm them as quickly as possible. Place cold hands under your armpits or bury them in your crotch. If your feet are cold, change your socks. If there's plenty of room in your boots, add another pair of socks. Do remember, though, that constricting your feet in tight boots can restrict blood flow and actually make your feet colder more quickly. Your socks need to have breathing room if they're going to be effective. Dead air provides insulation. If your face is cold, place your warm hands over your face, or simply wear a head stocking.

Should your skin go numb and start to appear white and waxy, chances are you've got or are developing frostbite. Don't try to thaw the area unless you can maintain the warmth. In other words, don't stop to warm up your frostbitten feet only to head back on the trail. You'll do more damage than good. Tests have shown that hikers who walked on thawed feet did more harm, and endured more pain, than hikers who left the affected areas alone. Do your best to get out of the cold entirely and seek medical attention—which usually consists of performing a rapid rewarming in water for 20 to 30 minutes.

The overall objective in preventing both hypothermia and frostbite is to keep the body's core warm. Protect key areas where heat escapes, like the top of the head, and maintain the proper nutrition level. Foods that are high in calories aid the body in producing heat. Never smoke or drink alcohol when you're in situations where the cold is threatening. By affecting blood flow, these activities ultimately cool the body's core temperature.

Altitude sickness (AMS). High lofty peaks, clear alpine lakes, and vast mountain views beckon hikers to the high country. But those who like to venture high may become victims of altitude sickness (also known as acute mountain sickness—AMS). Altitude sickness is your body's reaction to insufficient oxygen in the blood due to decreased barometric pressure. While some hikers may feel lightheaded, nauseous, and experience shortness of breath at 7,000 feet, others may not experience these symptoms until they reach 10,000 feet or higher.

Slowing your ascent to high places and giving your body a chance to acclimatize to the higher elevations can prevent altitude sickness. For example, if you live at sea level and are planning a weeklong backpacking trip to elevations between 7,000 and 12,000 feet, start by staying below 7,000 feet for one night, then move to between 7,000 and 10,000 feet for another night or two. Avoid strenuous exertion and alcohol to give your body a chance to adjust to the new altitude. It's also important to eat light food and drink plenty of nonalcoholic fluids, preferably water. Loss of appetite at altitude is common, but you must eat!

Most hikers who experience mild to moderate AMS develop a headache and/or nausea, grow lethargic, and have problems sleeping. The treatment for AMS is simple: Stop heading uphill. Keep eating and drinking water, and take meds for the headache. You actually need to take more breaths at altitude than at sea level, so breathe a little faster without hyperventilating. If symptoms don't improve over 24 to 48 hours, descend. Once a victim descends about 2,000 to 3,000 feet, his signs will usually begin to diminish.

Severe AMS comes in two forms: high altitude pulmonary edema (HAPE) and high altitude cerebral edema (HACE). HAPE, an accumulation of fluid in the lungs, can occur above 8,000 feet. Symptoms include rapid heart rate, shortness of breath at rest, AMS symptoms, dry cough developing into a wet cough, gurgling sounds, flu-like or bronchitis symptoms, and lack of muscle coordination. HAPE is life threatening, so descend immediately, at least 2,000 to 4,000 feet. HACE usually occurs above 12,000 feet but sometimes occurs above 10,000 feet. Symptoms are similar to HAPE but also include seizures, hallucinations, paralysis, and vision disturbances. Descend immediately—HACE is also life threatening.

Hantavirus pulmonary syndrome (HPS). Deer mice spread the virus that causes HPS, and humans contract it from breathing it in, usually when they've disturbed an area with dust and mice feces from nests or surfaces with mice droppings or urine. Exposure to large numbers of rodents and their feces or urine presents the greatest risk. As hikers, we sometimes enter old buildings, and often deer mice live in these places. We may not be around long enough to be exposed, but do be aware of this disease. Symptoms are flu-like and appear about two to three weeks after exposure. After initial symptoms, a dry cough and shortness of breath follow. Breathing is difficult. If you even think you might have HPS, see a doctor immediately!

Natural Hazards

Besides tripping over a rock or tree root on the trail, there are some real hazards to be aware of while hiking. Even if where you're hiking doesn't have the plethora of venomous snakes, poisonous plants, insects, and grizzly bears found in other parts of the United States, there are a few weather conditions and predators you may need to take into account.

Lightning. Thunderstorms build over the Uinta Mountains almost every day during the summer. Lightning is generated by thunderheads and can strike without warning, even several miles away from the nearest overhead cloud. The best rule of thumb is to start leaving exposed peaks, ridges, and canyon rims by about noon. This time can vary a little depending on storm buildup. Keep an eye on cloud formation, and don't underestimate how fast a storm can build. The bigger they get, the more likely a thunderstorm will happen. Lightning takes the path of least resistance, so if you're the high point, it might choose you. Ducking under a rock overhang is dangerous, as you form the shortest path between the rock and ground. If you dash below tree line, avoid standing under the only or the tallest tree. If you are caught above tree line, stay away from anything metal you might be carrying, Move down off the ridge slightly to a low, treeless point and squat until the storm passes. If you have an insulating pad, squat on it. Avoid having both your hands and feet touching the ground at once and never lay flat. If you hear a buzzing sound or feel your hair standing on end, move quickly, as an electrical charge is building up.

Flash floods. On July 31, 1976, a torrential downpour unleashed by a thunderstorm dumped tons of water into the Big Thompson watershed near Estes Park. Within hours, a wall of water moved down the narrow canyon, killing 139 people and causing more than $30 million in property damage. The spooky thing about flash floods, especially in Western canyons, is that they can appear out of nowhere from a storm many miles away. While hiking or driving in canyons, keep an eye on the weather. Always climb to safety if danger threatens. Flash floods usually subside quickly, so be patient and don't cross a swollen stream.

Bears. Most of the United States (outside of the Pacific Northwest and parts of the Northern Rockies) does not have a grizzly bear population, although some rumors exist about sightings where there should be none. Black bears are plentiful in the Uintas. Here are some tips in case you and a bear scare each other. Most of all, avoid scaring a bear. Watch for bear tracks (five toes) and droppings (sizable with leaves, partly digested berries, seeds, and/or animal fur). Talk or sing where visibility or hearing are limited. Keep a clean camp, hang food, and don't sleep in the clothes you wore while cooking. Be especially careful in spring to avoid getting between a mother and her cubs. In late summer and fall bears are busy eating berries and acorns to fatten up for winter, so be extra careful around berry bushes and oakbrush. If you do encounter a bear, move away slowly while facing the bear, talk softly, and avoid direct eye contact. Give the bear room to escape. Since bears are very curious, it might stand upright to get a better whiff of you, and it may even charge you to try to intimidate you. Try to stay calm. If a black bear does attack you, fight back with anything you have handy. Do not play dead. Unleashed dogs have been known to come running back to their owners with a bear close behind. Keep your dog on a leash or leave it at home.

Mountain lions. Usually elusive and quiet, lions rarely attack people. If you meet a lion, give it a chance to escape. Stay calm and talk firmly to it. Back away slowly while facing the lion. If you run, you'll only encourage the curious cat to chase you. Make yourself look large by opening a jacket, if you have one, or waving your hiking poles. If the lion behaves aggressively, throw stones, sticks, or whatever you can while remaining tall. If a lion does attack, fight for your life with anything you can grab.

Moose. Because moose have very few natural predators, they don't fear humans like other animals. You might find moose in sagebrush and wetter areas of willow, aspen, and pine, or in beaver habitats. Mothers with calves, as well as bulls during mating season, can be particularly aggressive. If a moose threatens you, back away slowly and talk calmly to it. Keep your pets away from moose.

Other considerations. Hunting is a popular sport in the United States, especially during rifle season in October. Hiking is still enjoyable in many areas during that time, so just take a few precautions. First, learn when the different hunting seasons start and end in the area in which you'll be hiking. You can check by visiting wildlife.utah.gov. During this time frame, be sure to wear at least a blaze orange hat, and possibly put an orange vest over your pack. Don't be surprised to see hunters in camo outfits carrying bows or muzzleloader rifles. If you would feel more comfortable without hunters around, hike in national parks and monuments or state and local parks where hunting is not allowed.

Navigation

Whether you are going on a short hike in a familiar area or planning a weeklong backpack trip, you should always be equipped with the proper navigational equipment—at the very least a detailed map and a compass.

Maps. There are many different types of maps available to help you find your way on the trail. Easiest to find are USDA Forest Service maps and BLM (Bureau of Land Management) maps. These maps tend to cover large areas, so be sure they are detailed enough for your particular trip. You can also obtain National Park Service maps as well as high-quality maps from private companies and trail groups. These maps can be obtained either from outdoor stores or ranger stations.

US Geological Survey topographic maps are particularly popular with hikers—especially serious backcountry hikers. These maps contain the standard map symbols such as roads, lakes, and rivers, as well as contour lines that show the details of the trail terrain like ridges, valleys, passes, and mountain peaks. The 7.5-minute series (1 inch on the map equals approximately 2/5 mile on the ground) provides the closest inspection available. USGS maps are available by mail (US Geological Survey, Map Distribution Branch, PO Box 25286, Denver, CO 80225), or online at USGS.gov.

The art of map reading is a skill that you can develop by first practicing in an area you are familiar with. To begin, orient the map so the map is lined up in the correct direction (i.e., north on the map is lined up with true north). Next, familiarize yourself with the map symbols and try to match them up with terrain features around you such as a high ridge, mountain peak, river, or lake. If you are practicing with a USGS map, notice the contour lines. On gentler terrain these contour lines are spaced farther apart, and on steeper terrain they are closer together. Pick a short loop trail, and stop frequently to check your position on the map. As you practice map reading, you'll learn how to anticipate a steep section on the trail or a good place to take a rest break, and so on.

Compasses. First off, the sun is not a substitute for a compass. So, what kind of compass should you have? Here are some characteristics you should look for: a rectangular base with detailed scales, a liquid-filled housing, protective housing, a sighting line on the mirror, luminous alignment and back-bearing arrows, a luminous north-seeking arrow, and a well-defined bezel ring.

You can learn compass basics by reading the detailed instructions included with your compass. If you want to fine-tune your compass skills, sign up for an orienteering class or purchase a book on compass reading. Once you've learned the basic skills of using a compass, remember to practice these skills before you head into the backcountry.

GPS. If you are a klutz at using a compass, you may be interested in checking out the technical wizardry of the GPS (Global Positioning System) device. A GPS device is a handheld unit that calculates your latitude and longitude. The Department of Defense used to scramble the satellite signals a bit to prevent civilians (and spies!)

from getting extremely accurate readings, but that practice was discontinued in May 2000, and GPS units now provide nearly pinpoint accuracy (within 30 to 60 feet).

There are many different types of GPS units available, and they range widely in cost. In general, all GPS units have a display screen and keypad where you input information. In addition to acting as a compass, the unit allows you to plot your route, easily retrace your path, track your traveling speed, find the mileage between waypoints, and calculate the total mileage of your route.

Before you purchase a GPS unit, keep in mind that these devices don't pick up signals indoors, in heavily wooded areas, or in ravines or deep valleys. They also rely on batteries. If you are counting on a GPS to protect your life, make sure you have extra batteries or map reading skills.

Pedometers. A pedometer is a small, clip-on unit with a digital display that calculates your hiking distance in miles or kilometers based on your walking stride. Some units also calculate the calories you burn and your total hiking time. Pedometers are available at most large outdoor stores.

Trip Planning

Planning your hiking adventure begins with letting a friend or relative know your trip itinerary so they can call for help if you don't return at your scheduled time. Always remember to let them know you have returned so Search and Rescue isn't sent into action looking for you. Your next task is to make sure you are outfitted to experience the risks and rewards of the trail. This section highlights gear and clothing you may want to take with you to get the most out of your hike.

Day Hikes

- camera/film/memory cards
- compass/GPS unit (extra batteries or charging device)
- day pack
- first-aid kit
- fleece jacket
- food
- guidebook
- hat
- headlamp/flashlight with extra batteries and bulbs
- insect repellent
- knife/multipurpose tool
- map
- matches in waterproof container and fire starter
- pedometer
- rain gear
- space blanket
- sunglasses
- sunscreen
- swimsuit
- watch
- water
- water bottles/water hydration system

Overnight Trip

- backpack and waterproof rain cover
- backpacker's trowel
- bandanna
- bear bell
- bear repellent spray
- biodegradable soap
- clothing—extra wool socks, shirt and shorts
- collapsible water container (2–3 gallon capacity)
- cook set/utensils
- ditty bags to store gear
- extra plastic sealable bags
- gaiters
- garbage bag
- ground cloth
- journal/pen
- long underwear
- nylon rope to hang food
- permit (if required)
- pot scrubber
- rain jacket and pants
- sandals to wear around camp and cross streams
- sleeping bag
- sleeping pad
- small bath towel
- stove and fuel
- tent
- toiletry items
- water filter
- waterproof stuff sack
- whistle

Equipment

With the outdoor market currently flooded with products, many of which are pure gimmickry, it seems impossible to both differentiate and choose. The only defense against the maddening quantity of items thrust in your face is to think practically—and to do so before you go shopping. The worst buys are impulsive buys. Since most name brands will differ only slightly in quality, it's best to know what you're looking for in terms of function. Buy only what you need. You will, don't forget, be carrying what you've bought on your back. Here are some things to keep in mind before you go shopping.

Clothes. Clothing is your armor against Mother Nature's little surprises. Hikers should be prepared for any possibility, especially when hiking in mountainous areas. Adequate rain protection and extra layers of clothing are a good idea. In summer, a wide-brimmed hat can help keep the sun at bay. In the winter months the first layer you'll want to wear is a "wicking" layer of long underwear that keeps perspiration away from your skin. Wear long underwear made from synthetic fibers that wick moisture away from the skin and draw it toward the next layer of clothing, where it then evaporates. Avoid wearing long underwear made of cotton, as it is slow to dry and keeps moisture next to your skin.

The second layer you'll wear is the "insulating" layer. Aside from keeping you warm, this layer needs to "breathe" so you stay dry while hiking. A fabric that provides insulation and dries quickly is fleece. It's interesting to note that this one-of-a-kind fabric can be made out of recycled plastic. Purchasing a zip-up jacket made of this material is highly recommended.

The last line of layering defense is the "shell" layer. You'll need some type of waterproof, windproof, breathable jacket that will fit over all of your other layers. It should have a large hood that fits over a hat. You'll also need a good pair of rain pants made from a similar waterproof, breathable fabric. Some Gore-Tex jackets are pricey, but you should know that there are more affordable fabrics out there that work just as well.

Now that you've learned the basics of layering, you can't forget to protect your hands and face. In cold, windy, or rainy weather you'll need a hat made of wool or fleece and insulated, waterproof gloves that will keep your hands warm and toasty. As mentioned earlier, buying an additional pair of light silk liners to wear under your regular gloves is a good idea.

Footwear. If you have any extra money to spend on your trip, put that money into boots or trail shoes. Poor shoes will bring a hike to a halt faster than anything else. To avoid this annoyance, buy shoes that provide support and are lightweight and flexible. A lightweight hiking boot is better than a heavy, leather mountaineering boot for most day hikes and backpacking. Trail running shoes provide a little extra cushion and are made in a high-top style that many people wear for hiking. These running shoes are lighter, more flexible, and more breathable than hiking boots. If you know you'll be hiking in wet weather often, purchase boots or shoes with a Gore-Tex liner, which will help keep your feet dry.

When buying your boots, be sure to wear the same type of socks you'll be wearing on the trail. If the boots you're buying are for cold weather hiking, try the boots on while wearing two pairs of socks. Speaking of socks, a good cold weather sock combination is to wear a thinner sock made of wool or polypropylene covered by a heavier outer sock made of wool. The inner sock protects the foot from the rubbing effects of the outer sock and prevents blisters. Many outdoor stores have some type of ramp to simulate hiking uphill and downhill. Be sure to take advantage of this test, as toe-jamming boot fronts can be very painful and debilitating on the downhill trek.

Once you've purchased your footwear, be sure to break them in before you hit the trail. New footwear is often stiff and needs to be stretched and molded to your foot.

Hiking poles. Hiking poles help with balance and, more important, take pressure off your knees. The ones with shock absorbers are easier on your elbows and knees. Some poles even come with a camera attachment to be used as a monopod. And heaven forbid you meet a mountain lion, bear, or unfriendly dog, the poles can make you look a lot bigger.

Backpacks. No matter what type of hiking you do you'll need a pack of some sort to carry the basic trail essentials. There are a variety of backpacks on the market, but let's first discuss what you intend to use it for. Day hikes or overnight trips?

If you plan on doing a day hike, a day pack should have some of the following characteristics: a padded hip belt that's at least 2 inches in diameter (avoid packs with only a small nylon piece of webbing for a hip belt); a chest strap (the chest strap helps stabilize the pack against your body); external pockets to carry water and other items that you want easy access to; an internal pocket to hold keys, a knife, a wallet, and other miscellaneous items; an external lashing system to hold a jacket; and a hydration pocket for carrying a hydration system (which consists of a water bladder with an attachable drinking hose).

For short hikes, some hikers like to use a fanny pack to store just a camera, food, a compass, a map, and other trail essentials. Most fanny packs have pockets for two water bottles and a padded hip belt.

If you intend to do an extended, overnight trip, there are multiple considerations. First off, you need to decide what kind of framed pack you want. There are two backpack types for backpacking: the internal frame and the external frame. An internal frame pack rests closer to your body, making it more stable and easier to balance when hiking over rough terrain. An external frame pack is just that, a frame attached to the exterior of the pack. An external frame pack is better for long backpack trips because it distributes the pack weight better and you can carry heavier loads. It's easier to pack, and your gear is more accessible. It also offers better back ventilation in hot weather.

The most critical measurement for fitting a pack is torso length. The pack needs to rest evenly on your hips without sagging. A good pack will come in two or three sizes and have straps and hip belts that are adjustable according to your body size and characteristics.

When you purchase a backpack, go to an outdoor store with salespeople who are knowledgeable in how to properly fit a pack. Once the pack is fitted for you, load the pack with the amount of weight you plan on taking on the trail. The weight of the pack should be distributed evenly, and you should be able to swing your arms and walk briskly without feeling out of balance. Another good technique for evaluating a pack is to walk up and down stairs and make quick turns to the right and to the left to be sure the pack doesn't feel out of balance. Other features that are nice to have on a backpack include a removable day pack or fanny pack, external pockets for extra water, and extra lash points to attach a jacket or other items.

Sleeping bags and pads. Sleeping bags are rated by temperature. You can purchase a bag made of synthetic fiber, or you can buy a down bag. Down bags are more expensive, but they have a higher insulating capacity by weight and will keep their loft longer. You'll want to purchase a bag with a temperature rating that fits the time of year and conditions you are most likely to camp in. One caveat: The techno-standard for temperature ratings is far from perfect. Ratings vary from manufacturer to manufacturer, so to protect yourself you should purchase a bag rated 10 to 15 degrees below the temperature you expect to be camping in. Synthetic bags are more resistant to water than down bags, but many down bags are now made with a Gore-Tex shell that helps to repel water. Down bags are also more compressible than synthetic bags and take up less room in your pack, which is an important consideration if you are planning a multiday backpack trip. Features to look for in a sleeping bag include a mummy-style bag, a hood you can cinch down around your head in cold weather, and draft tubes along the zippers that help keep heat in and drafts out.

You'll also want a sleeping pad to provide insulation and padding from the cold ground. There are different types of sleeping pads available, from the more expensive self-inflating air mattresses to the less expensive closed-cell foam pads. Self-inflating air mattresses are usually heavier than closed-cell foam mattresses and are prone to punctures.

Tents. The tent is your home away from home while on the trail. It provides protection from wind, snow, rain, and insects. A three-season tent is a good choice. These lightweight and versatile tents provide protection in all types of weather, except heavy snowstorms or high winds, and range in weight from 4 to 8 pounds. Look for a tent that's easy to set up and will easily fit two people with gear. Dome type tents usually offer more headroom and places to store gear. Other tent designs include a vestibule where you can store wet boots and backpacks. Some nice-to-have items in a tent include interior pockets to store small items and lashing points to hang a clothesline. Most three-season tents also come with stakes so you can secure the tent in high winds. Before you purchase a tent, set it up and take it down a few times to be sure it is easy to handle. Also, sit inside the tent and make sure it has enough room for you and your gear.

Cell phones. Many hikers are carrying their cell phones into the backcountry these days in case of emergency and to take pictures. That's fine and good, but know that cell phone coverage is often poor to nonexistent in valleys, canyons, and thick forest. More important, people have started to call for help because they're tired or lost. Let's go back to being prepared. You are responsible for yourself in the backcountry. Use your brain to avoid problems, and if you do encounter one, first use your brain to try to correct the situation. Only use your cell phone, if it works, in true emergencies.

Hiking with Children

Hiking with children isn't a matter of how many miles you can cover or how much elevation gain you make in a day; it's about seeing and experiencing nature through their eyes.

Kids like to explore and have fun. They like to stop and point out bugs and plants, look under rocks, jump in puddles, and throw sticks. If you're taking a toddler or young child on a hike, start with a trail that you're familiar with. Trails that have interesting things for kids, like piles of leaves to play in or a small stream to wade through during the summer, will make the hike much more enjoyable for them and will keep them from getting bored.

You can keep your child's attention if you have a strategy before starting on the trail. Using games is not only an effective way to keep a child's attention, it's also a great way to teach him or her about nature. Quiz children on the names of plants and animals. If your children are old enough, let them carry their own day pack filled with snacks and water. So that you are sure to go at their pace and not yours, let them lead the way. Playing follow the leader works particularly well when you have a group of children. Have each child take a turn at being the leader.

With children, a lot of clothing is key. The only thing predictable about weather is that it will change. Especially in mountainous areas, weather can change dramatically in a very short time. Always bring extra clothing for children, regardless of the season. In the winter, have your children wear wool socks and warm layers such as long underwear, a fleece jacket and hat, wool mittens, and good rain gear. It's not a bad idea to have these along in late fall and early spring as well. Good footwear is also important. A sturdy pair of high-top tennis shoes or lightweight hiking boots is the best bet for little ones. If you're hiking in the summer near a lake or stream, bring along a pair of old sneakers that your child can put on when he wants to go exploring in the water. Remember when you're near any type of water, always watch your child at all times. Also, keep a close eye on teething toddlers, who may decide a rock or leaf of poison oak is an interesting item to put in their mouth.

From spring through fall, you'll want your kids to wear a wide-brimmed hat to keep their face, head, and ears protected from the hot sun. Also, make sure your children wear sunscreen at all times. Choose a brand without PABA—children have sensitive skin and may have an allergic reaction to sunscreen that contains PABA. If you are hiking with a child younger than 6 months, don't use sunscreen or insect repellent. Instead, be sure that their head, face, neck, and ears are protected from the sun with a wide-brimmed hat, and that all other skin exposed to the sun is protected with the appropriate clothing.

Remember that food is fun. Kids like snacks, so it's important to bring a lot of munchies for the trail. Stopping often for snack breaks is a fun way to keep the trail interesting. Raisins, apples, granola bars, crackers and cheese, cereal, and trail mix all make great snacks. If your child is old enough to carry her own backpack, fill it with treats before you leave. If your kids don't like drinking water, you can bring boxes of fruit juice.

Avoid poorly designed child-carrying packs—you don't want to break your back carrying your child. Most child-carrying backpacks designed to hold a 40-pound child will contain a large carrying pocket to hold diapers and other items. Some have an optional rain/sun hood.

Hiking with Your Dog

Bringing your furry friend with you is always more fun than leaving him behind. Our canine pals make great trail buddies because they never complain and always make good company. Hiking with your dog can be a rewarding experience, especially if you plan ahead.

Getting your dog in shape. Before you plan outdoor adventures with your dog, make sure he's in shape for the trail. Getting your dog into shape takes the same discipline as getting yourself into shape, but luckily, your dog can get in shape with you. Take your dog with you on your daily runs or walks. If there is a park near your house, hit a tennis ball or play Frisbee with your dog.

Swimming is also an excellent way to get your dog into shape. If there is a lake or river near where you live and your dog likes the water, have him retrieve a tennis ball or stick. Gradually build your dog's stamina up over a two- to three-month period. A good rule of thumb is to assume that your dog will travel twice as far as you will on the trail. If you plan on doing a 5-mile hike, be sure your dog is in shape for a 10-mile hike.

Training your dog for the trail. Before you go on your first hiking adventure with your dog, be sure he has a firm grasp on the basics of canine etiquette and behavior. Make sure he can sit, lie down, stay, and come. One of the most important commands you can teach your canine pal is to "come" under any situation. It's easy for your friend's nose to lead him astray or possibly get lost. Another helpful command is the "get behind" command. When you're on a hiking trail that's narrow, you can have your dog follow behind you when other trail users approach. Nothing is more bothersome than an enthusiastic dog that runs back and forth on the trail and disrupts the peace of the trail for others. When you see other trail users approaching you on the trail, give them the right of way by quietly stepping off the trail and making your dog lie down and stay until they pass.

Equipment. The most critical pieces of equipment you can invest in for your dog are proper identification and a sturdy leash. Flexi-leads work well for hiking because they give your dog more freedom to explore but still leave you in control. Make sure your dog has identification that includes your name and address and a number for your veterinarian. Other forms of identification for your dog include a tattoo or a microchip. You should consult your veterinarian for more information on these last two options.

The next piece of equipment you'll want to consider is a pack for your dog. By no means should you hold all of your dog's essentials in your pack—let him carry his own gear! Dogs that are in good shape can carry 30 to 40 percent of their own weight.

Most packs are fitted by a dog's weight and girth measurement. Companies that make dog packs generally include guidelines to help you pick out the size that's right for your dog. Some characteristics to look for when purchasing a pack for your dog include a harness that contains two padded girth straps, a padded chest strap, leash attachments, removable saddle bags, internal water bladders, and external gear cords.

You can introduce your dog to the pack by first placing the empty pack on his back and letting him wear it around the yard. Keep an eye on him during this first introduction. He may decide to chew through the straps if you aren't watching him closely. Once he learns to treat the pack as an object of fun and not a foreign enemy, fill the pack evenly on both sides with a few ounces of dog food in sealable plastic bags. Have your dog wear his pack on your daily walks for a period of two to three weeks. Each week add a little more weight to the pack until your dog will accept carrying the maximum amount of weight he can carry.

You can also purchase collapsible water and dog food bowls for your dog. These bowls are lightweight and can easily be stashed into your pack or your dog's. If you are hiking on rocky terrain or in the snow, you can purchase footwear for your dog that will protect his feet from cuts and bruises.

Always carry plastic bags to remove feces from the trail. It is a courtesy to other trail users and helps protect local wildlife.

The following is a list of items to bring when you take your dog hiking: collapsible water bowls, a comb, a collar and a leash, dog food, plastic bags for feces, a dog pack, flea/tick powder, paw protection, water, and a first-aid kit that contains eye ointment, tweezers, scissors, stretchy foot wrap, gauze, antibacterial wash, sterile cotton tip applicators, antibiotic ointment, and cotton wrap.

First aid for your dog. Your dog is just as prone—if not more prone—to getting in trouble on the trail as you are, so be prepared. Here's a rundown of the more likely misfortunes that might befall your little friend.

Bees and wasps. If a bee or wasp stings your dog, remove the stinger with a pair of tweezers and place a mudpack or a cloth dipped in cold water over the affected area.

Porcupines. One good reason to keep your dog on a leash is to prevent it from getting a nose full of porcupine quills. You may be able to remove the quills with pliers, but a veterinarian is the best person to do this nasty job because most dogs need to be sedated.

Heat stroke. Avoid hiking with your dog in really hot weather. Dogs with heat stroke will pant excessively, lie down and refuse to get up, and become lethargic and disoriented. If your dog shows any of these signs on the trail, have him lie down in the shade. If you are near a stream, pour cool water over your dog's entire body to help bring his body temperature back to normal.

Heartworm. Dogs get heartworm from mosquitoes, which carry the disease in the prime mosquito months of July and August. Giving your dog a monthly pill prescribed by your veterinarian easily prevents this condition.

Plant pitfalls. Foxtails are pointed grass seed heads that bury themselves in your friend's fur, between his toes, and even get in his ear canal. If left unattended, these nasty seeds can work their way under the skin and cause abscesses and other problems. If you have a long-haired dog, consider trimming the hair between his toes and giving him a summer haircut to help prevent foxtails from attaching to his fur. After every hike, always look over your dog for these seeds—especially between his toes and his ears.

Other plant hazards include burrs, thorns, thistles, and poison oak. If you find any burrs or thistles on your dog, remove them as soon as possible before they become an unmanageable mat. Thorns can pierce a dog's foot and cause a great deal of pain. If you see that your dog is lame, stop and check his feet for thorns. Dogs are immune to poison oak, but they can pick up the sticky, oily substance from the plant and transfer it to you.

Protect those paws. Be sure to keep your dog's nails trimmed so he avoids getting soft tissue or joint injuries. If your dog slows and refuses to go on, check to see that his paws aren't torn or worn. You can protect your dog's paws from trail hazards such as sharp gravel, foxtails, lava scree, and thorns by purchasing dog boots.

Sunburn. If your dog has light skin, he is an easy target for sunburn on his nose and other exposed skin areas. You can apply a nontoxic sunscreen to exposed skin areas that will help protect him from overexposure to the sun.

Ticks and fleas. Ticks can easily give your dog Lyme disease, as well as other diseases. Before you hit the trail, treat your dog with a flea and tick spray or powder. You can also ask your veterinarian about a once-a-month pour-on treatment that repels fleas and ticks.

Mosquitoes and deerflies. These little flying machines can do a job on your dog's snout and ears. Best bet is to spray your dog with fly repellent for horses to discourage both pests.

Giardia. Dogs can get giardia, which results in diarrhea. It is usually not debilitating, but it's definitely messy. A vaccine against giardia is available.

Mushrooms. Make sure your dog doesn't sample mushrooms along the trail. They ould be poisonous to him, but he doesn't know that.

When you are finally ready to hit the trail with your dog, keep in mind that onal parks and many wilderness areas do not allow dogs on trails. Your best bet is t ke in national forests, BLM lands, and state parks. Always call ahead to see what th strictions are.

Hike Index

About the Authors

Jeffrey Probst is an outdoors writer who divides his time between writing about backpacking and programming computers. A lifelong resident of the state of Utah, he has backpacked in the High Uintas for more than thirty years and has written articles for outdoors magazines. His favorite place to backpack is the High Uinta Mountains, where he enjoys fishing, finding solitude, and taking photographs.

A native of northern Utah, **Brad Probst** spends much of his time exploring the wilderness. For more than twenty-five years, he and his brother, Jeff, have dedicated at least one trip a year to visit a new lake in the High Uintas, although he also enjoys solo expeditions. When he's not hiking, fishing, sketching, or taking photographs, he draws maps, writes outdoor literature, and prepares gourmet meals while watching football or the Utah Jazz.

Brett Prettyman was the outdoors editor for the *Salt Lake Tribune* for twenty-five years. He is the author of *Fishing Utah* (FalconGuides) and a frequent writer and blogger on outdoor sports. He grew up learning to fish in central Utah and in the high-elevation lakes of the Uinta Mountains, which he still visits frequently.